Palgrave Debates in Business History

Series Editors
Bradley Bowden, Brisbane, QLD, Australia
Michael Heller, Brunel Business School, Brunel University, London, UK

Scholarship in business history often produced divergent opinions that seldom engage with each other. Business historians have continued their scholarly endeavors with little obvious concern to the popular discontents around them. This book series will foster debate among business historians, bring together a variety of opinions from around the globe to confront the key issues of our time with the intent of becoming a fulcrum of debate. The series will use a broad understanding of "business history" so that it brings together work that is currently operating in tandem with each other without ever engaging with each other: work from business and management history, social history, economic history, cultural history, labor history, sociology, and political history whose focus is societal rather than personal or narrowly institutional. The series will focus on the following current debates in the field: the nature of globalization; the nature of capitalism; the nature and effects of western civilization (particularly as relates to industrialization); the mediatisation of business; gender, class and identity; and business and shifts in wealth, power and inequality. Within these topics there is passionate dissension, creating an opportunity engage multiple perspectives.

More information about this series at
http://www.palgrave.com/gp/series/16405

Elly Leung

The (Re)Making of the Chinese Working Class

Labor Activism and Passivity in China

palgrave
macmillan

Elly Leung
University of Western Australia
Crawley, WA, Australia

ISSN 2662-4362 ISSN 2662-4370 (electronic)
Palgrave Debates in Business History
ISBN 978-3-030-83312-1 ISBN 978-3-030-83313-8 (eBook)
https://doi.org/10.1007/978-3-030-83313-8

This Palgrave Macmillan imprint is published by the registered company Springer Nature Switzerland AG
The registered company address is: Gewerbestrasse 11, 6330 Cham, Switzerland

In memory of my mother and father

Series Editor's Foreword

This book by Elly Leung is the first in a new book series by Palgrave Macmillan, *Debates in Business History*. The purpose of this series is not one directed toward conventional business history studies that involve the study of individual firms or industries. Rather it aims to be a forum for debates that speak to the key business-related issues and concerns of our time.

Of the issues and concerns of our time arguably few are more important than China. A demographic and economic colossus, China is associated with three popular narratives. Long dominant is the belief that China's (supposed) embrace of Western economic principles will inevitably cause the society to transition toward a liberal democracy with all the personal liberties which that entails. A second narrative holds that although the Chinese Communist Party (CCP) is intent on maintaining its iron grip, that this will eventually loosen in the face of mass opposition. In other words, CCP control will collapse in ways similar to that witnessed in the Soviet Union and Eastern Europe. As Leung notes in her first chapter, it is this narrative which has long reigned supreme in Chinese labor studies. Seen from this perspective, every upsurge in workplace disputes is seen as evidence that another existential threat to the regime—similar to that associated with the Tiananmen massacre in 1989—is just around the corner. A third perspective, which Leung describes as a "counter-narrative", holds that not only is China the home of a brutal and exploitative dictatorship but also that the power of the CCP is not under serious threat. It is to this counter-narrative that Leung speaks, asking the following key question in relation to Chinese workplaces and the society more generally:

> What are the constraining factors that inhibit protest and facilitate conformity?

In seeking answers to this fundamental question, Leung's book does what all good academic studies do: it evaluates the academic literature in the field, explores statistics on employment and protest, and locates the reader within the dynamics of CCP-dominated China. What makes this book truly exceptional, however, is the nature of Leung's primary research. For extended periods, Leung not only observed and interviewed the industrial workers of six Chinese cities: Shenzhen, Hefei, Hangzhou, Panyu, Foshan, and Haizhu. She also lived alongside them, ate with them, and got to know her subjects on a personal basis as she recorded their fears and faded dreams. This is the description of the lodgings where Leung "randomly rented" a room, similar to all others, adjacent to the vast Foxconn factory in Shenzhen:

> The rooms of the lodging were small; old; filthy; smelly, dark and filled with mosquitos and cockroaches ...walls were broken or sagging; the bed frames were snapped or cracked ...there were no flush toilets in the stinky washrooms ...Externally, it was surrounded by the murky and smelly rivers of sewage; the streets were filled with piles of garbage alongside cockroaches and rats ...The streets were always crowded with workers. They all wore their work uniforms in a sloppy way with an unbearable smell of sweat, like they never showered ...They all looked angry; they never smiled.

In the pantheon of studies into the nature of business and management, Leung's book draws comparison to Whiting Williams's great classic, *What's on the Worker's Mind*. Published in 1921, Williams sought to understand the United States of his time by living and working alongside blue-collar workers in America's coal mines, steel plants, and shipbuilding yards. What emerged from Whiting's study was an uplifting tale. The idea that all workers wanted from a job "is in the pay envelope", Williams observed, was a fallacy. Rather, he concluded a worker's whole sense of identity and of individual worth derived from the job. And what workers valued most in a job was not the physical job tasks, but rather "the relationships that it provides".

For all its methodological similarities to Williams's classic, the tone and conclusions of Leung's work are fundamentally different. Where Williams's tale is an uplifting account of workplace pride and self-fulfillment, Leung's image of working life in modern-day China is Dickensian. Where the American workers that Williams talked to expected far more from work that what's "in the pay envelope", Leung's subjects invariably inform her that all that they hope to obtain from their job is a "subsistence" wage—and even that is often lacking. As one worker from the industrial city of Hefei tells Leung,

> I don't have choices …it's impossible for me to get a better job. We work because we have to live, and there's no point thinking about whether we like our conditions or not …everywhere is the same for us … uneducated people live like this.

In a similar vein, a private-sector worker from Shenzhen informed Leung,

> I know my future – I'll be poor for the rest of my life. Once we're poor, we are always poor …Illiterate people like me …can only get low-wage jobs …we have to suffer because we have no 'culture' in us …that's why we do whatever our leaders want.

The vaunted legal protections offered to such workers by the Chinese state are revealed as meaningless. Of the employment contract that workers at a Hangzhou garment factory were forced to sign, one employee recalls that,

> …there was nothing written on the paper. We signed the paper anyway … we didn't have to know what we'd signed because we must do what our leaders want anyway.

Many of the things which Leung describes will come as no surprise. We have all read the stories of the long hours, low wages, and the dormitory living conditions that have driven many Chinese workers to suicide. There were, however, two aspects of Leung's account that were a shock to me, as I suspect they will be for most readers.

The first surprise was the extent to which the Chinese regime has created a vast underclass of what is referred to—both by society at large and the workers themselves—as low *suzhi* or, literally, people of "low personal quality". Representing a majority of China's industrial workforce, low *suzhi* workers are described by Leung as people existing in a netherworld of "semi-citizenship". According to the CCP's mouthpiece, the *China Daily*, this teeming mass are "barbarians", people who need to "improve" themselves by following the advice and direction of their "high quality superiors at work in the cities". Composed of workers from peasant backgrounds, *they* have no right to reside in the cities under China's *Hukou* system, i.e. internal passport control. This means that they either reside in the cities illegally or, more commonly, are sponsored by an employer who obtains them a "temporary residence" permit. Invariably, the workers who "benefit" from such permits have the cost deducted from their wages, effectively turning them into "bonded labor". As temporary residents, *they* are denied access to benefits that accrue to permanent residents, such as health care and education. Where they do send their children to city schools, the average monthly fees amount to around 2000 Yuan. For workers whose monthly pay-packet is in the vicinity of 800 to 1500 Yuan, such costs present an insurmountable barrier. Accordingly, the children of many low *suzhi* families receive their education in rural schools that are characterized by what Leung describes as "low-quality teaching staff and poor facilities". Within such schools, moreover, the setting of conformist behavioral norms is given a higher priority than educational outcomes. As one Foxconn worker advised Leung, "It's about the behavior that our teachers wanted to see. If we behaved properly ...then we got better grades". The perhaps inevitable—and one suspects, intended—consequence of this is mass illiteracy and semi-literacy. Leung estimates that China now boasts 300 million adults who are illiterate or semi-literate, a total that equates to around a third of the current workforce (810 million). Even where they are able to obtain a reasonable level of functional literacy, low *suzhi* workers are seldom able to progress beyond an elementary education. In other words, the image that most of us have of China as a high-tech society that rivals the United States and Japan in its dynamism and educational achievements is myth.

The second surprise in Leung's study, one that goes to the core of her analysis, is the extent to which Chinese workers accept what most of us would regard as an intolerable situation with fatalism, or what they refer to as *Mingku* (literally, "bitter destiny"). Expressing a general view, a hotel cleaner from Hangzhou informs Leung,

> ...workers are just workers – we don't have any rights – because power and rights all belong to the leaders ...'low-quality' people are like that ... don't know a thing ...but to obey our leaders and do whatever we are told – so that we get our wages and keep our 'rice bowl' ...this is what are destiny [ming] is.

In Leung's estimation, it is the internalization of this sense of *mingku*—what she refers to as "self-regulation of a subservient status"—that underpins the CCP-regime and the "docile" supply of cheap labor upon which its economic achievements are built. And underpinning this internalized sense of a "subservient" self, Leung argues, is more than simply communist surveillance and censorship. Instead, Leung concludes, conformity and obedience to authority are deeply ingrained in Chinese culture. Indeed, since at least 1300 BC Chinese society has been built around *li* (literally, "proprieties") that demand not only respect for authority but also an acceptance of one's *ming*, or destiny. Reinforced by Confucian teachings, and mercilessly exploited by the CCP as a source of cultural and political control, the inevitable result of this historical legacy is found in a society of "docile bodies and minds".

In explaining the way in which historic cultural norms underpin conformity and acceptance in CCP-dominated China, Leung draws on a Foucauldian perspective. Chinese people accept their *mingku* (bitter destiny), it is convincingly argued, because of power-knowledge relationships that cause them to accept certain things—and certain social relationships—as unquestionable "truths". Many readers, I suspect, will not share Leung's Foucauldian perspective. In my own case, my antipathy to postmodernism is well known, evidenced in the publication (with this publisher) of *Work, Wealth and Postmodernism: The Intellectual Conflict at the Heart of Business Endeavour*. However, whatever you may think of Foucault, one must nevertheless recognize that—like Nietzsche before him—he placed individual freedom and self at the forefront of his life's work. It was in this that Foucault—like Nietzsche before him—made his great contribution to philosophy and politics. In recent years there has been a tendency to apply Foucault's principles largely through reference to sexuality and personal identity. With Leung's work, however, it is applied in ways that make Foucault relevant to a bigger story: the intellectual and cultural subjugation of an entire culture.

Leung's story is a powerful one. In reading it I was at times reduced almost to tears. At other times, I was enraged. What we have here, in short, is an exceptional work that speaks to one of the most important issues of our epoch: the future direction of Chinese society.

Controversy and Debate

Leung's book will be controversial. Born and bred in Hong Kong—although now an Australian citizen—her passion for her topic runs through every page. Not everyone will, however, share her antipathy for the CCP regime. Any critical analysis of China offends an array of vested interests, both within China and without. This book series, however, does not intend to shy away from controversy and debate. Along with my Co-Editor, Michael Heller (Brunel University, London, UK)—and my Associate Editors, Jeffrey Muldoon (Emporia University, Kansas, USA) and Gabrielle Durepos (Mount Saint Vincent University, Halifax, Canada)—this series seeks to confront debates germane to business history in an open, collegial but fearless fashion. Among the leadership team, it would be fair to say that some of us are sympathetic to postmodernist and/or critical perspectives, and some of us are not. Such variety of view, we believe, is not only useful. It is essential to our endeavors.

Currently, this series has a number of other studies in the pipeline. These include:

- *Business Practice in Socialist Hungary: From Chaos to Reform, 1945–1972*, an exploration into the nature of Eastern European communism and its legacy, by Phillip Scranton (Rutgers University, USA)
- *ANTi-History*, a theoretical study that builds on the work of the book's editors, Gabrielle Durepos (Mount Saint Vincent University, Halifax, Canada) and Albert Mills (Saint Mary's University, Halifax, Canada)
- *Business Endeavour and Western Civilization*, a study into the interrelationship between business and the rise of the modern iteration of Western civilization (by my good self).

Those wishing to know more about the series can find details at: https://tacitusforum.com/debates-in-business-history-book-series/.

In concluding this Foreword, I would like to not only acknowledge the extraordinary research efforts and, indeed, physical courage of Elly Leung—whose inquiries took her to places that few of us would wish to venture—but also the support of Marcus Ballenger, Palgrave Macmillan's New York-based Business Editor. Over the last few years, Marcus has provided a calm, quiet resolve in terms of bringing this book and this series to fruition. Without his efforts, Leung's powerful study would not be where it is: before a mass audience.

Hamilton, VIC, Australia
June 2021

Bradley Bowden

Acknowledgments

I would like to take this opportunity to acknowledge and thank those who have had a great impact on completing this Ph.D.-based book.

I am deeply thankful to the Chinese workers for sharing their personal stories with me at the interviews. I am also grateful to Apo Leung and Sally Choi at the Asia Monitor Resource Centre (AMRC); Kwan Ping at the Labor Action China (LAC); and workers (whose names cannot be disclosed) across several labor NGOs in China; Li Kungang at Anhui University; Jenny Chan at the University of Oxford, and Pun Ngai at Hong Kong Polytechnic University for helping me to gain access to a number of field sites.

I am forever indebted to my Ph.D. supervisor, colleague, and friend Donella Caspersz at the University of Western Australia. She provided me with invaluable insights and constantly pushed me to think critically and explore different perspectives. Without her guidance and encouragement, none of this work would have come into existence.

Special thanks go to Bradley Bowden for being an encouraging, supportive, thoughtful, and insightful mentor in creating numerous opportunities for me to develop my academic career. In addition, he polished one of the chapters with enthusiasm and precision to show me the ways to write it better. Thanks also to Marcus Ballenger and the publishing team for their patience and outstanding work in turning plain text into an actual book.

Warm thanks go to my beautiful friends Xinli Huang, Renata Casado, Marisa Duong, Sandra Martain, Catherine Leighton, Terence Chia, Leslie Howarth, Aleysha Howarth, Leanne Howarth-Gairen, Nonie Howarth, Daphne Wong, Steve Tien, Albert Tien, Mary Tien, Jong Liang Yuan, Hafizah Hsbollah, Caron Lim, Ian Tan, and Diana Timming for offering me their wise counsel and looking out for me.

I would like to thank my family, whom I owe a great deal. I want to thank auntie Mei Lei for supporting us to get through difficult times. Thank you to my sister Jessica N. T. Leung for always being there for me with unconditional love. My greatest thanks go to my late parents Ernie Su and Paul Y. C. Leung for their persistence and determination to stimulate my intellectual curiosity, which manifested my *Will to Knowledge*.

Parts of the book chapters have been published in "Chinese Workers History: Passive Minds Docile Bodies", *Journal of Management History* 25 (2019); "Exploring Worker Consciousness in China", *Labour & Industry* 26 (2016); "The Making of a Docile Working Class in Pre-Reform China", and "Governmentality and the Chinese Workers in China's Contemporary Thought Management System", *The Palgrave Handbook of Management*.

Contents

Abbreviations

ACFTU	All-China Federation of Trade Unions
AMRC	Asia Monitor Resource Centre
CCP	Chinese Communist Party
FDI	Foreign Direct Investment
FIE	Foreign Invested Enterprise
GDP	Gross Domestic Product
GNP	Gross National Product
I.T.	Information Technology
ILO	International Labour Organisation
LAC	Labour Actions China
MFN	Most Favored Nations
MNE	Moral and National Education
NGO	Non-Government Organisation
OHS	Occupational Health and Safety
SEZ	Special Economic Zone
SM	Sadomasochism
SOE	State-Owned Enterprise
U.K.	United Kingdom
U.S.	United States
USSR	Union of Soviet Socialist Republics
WTO	World Trade Organisation

List of Figures

List of Tables

CHAPTER 1

Introduction: Debates on Workers' Consciousness Development in China

This book assesses the potential for labor activism in China to develop into an organized worker's movement that is capable of challenging communist control.

The need for such an assessment is self-evident. Since the open market reforms of 1978, China has become a world factory and a global export leader. In the process, millions of Chinese peasants have been converted into urban industrial and service workers amid the dismantling of many State-owned enterprises (SOEs).

Understanding the political economy of these changes has dominated Chinese labor studies, especially in documenting incidents of worker protest actions triggered by labor abuses and poor working conditions. Since the involvement of industrial workers in the student-led Tiananmen Uprising of 1989, various studies have strived to demonstrate how the past experiences have stimulated worker consciousness and shaped the emergence of a self-conscious working class. In recent years, studies have increasingly interpreted these brutal working experiences as proof that workers have come to understand their class position at work and in society, forming themselves into a Chinese working class that continuously engages in collective actions to advance their work rights and benefits for themselves and others as a class (or groups) of *workers*. The term "rising class consciousness" (*yishi shangsheng* 意識上升) (Chan and

E. Leung, *The (Re)Making of the Chinese Working Class*, Palgrave Debates in Business History,
https://doi.org/10.1007/978-3-030-83313-8_1

Table 1.1 Trend of worker protests in China

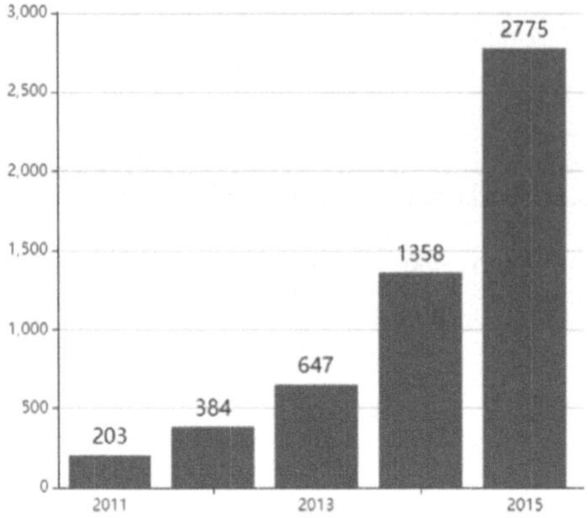

Source China Labor Bulletin (2021)

Pun 2009; Chan 2010a; Chan and Hui 2016; Chan and Selden 2016) has thus become a dominant discourse to describe workers' increased awareness of their common interests; an awareness grounded in brutal working experiences and exhibited in protest actions. Such actions are considered confrontational as they often face swift and sustained suppression both by the Chinese State[1] and entrepreneurs (Qi 2010); suppression facilitated by the absence of independent unions willing and able to support these struggles (Pringle and Clarke 2011; Hess 2013). Given these unfavorable conditions, non-government labor rights organizations (or labor NGOs) such as the Hong Kong-based China Labor Bulletin (2021) have reported that the number of worker protest actions increased from 203 incidents in 2011 to 2775 cases in 2015 (see Table 1.1).

The worker protests reported by labor NGOs are not the only evidence of discontent. Over the last two decades, we have often heard of 'mass incidents', popular protests inspired by environmental as well as workplace concerns (Friedman and Lee 2010). In 2004, there were 74,000 such incidents. In 2005, there were 87,000 (Leung and Pun 2009: 553; Estlund 2017). This evidence of popular discontent has caused many prominent Chinese labor studies experts (Chan and Pun 2009; Pun and

[1] A Chinese State is defined as a politically organised community living under the rules of different political leaders in history. The CCP is the political leader to rule China since 1949.

Lu 2010a, b; Chan and Hui 2016) to proclaim the existence of a "rising consciousness", one that has caused industrial employees to regard themselves as members of a self-conscious class of *workers* in China. Exponents of this view optimistically conclude that this heightened working "class" consciousness poses an existential challenge to not only business operations, but also—ultimately—the authority of the one-party State (Chan and Pun 2009; Chan 2010a; Chan and Hui 2016; Chan and Selden 2016).

Despite the optimistic predictions that work-based experiences will (or have) transformed Chinese workers into a proactive "working class" capable of mobilizing political actions for social change, this book suggests that Chinese reality is (unfortunately) very different.

The recent history of activism and worker militancy in China (see following sections and remaining chapters for details) differs in fundamental ways from that witnessed in South Korea and Tunisia during the so-called Arab Spring, and the former British colonial Hong Kong (1841–1997). Each of these countries has witnessed protests on a scale that far surpass anything seen in China. In Hong Kong, for example, the government's proposal in 2019 to amend the *Fugitive Offenders and Mutual Legal Assistance in Criminal Matters Legislation* (or Extradition Bill) so as to establish an extradition arrangement with China[2] triggered the largest wave of sustained anti-government and anti-China protests since the city was returned to Mainland China in 1997 (see Chapter 5). Joined by hundreds of thousands of people from different social classes across different occupational sectors—including medical professionals, social workers, teachers, and university and high-school students—the anti-Extradition Bill protests quickly evolved into a series of anti-China and anti-government movements, united under the slogans of "*Five Demands, Not One Less*" and "*Liberate Hong Kong, Revolution of Our Time*". Despite these movements appearing to "die down" in the face of both the coronavirus (COVID-19) pandemic and a draconian National Security Law (2020) on behalf of the Chinese Community Party (CCP), Hong Kong witnessed a continuance of collective resistance. To express their opposition to both the CCP and the Hong Kong government, citizens took to wearing black clothes and face masks (most notably

[2] The concern among the Hong Kong people with the Extradition Bill is that Hong Kong residents and has been the removal of the separation of the region's judiciary system from China under the "One Country, Two Systems" principle. See Chapter 5.

gas masks). They also created a so-called "yellow economic circle",[3] boycotting businesses that supported the HK Police Force (known as blue shops) and those affiliated with or owned by the Mainland Chinese (or Mainlanders) and the CCP (known as red shops). Among those to suffer from such popular ire were some of China's largest businesses, most notably the Bank of China (BOC).

In contrast to the mass opposition to communist rule evident in Hong Kong, my empirical findings suggest that the focus of Chinese worker protests is far narrower, posing little threat to the CCP-dominated regime. Rather than seeking transformative change, the protests in Mainland China are invariably driven by more prosaic concerns linked to individual economic need and everyday sustenance. Protests characterized by a strong sense of collective identity and solidarity are rare (see Chapters 3 and 4). It is for this reason that protest activities are largely unorganized and hence easily controlled. There is little evidence of the much touted "rising class consciousness" of workers as a class of *workers*. Instead, I argue, their capability of developing themselves into a proactive working class is constrained by their embryonic consciousness, one shaped by Chinese historical experience and Confucian culture.

In exploring the nature and extent of Chinese worker protests, this book seeks answers to fundamental questions, ones that go to the core of the long-term future of the CCP regime in China, namely:

1. How has worker consciousness been shaped in China?
2. How does the shaping of Chinese worker consciousness affect labor activism?
3. How does the shaping of worker consciousness affect their ability to develop themselves into an organized labor movement capable of improving living and working conditions for themselves and others?

[3] During the 2014 Umbrella Movement in Hong Kong, the song Tie a Yellow Ribbon Round the Ole Oak Tree was routinely performed by pro-democracy protestors as one of their protest songs. As a result, "yellow ribbons" have become a symbol of the movement as well as the self-identity of pro-democracy protestors and supporters. The yellow economic circle is created by the 'yellow ribbons' to support the livelihoods of pro-democracy businesses (or 'yellow shops').

The Marxian Theories on Worker Consciousness and Organized Labor Movement

Questions as to the nature of Chinese labor activism inevitably lead in the direction of controversial debates as to the nature of "class consciousness" and Karl Marx's (1844/2007) distinction between class-in-itself and class-for-itself. According to Marx (1844/2007), a "class-in-itself" was something created by economic relationships. A class-for-itself, however, was one created through the industrial and political struggles through which it derived a sense of its own distinct interests as well as a capacity to act upon those interests in transformative ways.

For Marx (1894/1992), worker awareness of their unique economic and social position as a "class" is the necessary basis of their power. It is only this consciousness that transforms struggles in a single factory, which are typically generated by prosaic bread-and-butter issues, into ones that unite across factories in the pursuit of common, "class" interests, i.e. to act as a "class-for-itself".

Since the twentieth century, exponents of Marx's class-for-itself theory have strived to develop strategies to shape workers' consciousness in ways that facilitate political struggles and the achievement of socialism (or communism). The Russian revolutionary leader Vladimir Lenin (1918/1992), for example, argued that the opportunities to transform a working class from a class-in-itself to a class-for-itself were rooted in the Socialist Revolutionary Party's (Bolshevik's)[4] decisive role as an intellectual and political leader. In doing so, Lenin identified three levels of workers' consciousness: individual consciousness, trade union consciousness, and revolutionary consciousness (1918, 1992). He insisted that workers' consciousness could only be raised from individual level—that focused upon wage maintenance for themselves—to the revolutionary level through the leadership posited intellectual vanguard, that is, the Socialist Revolutionary Party (1918, 1992). In other words, Lenin perceived that the maturation of working-class "consciousness" relied on the Party's action in providing them with a 'proper revolutionary education' that drew on party propaganda such as "*The Revolutionist... no*

[4] The Socialist Revolutionary Party was a faction of the Marxist Russian Social Democratic Party (RSDLP). The Party was founded by Vladimir Lenin and Alexander Bogdanov in 1905 which consisted of workers. See Shepley, Nick (2013) *Russia's Struggle With Modernity 1815–1929*, Bedfordshire: Andrews UK Limited.

private interests... property... of his own. His entire being is devoured by one purpose, one thought, one passion – the revolution" (Shepley 2013: 101). It is in this context that Lenin asserted that only the dictatorship of a single socialist party could effectively eliminate their exploitation by the capitalist class (1918, 1992).

For Lenin, economic and industrial struggles led by a "vanguard" party were the only sure pathway to socialism. Other Marxists, however, had other ideas. Karl Korschi (1938, 2016) and Louis Althusser (1965/2005), for example, noted that worker consciousness was not merely a reflection of their economic conditions. It was also the product of political ideology. They argued that it is only when workers developed a higher level of consciousness that they understood how the dominant (capitalist) political ideology had marginalized them. Only with this collective insight were workers able to form themselves into a class-for-itself. Antonio Gramsci (1988/2000) also placed the role of political ideology at the center of his analysis. According to Gramsci, the formation of a class-for-itself required intellectual-led (or 'organic intellectuals') political organizations able to shape workers' consciousness through a contestation over hegemony (or domination). For Georg Lukács (1968), however, it was the experiences generated in the production process that remained key. Even without a revolutionary vanguard, Lukács (1968) believed, such experiences were unique to a whole class, shaping consciousness and therefore the formation of a class-for-itself and its significant actions were determined by such a class consciousness.

In extending Lukács' debate around the relations between class experiences and consciousness, the English labor historian, E.P. Thompson (1966) emphasized the role of workers' culture and social relationships in his iconic study, *The Making of the English Working Class*. According to Thompson, the making of a class-for-itself was something that happened through lived experiences, both within and outside the production process. As Thompson (1966) expressed it,

> People find themselves in a society structured in determined ways [particularly] in productive relations, they experience exploitation... they identify points of antagonistic interest, they commence to struggle around these issues and in the process of struggling they discover themselves as classes, they come to know this discovery as class consciousness.
>
> (Thompson 1978: 149)

Thompson (1966) insisted that class consciousness emerged only through lived experiences as workers articulated the differences between themselves and the 'other' (ruling) class that was antagonistic to their interests. Working-class consciousness was not something imposed by a vanguard. Rather the *making* of a working-class consciousness arose organically through shared desires and actions. This meant that,

> ...class is defined by men as they live their own history, and, in the end, this is its only definition.
>
> (Thompson 1966: 11)

The Memories of Past Experiences and the Continuity of Class Consciousness

Thompson's concept of class consciousness arising organically from lived experience is one that many see as germane to the process of industrialization and societal change that occurred in post-1978 China.

Without doubt, the changes that occurred in this period were profound and far-reaching. Following the death of the CCP Chairman and founder of the People's Republic of China (PRC) Mao Zedong (1949–1976), the post-Mao CCP leader Deng Xiaoping (1976–1997) initiated an "*Open Door*"[5] policy. In doing so, Deng sought to transform China from a poor, rural, and revolutionary-based economy into a modern, industrialized "socialist market economy" (Leung and Caspersz 2016). The success of China's reforms repositioned the country, making it the world's factory and export leader (Leung and Pun 2009).

Central to Chinese success was its command of the world's largest and cheapest workforce. As of 2019, China boasted a workforce of at least 769 million (The World Bank 2019). In large part, this cheap labor force was created both by converting millions of peasants into urban industrial and service workers. At the same time, the CCP-dominated government dismantled the system of lifetime employment—the *iron rice bowl* (*tie fanwan* 鐵飯碗)—established in Mao's China for the millions of Chinese proletariats who worked in State-owned enterprises (SOEs)

[5] The 'Open Door' policy relates to a series of economic modernisation programmes that altered China's development strategy from one based on self-sufficiency in the Maoist state to one that actively participates in the world market. See Huan, Guocang (1986) 'China's Open Door Policy, 1978–1984', *China in Transition* 39(2): 1–18.

(Li and O'Brien 1996; O'Brien 1996; Chan 2001; Hurst and O'Brien 2002; Fan 2003, 2004; Pun 2007; Leung and Pun 2009; Pun et al. 2009; Pun and Lu 2010a, b). Once the pride of Mao's China, held up as the "masters of the State", it was these SOE workers who suffered most grievously in the post-1978 era. Reduced income and job losses were experienced almost everywhere as the post-Mao CCP leaders sanctioned a massive layoff (off-duty or *xiagang* 下崗) policy to restructure and privatize their SOE workforces (see Chapter 2). Subject to a relentless search in favor of efficiency and profitability, it was the SOE workers who were central to the wave of protests that reached a peak in 1988 and 1989. As such, they were seminal to the protests that culminated in the Tiananmen Square massacre (Walder 1991; Chen 2000; Lee 2000b; Hurst and O'Brien 2002).

Built around the Maoist concept that Chinese proletariats were the de facto "masters of the State", SOE protests were perceived by an array of Western scholars as a continuation of an historic class consciousness among the State workers, one that underpinned what was depicted as a conscious challenge to the CCP and its policies (Pringle and Clarke 2011). Tim Pringle and Simon Clarke (2011: 59), for example, claimed that despite large-scale redundancies, privatization, and even plant closures, SOE workers retained an awareness that they were the traditional Chinese working class (*gongren jieji* 工人階級), one that supposedly constituted the leading class in Mao's China. Post-Mao's economic reforms and eventual closure or restructure of SOEs, however, threatened this position and undermined workers' traditional job and economic security. Pringle and Clarke (2011) argue that these events stimulated the class consciousness developed in the Maoist period, fostering a supposed coalition among SOE workers intent on defending the survival of state enterprises. Protests involving SOE workers were thus generally described as reflecting an anti-privatization movement. It was also claimed that SOE worker agitation provided the seeds of a class-for-itself understanding that eventually found expression in the mass protests that coincided with the student-led Tiananmen movement in 1989 (Chan and Pun 2009; Pun et al. 2009).

In the wake of the 1989 student-led Tiananmen movement, a heightened level of working-class consciousness was detected by scholars such as Jude Howell (1998) and Malcolm Warner (1991). Warner (1991), for example, claimed that while workers were generally unwilling to voice their opinions or challenge either management or government officials, their discontent over poor labor protection, declining income, and increasing financial burdens was not without effect. The main outcome of this mass discontent was located in the formation of a number of independent workers' organizations (Walder 1991; Chan 1993; Walder and Gong 1993; Kent 2007; Lai 2010). The Beijing Worker Autonomous Federation (BWAF), for instance, attracted 20,000 workers to solidarity actions in 1989 (Goldman 2000: 122; Lee 2000a: 74; Potter 2001: 97). Organizations such as the 'workers' 'support team', the 'workers' 'picket team' and the 'dare-to-die' corps[6] (Walder 1991: 488) were also established at this time (Lorimer 2004: 22). It is certainly evident that these organizations represented more than a protest against growing inequality and declining working and living conditions. They were also a collective vote of no-confidence in the communist-sponsored All-China Federation Trade Unions' (ACFTU) ability to defend their rights and the long-term survival of the SOEs themselves. Whatever their actual objectives, it is clear that the CCP regarded these independent organizations with alarm, worried that their protests would turn political and threaten its one-party regime. Accordingly, these newly formed organizations were identified with the "counterrevolutionary riot" (i.e. Tiananmen) that promoted "bourgeois liberalization".[7] The People's Liberation Army (PLA)[8] was therefore ordered to kill, torture, arrest, and imprison the

[6] The function of the 'workers' support team' was to mobilize workers to participate in demonstrations while the 'workers' picket team' aimed to protect the protesters. The 'dare-to-die' corps shared similar tasks with the 'picket team' but travelled anywhere to block the retaliatory action by the Chinese military, that is, the People's Liberation Army (PLA), against the protesters during the 1989 Tiananmen movement. See Walder, Andrew (1991) 'Workers, Managers and the State: The Reform Era and the Political Crisis of 1989', *The China Quarterly* 127: 467–492.

[7] The term "bourgeois liberalization" is another label for "bourgeois rightists" that described the spreading of unwanted Western—particularly American—influences. During the Cultural Revolution (1966–1976), Mao used the label "bourgeois rightists" to attack his perceived capitalist enemies including Deng Xiaoping. See Chapter 2.

[8] The People's Liberation Army (PLA) was formerly called the Red Army prior to 1946. See Grasso, June, Corrin, Jay and Kort, Michael (2009) *Modernization and Revolution: From the Opium Wars to the Olympics*, New York: M.E. Sharpe, Inc. The Army consisted of Chinese workers and peasants (the masses) which had engaged battles against the Japanese troops during the Second World War (1937–1945) and the Kuomintang (KWT) party in the Chinese Civil War (1946–1949). See Chapter 2 and Li, Xiaobing (2012) *China at War: An Encyclopedia*, California: ABC-CLIO, LLC.

activists involved in these organizations and the protests they promoted (Amnesty 2019).

The hardline response that followed the Tiananmen Massacre was tempered by the international reaction, both by human rights groups such as the International Labor Organization (ILO) and foreign states with the United States (U.S.) revoking China's Most Favored Nations (MFN) trading status (The Washington Post 1989). Under these international pressures, the CCP was also compelled to enact the *Labor Law* (1995) and, subsequently, an updated version of the *Labor Contract Law* (2008).[9] Other supplementary legislation also provided works with theoretical protection in relation to labor contracts, reasonable working hours and rest days, overtime penalty rates, social insurance, and labor disputes resolution. The laws also mandated that the ACFTU defends workers' rights. However, the capacity of the official trade unions to protect workers was constrained by other laws, most notably the *Assembly Law* (1989) and the *Criminal Law* (1987).[10] The regime's unwillingness to

[9] Following the State workers' protest involvement in the 1989 Tiananmen movement, the CCP leaders enforced the labour standards provisions, including working hours, rest days, minimum wages and overtime penalty rates, to govern the rights and duties between employers and workers under the *National Labour Law* (1995). In 2008, the CCP enacted the *Labour Contract Law* (2008) to further regulate the use of employment contracts and also outlined the procedure for collective bargaining and labour dispute resolution. See ACFTU (1997) Labour Law of the People's Republic of China, http://www.acftu.org.cn/template/10002/file.jsp?cid=56&aid=31, accessed 10 September 2012, Lehman (2008) Labour Contract Law of the People's Republic of China, http://www.lehmanlaw.com/fileadmin/lehmanlaw_com/laws___regulations/Labor_Contract_Law_of_the_PRC__LLX__06292007_.pdf, accessed 12 October 2010, Su, Yang and He, Xin (2010) 'Street as Courtroom: State Accomodation of Labor Protest in South China', *Law & Society Review* 44(1): 157–184.

[10] These laws were used during the 1989 Tiananmen protests to suppress workers' attempts to organise an independent labour movement under the twin doctrines of "no crime without a law" and "no punishment without a law" Keith, Ronald and Lin, Zhiqui (2003) 'The "Falun Gong Problem": Politics and the Struggle for the Rule of Law in China', *The China Quarterly* 175: 623–642, Merchant, Toby (2004) 'Recognizing ILO Rights to Organize and Bargain Collectively; Grease in China's Transition to a Socialist Market Economy', *Case Western Reserve Journal of International Law* 36(223): 223–253, ITUC (2010) Internationally Recognised Core Labour Standards in the People's Republic of China: Report for teh WTO General Council Review of the Trade Policies of the People's Republic of China, http://www.ituc-csi.org/IMG/pdf/Chinal_Final-2.pdf, accessed 2 November 2012. *The Criminal Law of 1987*, for example, defined 'a criminal group' as a group of three or more people forming a criminal or an illegal organisation to carry out joint criminal activities to harm the society (*Articles 14 and 26*) UNHRC

allow meaningful defense of worker rights through both trade unions and other representative organizations was demonstrated by the CCP's refusal to ratify core ILO's labor standards,[11] that is, the *Freedom of Association and Assembly* (1948, No.87) and the *Right to Organize and Collective Bargaining* (1949, No.98); (ITUC 2010; Jantz 2010). Thus, even when the *Trade Union Law* (1992 & 2001) was enacted to strengthen the representation rights of the ACFTU, there is no evidence that this meaningfully benefited worker interests. Nor was there any evidence of the ACFTU mobilizing its workplace members through organized action against employers or employer organizations (Chan 2010a).

The fact that Chinese workers gained little from the strengthened role of the ACFTU is found in the fact that trade union officials at the enterprise level in China are largely appointed, rather than elected. Invariably, therefore, ACFTU-affiliated officials and the associated array of CCP cadres sided with employers/management—and the CCP government—in any workplace dispute (Howell 2008; Chen 2009, 2010). Today, the ACFTU remains what it always has been: an officially sanctioned organization that acts as a transmission belt to implement directives from the CCP, rather than being the representative of Chinese workers (Pringle 2011).

Given both the weak enforcement of the *Labor Laws* (1995 & 2008) and the ACFTU's unwillingness to challenge management, labor NGOs have played a significant role in representing Chinese workers since the mid-1990s (Chan 2012). Invariably, these labor organizations had been sponsored and funded by outside NGOs such as Oxfam Hong Kong.

(1997) Criminal Law of the People's Republic of China, http://www.unhcr.org/cgi-bin/texis/vtx/refworld/rwmain?docid=3ae6b5cd2&page=search, accessed 31 October 2012.. In addition, while the new *Labour Contract Law* (2008) did not specify whether striking was a legal action Wang, Tianyu and Cooke, Fang-Lee (2016) 'Striking the balance in industrial relations in China? An analysis of court decisions of 897 strike cases (2008–2015)', *Journal of Industral Relations* 59(1): 22–43., the regulations under the *Assembly Law* of 1989 stated that demonstrations or assembly activities must not "impair state, public or collective interests" (*Article 4*) UNHCR (1989) Law of the People's Republic of China on Assemblies, Processions and Demonstrations, http://www.unhcr.org/refworld/docid/3ae6b592e.html, accessed 22 October 2012..

[11] China has ratified only four of the eight core ILO's labour standards, namely the *Minimum Age* (1973, No.138), *Worst Forms of Child Labour* (1999, No.182), *Equal Remuneration* (1951, No.100), *Abolition of Forced Labour* (1959, No.105) and *anti-discrimination* (1958, No.111) conventions.

To legally operate within China, however, such bodies need to collaborate with local government in officially recognized labor projects (Lu 2009). Hence, the operations of the labor NGOs or any social organizations were subject to their ability to obtain a 'business supervisory unit' from the authorized government organizations (Chan 2012). In this context, NGOs have had a diversity of legal statuses. Some were registered as popular organizations (*minban* 民辦 or organized by citizens). Others were legally regarded as business enterprises. Given the difficulties in gaining legal recognition, many remained unregistered (or illegal) organizations (Lu 2009). It was rare for NGOs to be registered as actual labor organizations. Even if this was achieved, Chinese law banned NGOs from receiving membership-based funding. Now were labor NGOs able to represent specific social groups, such as migrant workers or laid-off workers. The clear intent of such restrictions was one of constraining the growth of NGOs in order to prevent both public protests and labor disputes (Biddulph 2015). As a result, the scope of NGO activities was limited to one of defending workers' legal rights (*hefa quanyi* 合法權益); initiatives undertaken along with international campaigns for law-oriented labor rights protection programs (*weiquan* 維權) (Benney 2013).[12]

With both international funding organizations and the CCP backing legalistic *weiquan* approaches, most labor NGOs restricted their activities to legal advice and training. Within the scope of such endeavors, activities to improve occupational health and safety (OHS) were commonplace (Chan and Siu 2012). Chris Chan (2012) notes that most labor NGOs were essentially service providers. At these NGO service centers, workers were provided with free newspapers and educational classes that promoted legal awareness and understanding. These labor NGO centers also offered free legal hotlines and consultation, providing workers with after-the-fact legal advice on resolving grievances through mediation, arbitration, and litigation (Friedman and Lee 2010). Despite their focus on free services, Eli Friedman and Ching Kwan Lee (2010: 524) note that in fact, many labor NGOs began to operate as businesses, or what were referred to

[12] Chinese discourse of rights protection is characterized by the acceptance of the laws as the standard by which the clauses such as working conditions and minimum wages have been set. See Benney, Jonathan (2013) *Defending Rights in Contemporary China: Reserving the Right*, New York: Routledge. See Chan, Anita and Siu, Kaxton (2012) Chinese Migrant Workers: Factors Constraining the Emergence of Class Consciousness. in Beatriz Carrillo and David Goodman (eds.) *China's Peasants and Workers: Changing Class Identities*. Massachusetts: Edward Elgar Publishing Ltd.

as "citizen's agents" (i.e. legal-aid agencies). This meant that they operated on a fee-for-service basis. A range of services were provided on this basis: preparing and filing legal complaints with the local labor bureaus,[13] acting as legal representatives in dispute resolution, and pursuing court action over matters such as back-pay and workplace injury compensation. As a result, these legal-aid *weiquan* programmes were exercised only when workers' legal rights were violated. There was little focus on proactively advancing rights and interests that were beyond the legal standards (Chan and Siu 2012; Benney 2013; Hui 2020).

Although largely reactive, Mary Gallagher (2005, 2006, 2007; Gallagher et al. 2013) maintains that legal-aid *weiquan* services provided by the labor NGOs have been a critical instrument in raising legal rights consciousness (*falu quanli yishi* 法律權利意識). Although legal consciousness was profoundly shaped by the heavy hand of the State through the *pufa* campaign (see Chapter 2), Gallagher claims that the slogan "use law as a weapon"—popularized by both the National's People Congress and the media—provided workers with a strategic justification for legal action to sue their employers under the discourse of *weiquan* (2006). In her study of a labor NGO in Shanghai, Gallagher also notes that the official propaganda about using "legal weapons" created expectations that motivated workers to use the law to protect their rights even without substantive legal knowledge (2005, 2006: 799). Despite confusion as to what the legal responsibilities of their employers actually were, a sense of entitlement nevertheless emerged that encouraged the use of "legal weapons". This drove a desire to acquire a better knowledge of laws, regulations, legal procedures, and the use of evidence, objectives that underpinned increased participation in the legal consultation services offered by the labor NGO (Gallagher 2005, 2006). Gallagher also concludes that workers' engagement in the legal consultation and discussion was both a learning and corrective process, one associated with the emergence of a critical legal rights consciousness. This caused workers to believe that the standards provided in law were not only meaningful, but also that they themselves could defend their legal rights (*weiquan*) for themselves (2006).

[13] Filing labour dispute arbitration with the local labour bureau is the prerequisite for filing civil lawsuits. See Friedman, Eli and Lee, Ching Kwan (2010) 'Remaking the World of Chinese Labour: A 30-Year Retrospective', *British Journal of Industrial Relations* 48(3): 507–533.

As a consequence of the CCP's promotion of *weiquan* programs through government and non-government organizations (Benney 2013), the number of formal dispute cases over work-related issues heard by the *Labor Arbitration Committees*[14] has progressively increased since the 1990s (2015).

Eli Friedman and Ching Kwan Lee (2010: 517) note that thirty percent of the dispute cases as of 2010 were about unfair dismissal. By contrast, fifty percent of cases involved wage arrears, non-payment of *xiagang* pension benefits and social insurance (see Chapter 2). Most of these latter cases involved SOE workers. Friedman and Lee also reveal that SOE workers accounted for thirty-four percent of the official disputes filed with the labor bureaus. Workers in private enterprises and those characterized by foreign investment accounted for ten percent and twenty-one percent, respectively, of the 48,121 cases filed in 1995 alone; a litany of cases that involved 189,120 workers (2010: 517). New cases continued to rise. Whereas 520,000 cases were filed in 2008, by 2014 there were 715,163 cases (Friedman and Lee 2010: 518). Such figures, however, should not be regarded as evidence of an improvement in worker circumstance. Instead, labor bureaus were overburdened, unable to efficiently resolve workers' grievances. The effectiveness of the labor law provisions associated with *weiquan* discourse was also rendered insignificant by the absence of any independent working-class organization that could constitute its own union membership as a collective force (Friedman and Lee 2010).

From the mid-1990s, the inability of the legal system to redress workers' grievances in accordance with the *weiquan* discourse fostered increasing levels of worker protest, whether measured by frequency or intensity (Lee 2002a; Chen 2003; Benney 2013). Behind this upsurge was a deterioration in working conditions as SOE workers experienced layoffs, increased precariousness, reduced wages, unpaid wages, and reduced

[14] In accordance with Article 81 of the *Labour Contract Law* (2008), the *Labour Arbitration Committee* is established at the county, municipality and district levels. See Chen, Ke (2011) *Labour Law in China*, The Netherlands: Kluwer Law International BV. The Labour Arbitration Committee is composed of representatives of the local Labour Bureau (or labour administrative department) and the trade union as well as the government staff and lawyers as full-time or part-time arbitrators where the Committee is chaired by the responsible person in charge of the local labour administrative department. See Hunter, Christopher, Lam, Louisa and Lin, Ketong (2008) *Employment Law in China*, Hong Kong: CCH Hong Kong Limited.

xiagang benefits (Friedman and Lee 2010). Feng Chen's (2000) early study of worker protest activities in a medium-sized SOE in North China's Henan province is illustrative of these trends.[15] In this study, Chen reveals a tale of wage and pension arrears as well as growing numbers of layoffs. Chen also found that these Henan workers were drawing on their own *weiquan* concept in defense of their 'right to subsistence' (*shengcun quan* 生存權) (2000). Of particular concern was the prospect, or reality, of having to survive after being laid off for months or years without any income (2000). Protests by laid-off workers were, however, essentially spontaneous, leaderless, and largely motivated by demands for "some subsistence aid from local authorities" (Chen 2003: 242). Given their limited demands, such protests by SOE workers were not repressed by the local authorities as their actions were "easily defused by a government promise of a couple of hundren yuan as compensation" (Chen 2006: 47). Chen thus argues that these SOE workers' actions remained passive and reactive, submitting themselves to the mandated changes until they could not subsist (Chen 2000: 62). Their incapability to define any interest beyond the 'right to subsistence' led Chen to conclude that the Chinese working class remained at the level of a class-in-itself,[16] rather than a class-for-itself. In order words, their rather embryonic consciousness had not matured to a level capable of taking action for the 'wider good'.

In considering the same phenomenon, Lee (1999) argues that the emphasis by SOE workers on a subsistence ethic was shaped by the Chinese *Labor Contract Reform* policy (1986) and the *Labor Law* (1995).

[15] Henan province was one of the top four provinces (next to the three other SOE concentrated locations of Liaoning, Heilongjiang and Jilin provinces) in terms of the number of SOE workers that faced with wage arrears. With 640,000 of 4.13 million SOE workers laid off, Henan's province's unemployment rate was reported as the third highest in the country, next to Liaoning and Heilongjiang. See Chen, Feng (2000) 'Subsistence Crises, Managerial Corruption and Labour Protests in China', *The China Journal* 44: 41–63.

[16] Contrary to a class-for-itself, a class-in-itself is constituted by the production structure without becoming discursively aware (or conscious) of its own position (or identity) within the capitalist system. Thus, it is argued that a class-in-itself is formed without class identity and hence is incapable of engaging in class-based action to defend the rights and interests of workers. See Research Background, p. 23 and Haugaard, Mark (1997) *The Constitution of Power: A Theoretical Analysis of Power, Knowledge and Structure*, Manchester: Manchester University Press.

Significantly, the *Labor Law* (1995) allowed enterprise-based management to engage in no-fault dismissal of SOE workers. New labor contracts also strengthened managerial power to fire SOE workers, particularly in less competitive and older industries (1999). In Guangdong, for example, the legal enhancement of managerial autonomy within SOEs thus led to a steadily increased *xiagang* (stood down) rate, which grew from 0.7% in 1988 to 10% in 1994, before reaching a staggering 35.8% in 1996 as privatization accelerated (Lee 1999: 55–56). In 1997, the number of unemployed workers together with *xiagang* workers in Guangzhou province alone amounted to approximately 103,000 (Lee 1999: 56). Lee (1999) perceives that this enhanced managerial power to make workers redundant, or unilaterally dismiss them, placed particular pressure on those who were less competitive in the labor market such as the old and the sick, pressures that caused them to become submissive or quiescent because they continued to receive *xiagang* benefits and were formally still attached to SOE work units (*danwei* 單位) (1999). This weakened their capacity to act collectively even when their subsidies (or *xiagang* benefits) were inadequate or remained unpaid. In a sense, the series of labor laws and regulations were implemented not to strengthen workers' legal rights, but rather to construct a level of what Mary Gallagher (2005, 2006) refers to as legal consciousness among the workers that was aligned with a sense of individualized legal rights. It is this consciousness that manifested itself in passive, spontaneous, and sporadic protests by SOE workers. By contrast, collective and organized protests remained rare, even though the workers concerned were often desperate and had very little to lose (Lee 1999: 68).

While protests by SOE workers were characterized by passive forms of resistance, Lee (2000b) envisages that their collective memories of Maoist socialism provided desperate *xiagang* workers with a strong sense of class solidarity. In her research in Liaoning, a declining SOE industrial district in a northeastern province, Lee finds that worker discourses were sprinkled with references to their past experiences of the socialist system. In protest actions, such sentiments were expressed in slogans such as, '*Workers are masters of the state*', '*Yes to socialism, No to capitalism*', and '*Long live the working class*' (2000b: 220). Lee also notes that the sense of class, which workers developed in their socialist past, was evident in their discourse when defending what they understood as their class interests; a discourse expressed in demands that included:

> 'We want to work', 'Our children want to go to school'... 'Not a yuan [Chinese dollar] in six months, we want to eat'... 'Down with the newly emerging nobility', 'Eradicate the new bureaucratic bourgeoisie'... 'Save the factory, save the people'...
>
> (Lee 2000b: 219–220)

Drawing on protest slogans such as those noted above, Lee argues that class consciousness was increased through the direct experiences of working under market conditions. It was also observed that their sense of their 'right to subsistence' was strongly related to the Maoist past, embedded in their previous lifetime SOE employment and guaranteed welfare and pension (or iron rice bowl) (Lee 2000b). Accordingly, Lee argues, (2000b, 2002a) it was their loss of permanent jobs as a result of SOE restructuring—coupled with the failure of local government to implement central policies of *xiagang* benefits—that triggered months and years of collective actions by SOE workers to safeguard the Maoist ideal of their basic livelihood (or subsistence); ideals that Lee perceives as having a clear class dimension grounded in collective memories of Maoist socialism (2000b).

Building on Lee's perspective, Chen's later work on SOE protest also identifies collective memories of the socialist past as central to a supposed sense of class solidarity among those employed in SOE factories (2006). Drawing on case studies of three SOE factories that were merged with private enterprises in Liaoning, Chen records how the workers from these factories staged protests against these mergers, which were de facto SOE privatization schemes (2006). Chen (2006: 44) argues that in these workers's minds, privatization of SOEs reflected "class-conflict" between themselves and capitalists. This mindset, according to Chen, was cultivated among SOE workers through decades of indoctrination in socialist and anti-capitalist ideologies (or Maoism) during Mao's period (2006: 44). These memories inspired the use of class discourse by workers and slogans such as:

> We are no longer the master of the factory. We are now an oppressed class. There are now a lot of incidents of oppressing workers... Our struggle [against privatization] is a manifestation of class struggle. Oppression and polarization inevitably lead to class struggle.
>
> (Chen 2006: 49)

Chen (2006) also notes that the slogans used by SOE workers in their anti-privatization protests were mixed with an anti-bourgeois tone that promoted the Maoist doctrine about the superior status of the Chinese working class. This had been made popular during the Cultural Revolution (see Chapter 2). For Chen, workers' reappropriation of the old ideological rhetoric in describing the impact of privatization on their lives reflected their proclivity for class-conscious action was largely a consequence of a collective class consciousness developed among SOE workers since Mao period (2006). Chen subsequently argues that the comprehension of the SOE privatization in class terms by workers drawing on past experiences of socialism indicates a possibility to forge strong collective class movements in response to proletarianization (Chen 2006). The success that the workers in these three factories had in halting the process of privatization adds support to Chen's claim that workers were capable of taking effective class action. However, Chen's case studies stand in contrast to the overall effect of the CCP's privatization agenda for SOEs, which decimated the potential for SOE workers to coalesce into a class-for-itself. That is, while the cultivation of class ideologies in workers in the Maoist past had presented the possibility for class consciousness development among SOE workers, the post-Maoist State acted decisively to quell any potential for this to mature further.

At the same time as initiating the layoff of tens of millions of SOE workers during the 1990s, the State simultaneously recruited large numbers of new workers to work within the SOEs (Lin 2015). These workers were mostly peasant workers who faced more precarious labor conditions than did the earlier generation (Lin 2015). For instance, peasant workers were forced to work an additional 20 h of compulsory unpaid or underpaid overtime work each week in addition to their basic 40 h work week (Lin 2015: 75). By substituting the older generation of working-class SOE workers with a new class of peasant workers, the post-Maoist State was able to effectively replace an entire generation of workers who had shown evidence of class-based interests with those who had little or no history of class, and whose very existence was even more precarious because of their working conditions. Therefore, it is no surprise that protest actions by SOE workers decreased dramatically from over 80% of all 'mass incidents' to 20% between 2000 and 2010 (Lin 2015: 81–82). For SOE workers there was effectively nothing left to defend following the period of privatization and reconstruction of SOE workforces in the 1990s. Accordingly, the CCP had effectively quelled the potential for the 'old' group of SOE workers who had been prominent in the Tiananmen movement to continue along a pathway of increasing class consciousness in ways that threatened regime survival.

Brutal Experiences, Kinships, and Class Consciousness Development

Although the conditions of peasant workers in the State sector differed from those of earlier generation of SOE workers, Lin reveals that SOE peasant workers perceived themselves as having better conditions than those in the export-oriented, foreign-invested enterprises (FIEs) who had to work approximately 30 hours of overtime a week (2015: 75). As SOE protest actions declined, therefore, those emanating from the FIE sector increased. Yanqi Tong and Shaohua Lei (2010: 490), for example, note that protests by peasant workers in FIEs constituted 45% of mass incidents in China between 2003 and 2009. A series of studies since the 1990s (Chan and Li 1999; Mallee 2000; Bao et al. 2002; Fan 2003, 2004) have highlighted the experiences of this new peasant workforce who were pushed by rural poverty, and pulled by the growing urban economy. While their city earnings were higher than their rural incomes, Lee (2002b) notes that their wages were as little as only one-sixth of those of Mexico and one-fortieth that of the U.S. This contradiction between rapid growth of economy and cheap labor costs attracted criticism about China's role in driving a global 'race to the bottom' (Li 2006; Silver and Zhang 2009; Pringle 2011). Anita Chan (2001) and Pun Ngai (2005), for example, found that peasant workers in FIEs experienced extreme levels of employment exploitation, including low wages and long working hours. These conditions were exacerbated by the household registration system (*hukou*户口) (see Chapter 2), which intentionally put peasant workers in a vulnerable position in exchange for subsistence urban wages (Chan 2001). Under this system, whereby peasant workers were employed in regions where they had no legal right to reside, employment remained inherently precarious. Indeed, according to Pun (2005), the *hukou* system enabled management in FIEs to facilitate an extreme form of class domination, even imposing restrictions on toilet-going.

The studies which we have discussed so far have largely focused on the ways in which worker consciousness was shaped by collective memories and the past experiences of Mao's socialism. Since 2000, however, other studies have drawn on Thompson's (1966) constructivist and agency-oriented conception of class, focusing on the relations between workers' experiences and protest activities.

As noted above, in the post-2000 era, it was the new workforce drawn from peasant areas that increasingly acted as the social base for workplace protests. Lacking effective workers' organizations to voice their grievances, peasant workers also began to bypass the state-sponsored trade unions (Howell 2008; Chen 2009, 2010). Although Smith and Pun (2006) among others recognize the weakness of the resistance pattern among peasant workers as compared with SOE workers, they nonetheless argue that they also shared attributes that favored sustained protest. Chief among these were networks of kinship and historic friendships. On occasion, even their original home-place was physically close to the factory that employed them, allowing them to draw upon community support networks. Above all, it is suggested, their collective existence in the factory dormitory provided a platform for workers to begin to identify their common interests as a class.

In their study of Shenzhen in South China, Smith and Pun (2006) conceptualize the dormitory regime as a peculiar form of labor process that embedded both management control and workers' resistance. Their study reveals that the dormitory compound consisted of both manager and worker accommodation located in close proximity; a circumstance that facilitated the imposition of systems of discipline and punishment to regulate the dormitory behavior of the workers in terms of sleeping, eating, and bathing (Smith and Pun 2006: 1464). Close proximity, however, also facilitated resistance to management. In the enterprise that was the focus of Smith and Pun's study, overt protest resulted from management's decision to relocate its production lines and dismiss 600 workers without compensation (Smith and Pun 2006: 1465–1466). This incited another 1000 workers who also faced dismissal to organize actions in the dormitory prior to the second wave of redundancy in 2002 (Smith and Pun 2006: 1465–1466). Smith and Pun argue their everyday life in the dormitory and factory nurtured a solidarity between these workers, which motivated them to act collectively to demand layoff compensation through demonstrations (2006).

Others (Cai 2002; Leung and Pun 2009) argue that class actions were also formed through the coordination of cross-enterprise action developed outside of living and working environments. Cai (2002), for example, suggests that cross-factory action was generated from a working-class shared perception of enterprise-specific grievances. Similarly, Pak Nang Leung and Pun Ngai (2009) argue that by sharing their bitter experiences and lessons with each other, workers also came to support each other in cross-enterprise collective action. In their case study (2009) of the struggles of silicosis-afflicted gemstone workers, Leung and Pun find that workers' resistance developed from engaging in single- and cross-factory legal actions with other victimized workers across the gemstone industry. Collective actions, including road blockages and demonstrations at government buildings, were also undertaken to demand economic compensation for other workers following their illness. Leung and Pun view this as illustrative of a developing class consciousness among workers who shared a collective identity, both as peasant workers and as occupational diseases victims, shared identities that transformed them from being "atomized workers in a single factory into a collective social force" (2009: 564).

Although peasant workers were not constituted as a working class in Mao's period, scholars such as Pun (2005) suggest that their class consciousness emerged in the reform era through their work-based experiences in the cities. In support of this argument, we read in the comments made by these workers at the time that:

> We are not treated as human beings... We work like dogs and never stop. When the superior asks you to work, you have to work no matter when and where... *Dagongzai* [or working men] is worth nothing. *Dagongzai* is only disposable stuff.
>
> (Pun 2005: 23–24)

Drawing on the comments above, Pun (2005) stresses that self-understanding among peasant workers of themselves as a class of workers was generated through their prolonged exploitative *dagong* experiences in the cities. From this perspective, their accumulated negative class experiences were fundamental to foster workers' consciousness and the subsequent class formation and actions against exploitation.

Recent studies by Pun and Hulin Lu (2010b) and Kam Wing Chan (2010b), among others, stress that the accumulated painful *dagong* experience of the first generation of peasant workers (born between the late 1960s and early 1970s) evolved into the anger and action of the second generation (born after the late 1970s and 1980s). Shared feelings and experiences between two generations were articulated as a particular element shaping consciousness of the younger generation, leading led them to change their perception and life expectation in the cities (Chan 2010b; Pun and Lu 2010b). Kam Wing Chan (2010b) notes that the younger workers were better educated and more rights-conscious, and therefore they were less tolerant of abuse and injustice than their elders. Pun and Lu (2010b) explain that because the move to *dagong* by young workers was not driven by economic needs, but rather by their 'dreams' of pursuing personal development and freedom in the urban consumer culture, they refused to tolerate their plight in silence. In their detailed study of the life struggles of one *dagongzai* in Shenzhen, Pun and Lu show how his anger and frustration over the factory's decision of relocation reinforced him to mobilize four other co-workers to take legal action against issues such as years of unpaid overtime wages (Pun and Lu 2010b; Pun 2019). It is in this context they describe the anger and resentment among the second generation of peasant workers experienced in their painful *dagong* lives as a fundamental element to nurture a new working class (Pun and Lu 2010b; Pun 2019).

Studies of the *dagong* life of student interns (or student workers) (Pun and Chan 2012; Chan 2013; Chan et al. 2013; Smith and Chan 2015; Pun et al. 2016) also highlight the ways in which anger and resentment motivated the actions of the second generation of peasant workers to defend their dignity and rights (Wong 2011). In particular, these studies reveal how peasant-student interns 'dispatched' by their vocational schools suffered from heightened feelings of desperation in one of China's biggest manufacturing FIEs—Hon Hai Precision Industry Company (commonly known as Foxconn) (Pun and Chan 2012). In one analysis (Smith and Chan 2015), student-internship is described as a form of forced labor that assigns students to jobs that are irrelevant to their educational qualifications or vocational training. Another study (Pun and Chan 2012) reports that student workers maintained a student identity that disqualified them from labor protection because internship was not considered employment in China. Moreover, student workers were subjected to "super-exploitation" and tight control and discipline, both by their school teachers and work supervisors, who dominated their lives within a highly centralized and hierarchical production system (Pun and Chan 2012: 392; Smith and Chan 2015). In the case of Foxconn, a repressive and inhumane mode of management had pushed student workers to their "physical and psychological limits", leading to daily resistance in the form of slow-downs, stealing, and stoppages (Pun and Chan 2012: 388). Some vented their frustration by smashing security offices and production facilities (Chan et al. 2013). Others threw fireballs at the dormitory (Smith and Chan 2015). Tragically, multiple workers committed suicide in what has been described as an extreme expression of anger, anxiety, alienation, and frustration (Chan et al. 2013; Pun et al. 2016). What we have here, in short, is the shattering of the hopes and dreams of the new generation of peasant workers by their desperate *dagong* experience in the cities.

Besides the extreme manifestation of suicide, Chris Chan and Elaine Hui (2012, 2016), and Kelvin Gray and Youngseok Jang (2015) conclude that workers' anger and frustration about their daily *dagong* experience contributed significantly to a growing level of class consciousness. This manifested itself in large-scale, organized, interest-based actions among the new generation of peasant workers. Thus, while protest actions by peasant workers were almost absent during the early 1990s (Lee 2002b), Chan and Hui's detailed study of the 2010 student workers' action at Honda's transmission and engine parts factory in Foshan, Guangdong Province, suggests growing intolerance of unfair income distribution. In the case of the Honda works, this resulted in a 17-day protest involving 1,800 workers (2012: 656; 2016). Unlike the situation at low-skilled exporting factories, Chan and Hui (2012, 2016) assert that the effective mobilization responsible for the Honda protest was grounded in peer networks previously established at vocational schools. The organizing capacity of this comparatively well-educated workforce was also fostered through their familiarity with electronic communication technologies, such as mobile text messaging and the internet. Significantly, this 'internet activism' was fostered by a high level of direct support from national and international intellectuals, as well as Hong Kong trade unions and NGOs (Xu 2013). The result of the coordination between the NGOs and Honda workers was a protest that forced the company to close four assembly plants, which immediately crippled Honda's auto production in China (Chan 2010a; Chan and Hui 2012, 2016; Gray and Jang 2015). While factory management had only partially redressed workers' protest demands (see below section and Chapter 4), studies describe this event as a watershed in workers' consciousness as they seized opportunity to demand an 80% (or 800 yuan) of 'big pay-rise' (Gray and Jang 2015: 602). Despite this, they also demanded a reform of trade union representation and the establishment of a system of workplace collective consultation (Chan and Hui 2012, 2016). In drawing wider lessons from this dispute, it is argued that the collective and sustained nature of the Honda dispute was indicative of workers forming themselves into a class-for-itself; an outcome that reflected their accumulated ***dagong*** experiences experienced over decades of working life (Smith and Pun 2006; Chan and Pun 2009; Leung and Pun 2009; Pun et al. 2009; Chan 2010a; Pun and Lu 2010a, b; Pringle 2011; Chan and Hui 2012, 2016; Pun et al. 2016).

Problems with the Working-Class Consciousness and Actions in China

For many, the increased volume of Chinese protest activities is proof of a "rising class consciousness" (Chan and Pun 2009; Chan 2010a; Chan and Hui 2016; Chan and Selden 2016). However, alternative studies (Lee 1999; Chen 2000; Blecher 2002; Chan 2011; Chan and Siu 2012; Chen 2006, 2016; Lee 2007; Cooke et al. 2016; Franceschini et al. 2016) highlight the quiescence of labor as a factor constraining workers against their exploitative conditions.

In arguing that quiescence is the defining characteristic of Chinese labor, Lee (1999) claims that a system of what they refer to as disorganized despotism has produced labor subordination through the flexible recruitment and dismissal of workers from a disposable labor market. Lee also argues that protests by peasant workers occurred only when the arbitration procedure failed to protect their legal rights. Similarly, their solidarity peaked only at the point of "collective exit from the factory, occasioned by plant closure or relocation" (2007: 175). In the wake of layoffs and plant closures, peasant workers also typically disperse into different locations to work without necessarily contacting one another again (Lee 2007). Thus, peasant workers were unable to develop much "workplace or associational bargaining power" to then form themselves into a *class-for-itself* (2007: 24). To substantiate this argument, Lee uses three insurgent identities of 'proletariat', 'citizen', and 'subaltern' to analyze the protests by both laid-off SOE workers and peasant workers, observing:

> I have found that class identity is more muted and ambivalent among migrant workers than among rustbelt [northern SOE] workers, whereas claims made on the basis of equality before the law and of citizens' right to legal justice are impassioned and firm, as in the Sunbelt [South China].

> Workers also identify themselves as the marginalized and the subordinate in society.
>
> (Lee 2007: 195)

Lee (2007) privileges the full citizenship status of SOE workers over the semi-citizenship status of peasant workers to explain their (perceived) higher level of class consciousness. This idea is indicated in Lee's concept of the 'protest of desperation' by laid-off SOE workers in relation to their unpaid pensions and *xiagang* payments. What linked this specific protest behavior to a wider consciousness was their sense of cultural and societal grievances related to the commodification of their daily lives in post-Mao China (Lee 2007). In Lee's estimation, therefore, the resistance patterns of SOE workers were underpinned by 'collective memories' of the 'socialist spirit' they associated with the Maoist era. As a result, layoffs generated a shared feeling of being 'betrayed by the Chinese capitalist-State' (2007: 71). This attitude stood in contrast to that of the peasant workers who lacked the past 'socialist spirit' as a Chinese working class, having come of age competitive and fragmented labor market that provided little in the way of either security or subsistence (Lee 2002b). It was in this context, Lee maintains, that the 'compromised' collective interests of peasant workers constrained their capacity to act collectively in the fragmented market (2000a).

Anita Chan and Kaxton Siu (2012) also point to the limited objectives and scope of even some of the largest and most successful strikes, such as that which occurred at the Honda plant (see previous section). As with disputes at SOEs and other export-oriented factories, the Honda dispute on serious and immediate economic grievances impacted workers at an individual level. Despite (largely temporary) successes at the factory level, there was no cross-over to coordinated action at a higher, cross-sectoral, cross-regional, or national level to consolidate and achieve further victories. As Chan and Siu observe,

> there have [been no] large-scale, coordinated and organized labor protests... nor have groups of workers from different factories made any collective demands on the local or central Chinese governments, nor have workers attempted to set up any independent trade unions at the workplace or multi-workplace level... [They] are cautious not to overstep the scope of their activities beyond economic rights-based demands.
>
> (Chan and Siu 2012: 84–99)

While the strikes and protests undertaken by Honda's workers, as well as other peasant and SOE workers, were viewed by many (Chan 2010a; Chan and Hui 2012, 2016; Gray and Jang 2015) as a class-based action, this view is hardly universal. Chan and Siu (2012) and Steve Hess (2013), for example, observe that the gains won by workers remained minimal. Honda's protest action, for example, was abandoned by groups of workers when they learned that they could receive individual wage increases as soon as they returned to work (Hess 2013). Worker disunity consequently destabilized the strike action. Although a wage increase of 24 to 32% was granted to the Honda workers, this was far less than what they had initially demanded (Hess 2013: 97). There is little evidence that the Honda workers understood the mechanics of workplace power, or that a permanent change to their condition involved a reconfiguration of trade union representation within the factory (Chan and Siu 2012: 91). In summing up the achievements and failings of the Honda workers, Chan and Siu conclude,

> Once satisfied that their economic demands had been met, they did not press for the immediate election of a new trade union committee. Thus, when the provincial trade union took several months to organize the first round of elections for 30 trade union representatives, workers' enthusiasm and sense of solidarity dissipated, along with their willingness to struggle for genuine representation.
>
> (Chan and Siu 2012: 91)

In her comparative study of labor protests in East Asian countries (2011), Anita Chan also highlights the differences between workers' grievances and industrial protests in Vietnam and China. Chan (2011) notes that while protest actions in both countries were spontaneous, unorganized, and lacked official union representation, the Vietnamese workers typically went on strike for *better* employment conditions. For example, they sought reduced work hours with better pay. In contrast, Chinese workers normally took action so as to *maintain* their previous employment conditions. Typically, they sought to restore wage rates and payment for overtime after these benefits had suffered managerial cutbacks. According to Chan, Chinese protests were also generally restrained by their confused understanding of the integral relationship between wages and work hours. They also lacked understanding of the kind of demands that needed to be made to improve their wages and overall employment conditions, e.g. improved representation rights, long-term labor contracts (2011: 35).

It has been accurately recorded that Chinese protest actions were generally characterized by limited coordination and commitments. Invariably, protests were isolated and directed toward specific, personalized objectives that individuals hoped to achieve collectively. These led to waves of protest actions that produced varying outcomes for the workers involved. Some returned to work with better gains, others with partial gains, and others failed to redress their economic grievances at all (Hess 2013: 99). Chan and Siu (2012: 89) note that, unlike their Western counterparts, Chinese workers lacked the accumulated historical experiences and traditions necessary to voice their collective interests in ways that permanently changed the industrial or legal landscape. We do not witness, for example, class-based struggles that led to improvements in legal minimum wages. Nor do we witness attempts to impose legal restructures on the hours of overtime that could be worked. Instead, collective actions occur only when employers breach the legal standards set for them (Chan and Siu 2012: 89). As a result, workers primarily fought for their 'right to subsistence'; a right which they were constantly under managerial assault (Chen 2000: 44). Where protests did extend beyond a single factory or company, they were invariably confined within specific occupational sectors (Hess 2013: 83). Hence, where labor actions did spread to multiple workplaces, these did not evolve into sustained organized action. Nor do we witness attempts to improve their bargaining position by forming organizational linkages with other workers on a regional or national level (Hess 2013: 88–99). A key factor behind the often directionless nature of Chinese protests was the restricted information available in the CCP's one-party authoritarian state; one characterized by an absence of reading materials on trade unions and labor movements, leading Chinese workers to have "little to inspire them to understand their own class position" (Chan and Siu 2012: 99).

In summing up the Chinese norm, Ivan Franceschini et al. (2016: 440) note that the wages typically demanded "are lower than the amount they are legally entitled to and for which they work more hours than the legal limits". Yanhua Deng and Jonathan Benney (2017: 92–99) describe this tendency as the 'misframing' of demands in ways that conform to the

Chinese concept of 'rightful resistance'.[17] As such, their protests align with—rather than confront—the existing political structure. Deng and Benney (2017) also note that the popular tendency to operate within a conformist mindset is one reinforced by China's hierarchical political structure. Within this structure, the different levels of government pursue differing operational objectives that have the effect of reinforcing the regime's overall power (2017). For example, the central government values the maintenance of social stability and harmony (*hexie*和諧) (see Chapter 2). In line with this objective, local governments are required to prevent "all visible forms of protest (the so-called 'zero target' model)" while, at the same time, ensuring regional economic development in different localities (Benney and Marolt 2015: 94). To achieve these objectives, local governments threaten severe penalties, ranging from fines to criminal prosecution (Benney 2016). In this content, so Deng and Benney note, the 'misframing' of demands causes protesters to ask "for something that is not actually what they 'want'" in hope of achieving partial gains within the perceived confines imposed by the regime (2017: 92). This suggests that workers are cautious to locate their protest demands within what they know of the *hefa quanyi* 合法權益 (legal rights) framework. Thus, the 'misframing' of demands illustrates a culture of silence that is reinforced by worker hesitancy when it comes to expressing their real grievances or concerns in protests.

Counter-Narratives

In countering the mainstream narrative in Chinese labor studies that highlights protest and resistance, the canon of alternative studies that highlights acquiescence and silence implies the existence of non-work mechanisms as well as workplace experiences that constrain the emergence of a proactive working class (or a *class-for-itself*).

While the Marxist enthusiasts have provided rich empirical narratives about the brutal work-based experiences of the Chinese working class, their ongoing discourse of "rising class consciousness" is constructed by narrowly focusing on protest activists in one or two large-size factories and even one individual worker. I regard their over-reliance on data that

[17] The concept of 'rightful resistance' is originally developed by Kelvin O'Brien to describe legal rights defense by Chinese protesters. See O'Brien, Kevin (1996) 'Rightful Resistance', *World Politics* 49: 31–55.

relates solely to protests and labor disputes as inappropriate. It assumes class antagonism, class consciousness, and class actions emerge *automatically* as the natural response to exploitation. If we look to the alternative literature, however, we are confronted with case studies and analyses that highlight the same intensity of exploitative conditions but different outcomes; ones characterized by conformity, silence, and protests that tend to be both spontaneous and narrowly focused.

What are the constraining factors that inhibit protest and facilitate conformity?

Some, such as Jake Lin (2017, 2019) suggests that patterns of silence and conformity occur because workers accept inequality as transitory, as part of China's transition from capitalism to socialism. Dorothy Solinger (2002, 2012), in contrast, suggests that Chinese workers are generally dissuaded from participating in protest activities by their prevailing day-to-day survival needs. If they decide their current circumstances are intolerable, then they prefer to expend their energies in seeking employment elsewhere. Adopting a Gramscian perspective, Marc Blecher (2002: 288) argues that workers' absorption of the hegemonic values of the free market has caused them to believe that their employment conditions are both acceptable and inevitable; beliefs that deter them from collective action. In William Hurst's (2008) estimation, it is regional disparities that act as the main barrier to a common working-class consciousness. Seen from this perspective, the uneven opportunities in China's different regional political economies inhibit coordinated protest actions. Not only is the bargaining power of workers highly variable from region to region, so too are immediate interests and grievances. In yet another explanation, Peter Ho (2007), and Eli Friedman and Lee (2010), believe that the CCP's careful toleration and restriction of labor NGOs' activities have guided workers toward non-confrontational acts when it comes to the State and its central agencies. In other words, they only seek what is allowed. Viewing matters from a wider perspective, John Hassard et al. (2007) assert that it is the sociocultural and institutional elements of Chinese society that have constrained class consciousness, causing works to confront their employers *as individuals* in the disorganized protest activities.

Exploring the Work and Non-Work Lives of Workers in China

The narratives of this book support the alternative view that the possibilities for class consciousness development are dependent on non-work-based factors that mediate between work-based experiences and consciousness. In doing so, it gives emphasis to the importance of place and of the cultures that are derived from place.

In her comparative study, for example, Elizabeth Perry (1993: 30) notes that workers' (re-) actions to their conditions in China—as with those in other East Asian societies—underline the importance of 'place' over 'class'. Although her definition of 'place' is wide-ranging, Perry regards the cultural traditions of Confucianism within the 'native place' (or 'original place') as a major element shaping workers' consciousness in China and East Asian countries that cannot be "fully explained by the familiar models of class consciousness inherited from the analysis of [Western] capitalism" (1996: 3). Hence, unlike their Western counterparts who turned localized protests into social movements, the non-class Chinese protests are generally limited in size, scale, and scope. Their objective is not social transformation but one of bettering one's status in ways that are informed by their 'older rules consciousness' (Perry 2009) or 'status consciousness' (Koo 2001). It is this consciousness that is deliberately constructed and retained through China's thought management (*sixiang guanli* 思想管理) (Brady 2008; see Chapters 2–4). It is within this system that the thoughts and behaviors of the Chinese working class are guided by their sense of the righteousness of moral actions grounded in their historical and cultural experiences.

In looking at class, conflict, and power in China, this book argues that it is wrong to perceive Chinese circumstances through the prism of Western historical experiences. Instead, the Chinese working class was born in the absence of many cultural and institutional factors identified as crucial to the formation of workers' class consciousness in the West. During the early days of industrialization in England, for example, labor struggles were led by artisans (or craftsmen) who considered themselves as skilled workers (Thompson 1966: 234–240). Later, as the factory system arose throughout the Industrial Revolution in the nineteenth century, factory workers inherited this tradition of class struggle (Thompson 1966: 243–268). Contrary to the English counterparts, artisans (*gongren* 宫

人)[18] in China occupied a very low societal status (Grasso et al. 2009). Many were originally slaves to manufacture iron weapons, paper and textile products for Chinese Emperors in Imperial periods (Zhang 2015). Without a historical and cultural history that was in anyway comparable to that enjoyed by the English working class had in which to form a class consciousness, generations of Chinese workers experienced proletarianization as atomized (or isolated) workers. Consequently, they endured social and political changes with little in the way of either expectations or a positive sense of identity as a Chinese working class (Wu 2016).

Aligned with the latter body of alternative literature, I propose that the consciousness, identity, and thus their activism of Chinese workers is (re-) shaped by Confucian values entrenched in cultural and historical. This perspective leads to the following propositions that inform the focus of this study:

1. Worker activism in China is influenced by a status consciousness (or 'older rules consciousness')
2. The 'older rules consciousness' has affected their willingness to engage in acts that are perceived as contradictory to their cultural (or social) practices in China
3. Workers' consciousness and their resistant activities are influenced by 'older rule consciousness', rather than work-based experiences alone

Recruitment of Everyday Workers in China

The originality of this research project resides in substantiating the above propositions, which are supported by original interviews with everyday workers[19] conducted between 2011 and 2014 across two phases of data

[18] Government slaves were referred to as *gongren* 宫人 in Imperial China. See Wagner, Donald (1998) *A Classical Chinese Reader: The Han Shu biography of Huo Guang*, New York: Routledge.

[19] The term everyday workers refers to those who sell their labour in exchange for a living wage. The term is interchangeable with that of ordinary workers, see Munck, Ronaldo (2004) Introduction: Globalisation and Labour Transnationalism. in Ronaldo Munck (ed.) *Labour and Globalisation: Results and Prospects*. Liverpool: Liverpool University Press. Ordinary workers refer to those skilled and unskilled wage labourers, male or female, across different occupations and industry types and sizes in the labour market. I chose to use the term everyday workers for this study to emphasize the lived experiences of workers, that is, their everyday experiences within and outside the production

collection in several locations in China. Growing up in Hong Kong, I am linguistically fluent in Cantonese and Mandarin[20] (or Putonghua). My linguistic abilities are crucial to the discovery of cultural meanings and perspectives that Chinese workers bring to bear on their daily lives in China.

To understand the basis upon which Chinese working-class formation was developing—and the opportunity this presents for resistance activity by workers to improve their living conditions—this project embraced an ethnographic fieldwork approach. Crucial to the success of ethnographic research is a bond of trust between the researcher and the community under study (Brewer 2000). Crafting this bond in China presented difficulties for a number of reasons. Foremost is the fact that conducting research in China is subject to a number of unspecified political restrictions. It was difficult to predict whether or not the research would encounter these and, if so, to what extent. Social polarization and diversification in Chinese society have also constrained access to certain communities (Thogersen and Heimer 2006). In my own case, this created difficulties in being able to initiate interviews and dialogue with workers for the data collection in China. This prompted the use of two key strategies. The first was spending time to establish a positive relationship with key informants (or primary sources)—for instance, labor activists, academic contacts, and labor NGOs—to develop an understanding of my research context and the cultural and social norms as well as to gain access to workers through their existing networks. Through these networks, I was able to build snowball contacts and organize interviews with everyday workers. These were carried out at NGO offices and at other locations where they provided legal consultations for workers, including Labor Bureau. Interviews were also undertaken at community-based service centers that provided workers with computer facilities, book

process as being the workers, to understand both their work and the way workers live. See Thompson, E.P. (1966) *The Making of the English Working Class*, New York: Vintage Books..

[20] Mandarin (or Putonghua) and Chinese simplified character is the only official form of Chinese language that acknowledged by the CCP in China; while Chinese Cantonese is the official spoken Chinese language with Chinese traditional character as the official form written language in Hong Kong that is used in education, broadcasting, government administration as well as daily communication. Apart from Cantonese, I learnt Mandarin from my parents. They were born in Indonesia where Mandarin was their native language used in Chinese community before migrating to Hong Kong.

lending services, interest classes, and recreational activities, and even at hospital wards that catered for work-related injuries. A second way in which interviews were obtained was through residence in the communities where workers were located. By residing where workers lived, I was able to develop familiarity with workers, observe and engage in their behavioral patterns by dining at the same eateries, and doing what workers generally did in their naturalistic setting.

Even in residing among communities of industrial laborers and artisans there still remained the dilemma of recruiting workers for interviews. As a result, part of the study was drawn on the technique of a 'guerrilla street interview'. Thomas Gold (1989: 180) describes this as "unchaperoned, spontaneous but structured participant observation and interviews as opportunities present themselves". Thus a 'guerrilla street interview' involves the process of observing people's daily behaviors and 'picking persons for research interviews by spontaneously engaging in seemingly idle, friendly conversation [with] people... on the streets' (Gold 1989; Solinger 2006: 161). In conducting the 'guerrilla street interview' in the sites I studied, I spent many hours on the streets in an attempt to speak to factory workers who were recognizable either by their clothing or appearance. Quite naturally, workers were either fearful, unwilling to talk to a stranger, or were in a rush going to work or on the way 'home'. Therefore, interviews were initially carried out in employment centers, known as Talent Markets (*rencai shichang* 人才市場), by approaching workers who were reading postings about employment opportunities with queries such as, 'What sort of jobs are you looking for?', 'Where are you from?', or 'How long have you been here?' After establishing this minimal level of trust, I presented these workers with my research *bona fides* and then conducted the 'street interviews' if they agreed. I also approached other workers outside of the Talent Markets with a friendly greeting, such as 'How are you?', presented my *bona fides,* and requested an interview. This approach enabled me to recruit *everyday* workers such as hotel cleaners, waitpersons of the small eateries, hawkers on the streets, and taxi drivers as well as factory workers. It also enabled me to include a wider group of workers in different age and gender groups with different work and non-work experiences across industries to gather a reservoir of rich ethnographic details and uncensored personal opinions and life stories that have subsequently informed the study.

Multiple Field Locations in China

Two phases of data were conducted in multiple locations. The first was in Shenzhen in Guangdong Province; Hefei city in Anhui Province; and Hangzhou in Zhejiang Province between 2011 and 2012. The second was in Panyu, Foshan, and Haizhu cities in Guangdong Province between 2013 and 2014. Figure 1.1 depicts the precise locations of these on a map of China:

Shenzhen was chosen because of its special economic zones (SEZs) which attract significant foreign investment (Harvey 2005). A 'flood' of peasant workers, nationwide have migrated here, providing the SEZs with cheap labor for their export factories (Harvey 2005). Resistance by these Shenzhen factory workers is a documented phenomenon (Chan and Pun 2009). Unlike Shenzhen, Hefei is an underdeveloped region with a large number of state-owned enterprises (SOEs), staffed largely by local workers (National Bureau of Statistic's Database 2011). By contrast, Hangzhou is one of the most developed regions with the largest number of domestic (or private) enterprises in China (National Bureau of

Fig. 1.1 Map of China

Statistic's Database 2011). As is the case with Shenzhen, this region has attracted a mixture of local and migrant peasant workers.

These three initial sites covered a spectrum of industry type, size, and worker occupation, enabling exploration of the research focus with everyday workers. However, the findings suggested that workers in these sites were relatively quiescent, as they appeared to have consented themselves 'voluntarily' to their exploitative conditions (Personal Interviews; Shenzhen, Hefei, Hangzhou, 2011 & 2012). Given the focus of this study was to understand how everyday-workers' lived experiences have influenced them to campaign against their employment conditions, it was decided to interview two additional groups of workers. In so doing, workers who had participated in protest actions were deliberately contacted in the second phase of data collection to explore the difference between those engaging in protest action and those who had not. This latter body of data was gathered in Panyu, Foshan, and Haizhu districts in Guangdong Province (Personal Interviews: from October 2013 to January 2014). Due to the sensitivities of workers engaging in protests in China, these workers were primarily organized through contacts with labor NGOs, including Asia Monitor Resource Centre (AMRC) and Labor Action China (LAC).

Worker Samples

A total of seventy-four interviews (n = 74) were conducted across the two phases of data collection. Table 1.2 summarizes the details of interviewees:

The findings are divided into two groups. Group One consists of fifty-two (n = 52) interviewees who had never participated in protests while twenty-two (n = 22) were in Group Two, that is, those who had engaged in protest action as summarized in Table 1.3.

Table 1.2 Profile of interviewees

	Phase 1 (2011–2012)	*Phase 2 (2013–2014)*	*Total*
Interviews	53	21	74
Gender	26 Females 27 Males	10 Females 11 Males	
Age	17–50	17–40	

Table 1.3 Interviews groupings

	Group 1 (Never engaged in protest activities)	*Group 2 (Engaged in protest activities)*	*Total*
Interviews	52	22	74
Gender	26 Females 26 Males	11 Females 11 Males	
Locations	Shenzhen Hefei Hangzhou	Shenzhen Hangzhou Panyu Haizhu Foshan	

In establishing a relationship between specific events in the stories to inform the techniques of narrative and discourse analysis, all interviews were translated and transcribed where Nvivo 12 Plus text analysis software was used to identify and code the narrative themes. The coding was a summary of each paragraph of interview transcripts that emerged from the data itself in a bottom-up fashion. Table 1.4 illustrates the coding.

Pseudonyms were assigned to all interviewed workers to protect their identities.

Taken all together, my interviews with both groups of everyday workers who had been either involved in worker protest action ($n = 21$) or not involved in worker protest action ($n = 53$) exposed a counter-factual: that is, despite having the world's largest workforce (Fujita and Hu 2001), the opportunity for Chinese workers to develop a level of individual consciousness that matures into a collective consciousness as a class of workers to willingly improve their living and working conditions remains limited. The findings suggest that while work-related experiences

Table 1.4 Coding example: 'Workers' Practices'

At the factory, I only obeyed and followed what I was told; brains were useless at a factory (Xiaoyuan)
We just won't do that because we won't want to go against our work leaders (Xiaoxin)
I can't talk to my boss because he hires me to do the job not to complain about the workload (Yaxing)

may have incited workers to engage in protests, class consciousness development among *everyday* workers has been severely constrained by factors rooted in their historical and cultural experiences (see Chapters 2–4).

From '*Class*' Power to Power-Knowledge Relations

The presentation of this alternative perspective requires different theoretical lens.

Departing from a Marxist framework that associates worker consciousness with experiences located in the capitalist structure of production relations, this book engages with the works of the French philosopher and historian Michel Foucault (1926–1984) to explore how workers' consciousness and experiences are constructed through the power-knowledge relations (or social relations). These relations, for Foucault and Rabinow (1991: 194), are inseparable as power produces reality and 'domains of objects and rituals of truth', that is, knowledge (or discourse). Such knowledge-power relationships are reinforced at the individual level through the work and non-work relations that they engage in: for example, relationship with work supervisors, co-workers, teachers, and parents in their power-knowledge relations. It is these human relationships with bodies of knowledge that categorized people into different societal positions, forming the basis of control and regulation by and among individuals in a particular culture (Foucault 1980b). Foucault would ask, for example, how do we know a parent as a parent and a child as a child? And would respond that we know this because of the construction of a truth about what constitutes a parent or child; a truth which is then circulated through discourse or speaking to become the dominant thought or knowledge about what constitutes a parent or child. When studying discourses, Foucault therefore focuses on how the truth affects individuals in their social relationships and the effects of that truth on their social world (1982). Foucault is especially interested in how the 'truth' about themselves affected an individual's notion of subjectivity, that is, how they behaved or acted in their world (1980b, 1982, 1997). Ideas about 'madness', for example, not only represent what we come to know as a mental illness, but also reflect the norms that wider society uses to judge what is normal and abnormal thinking and acting (Foucault 2001, 2006). It is the emergence of the form of normalizing judgment (or examination) across different institutions, such as schools and hospitals, that has guided the individual to spontaneously conform to the norm of behavior of their society (Smart 1985).

Given this general understanding of the relations between power-knowledge, discourses, and subjectivity, Foucault and Kritzman (1988) further develops the notion of governmentality to describe his work on rethinking the concept of governmentalization. Defined as 'the conduct of conduct', Foucault's concept of governmentality is characterized as subtle forms of governmental strategies, using particular types of knowledge (or truths) to govern the population (1980a). Thus, 'governmentality' relates to the how of governing: how we govern, how we are governed, and the relation between the government of the State, the government of ourselves and others, with particular *mentalities of government* that have emerged in particular societies (Dean 2010: 2). These mentalities are forms of knowing and thus become the rationalities by which we come to know an event or even people as true, that is, these rationalities help us to make meaning of the world. But, Foucault argues that our rationalities are constituted by a multitude of government apparatuses, such as schools and families, and practices (Foucault 2001; Skålén et al. 2008: 27). From this perspective, governmentality is thus a study of the collective and taken-for-granted discourses (truths or knowledge) regarding how we should behave in a particular social network or time (Dean 1994, 2010). Because these rationalities are embedded in our psyche or mentality, the truth of these rationalities in prescribing our behavior or even our social status is rarely questioned or problematized (Downing 2008: 17–18).

Organization of the Book

In the following chapter, I turn to Foucault and Rabinow (1991) methodology of genealogy (or historicalization method) that he employs to analyze how governmentality, or a certain knowledge, is established to govern subjects (or people) throughout history. This historicalization method is used to first identify important features of the present, and then examine the past to discover how knowledge was historically constructed through a series of events that have influenced our thoughts and hence behavior in the present day. This result is what Foucault refers to as a 'history of the present'. The chapter begins with a discussion of his way of using history as an analytical tool to question and analyze the problems of the development of thought, and to explore the historical forces of control that are exercised externally and internally upon individuals in shaping their consciousness to one that guides their behavior in the present day. The chapter then applies Foucault's genealogical account to trace the key historical events that spiritually and bodily made a docile working class since the Imperial China. The chapter argues that this mindset is a central component to (re-) make the Chinese working class continue subordinating themselves to the Chinese rulers in the past and even today's China.

In Chapter 3, "*Automictic Docility in Market Socialism*", I present the two phases of original field data elicited from 53 everyday workers in Group One—*who had never engaged in any protest activities*—that were gathered at a wide range of industries and occupations in multiple locations of China between 2011 and 2014. The chapter illustrates that, while the workers in this group had experienced prolonged exploitative conditions, their discourses reflected that the possibility of class consciousness development and class formation was undermined by the 'social truth' about their status (or identity) in the hierarchical relationships. This particular 'self-knowledge' reflects the effectiveness of Chinese governmentality in the *making* of automatic docile bodies and minds to serve the interests of their employers and the Chinese State.

Chapter 4 analyzes the two phases of empirical data elicited from 21 everyday workers in Group Two—*who had engaged in protest activities*—that was collected at multiple locations, mainly through contacts with labor NGOs in Hong Kong and Guangzhou Province in China between 2011 and 2014. This body of data illustrates that, while protest activities by this group of workers have seemingly opened up a space of possibility to transform the way they relate to themselves and to each other and to their conditions, these 'possibilities' are confined by their cultural knowledge within the 'social truth' about themselves. Thus, while the experiences of these workers have incited them to engage in protest activities, their actions are grounded in their immediate economic needs, and limited to 'prescribed' conditions in accordance with their *given* positions. This automatic compliance demonstrates their internal willingness to become the agents of maintaining the power-knowledge framework—consciously and subconsciously—by self-regulating themselves to attain a level of internal 'docility' to their *given* status.

Chapter 5 concludes this study with a discussion of the similarities between the two groups of everyday workers by illustrating the effects of governmentality as a result of the CCP's continuous efforts to internalize the "social truth" of Confucian knowledge about *being* the workers in their mindset so as to regulate their lives and *make* them serve as an instrument of the State for China's ongoing economic development. The implications of this will be reflected in the recent movements of resistance to the CCP in the post-colonial Hong Kong.

Bibliography

ACFTU. 1997. Labour Law of the People's Republic of China. http://www.acftu.org.cn/template/10002/file.jsp?cid=56&aid=31. Accessed 10 September 2012.

Althusser, Louis. 1965/2005. *For Marx*. New York: Verso.

Amnesty. (2019) 1989. Tiananmen Square Protests. https://www.amnesty.org.uk/china-1989-tiananmen-square-protests-demonstration-massacre. Accessed 11 August 2020.

Bao, Shuming, Gene Hsin Chang, Jeffrey Sachs, and Wing Thye Woo. 2002. Geographic Factors and China's Regional Development under Market Reforms, 1978–1998. *China Eocnomic Review* 13: 89–111.

Benney, Jonathan. 2013. *Defending Rights in Contemporary China: Reserving the Right*. New York: Routledge.

Benney, Jonathan. 2016. Weiwen at the Grassroots: China's Stability Maintenance Apparatus as a Means of Conflict Resolution. *Journal of Contemporary China* 25 (99): 389–405.

Benney, Jonathan, and Peter Marolt. 2015. Modes of Activism and Engagement in the Chinese Public Sphere. *Asian Studies Review* 39 (1): 88–89.

Biddulph, Sarah. 2015. *The Stability Imperative: Human Rights and Law in China*. Toronto: UBC Press.

Blecher, Marc. 2002. Hegemony and Workers' Politics in China. *The China Quarterly* (170): 283–303.

Brady, Anne-Marie. 2008. *Marketing Dictatorship: Propaganda and Thought Work in Contemporary China*. Maryland: Rowman & Littlefield Publishers.

Brewer, John. 2000. *Understanding Social Research: Ethnography Alan Bryman*. Buckingham: Open University Press.

Cai, Yongshun. 2002. The Resistance of Chinese Laid-Off Workers in the Reform Period. *The China Quarterly* 170: 327–344.

Chan, Anita. 1993. 'Revolution or Corporatism? Workers and Trade Unions in Post-Mao China. *Chicago Journals* 29: 31–36.

Chan, Anita. 2001. *China's Workers Under Assault: The Expoitation of Labour in a Globalizing Economy*. New York: An East Gate Book.
Chan, Anita. 2011. Strikes in China's Export Industries in Comparative Perspective. *The China Journal* 65: 27–51.
Chan, Anita, and Kaxton Siu. 2012. Chinese Migrant Workers: Factors Constraining the Emergence of Class Consciousness. In *China's Peasants and Workers: Changing Class Identities*, ed. Beatriz Carrillo and David Goodman. Northampton, MA: Edward Elgar Publishing Ltd.
Chan, Chris. 2010a. Class Struggle in China: Case Studies of Migrant Worker Strikes in the Pearl River Delta. *South African Review of Sociology* 41 (3): 61–80.
Chan, Kam Wing. 2010b. The Global Financial Crisis and Migrant Workers in China: 'There is No Future as a Labourer; Returning to the Village Has No Meaning. *Internaltional Journal of Urban and Regional Research* 34 (3): 659–677.
Chan, Chris. 2012. Community-Based Organizations for Migrant Workers' Rights: The Emergence of Labour NGOs in China. *Community Development Journal* 10: 1–17.
Chan, Chris, and Elaine Hui. 2012. The Dynamics and Dilemma of Workplace Trade Union Reform in China: The Case of the Honda Workers Strike. *Journal of Industrial Relations* 54 (5): 653–668.
Chan, Chris, and Elaine Hui. 2016. Bringing Class Struggles Back: A Marxian Analysis of the State and Class Relations in China. *Globalizations* 14 (2): 1–13.
Chan, Chris, and Ngai Pun. 2009. 'The Making of a New Working Class? A Study of Collectvie Actions of Migrant Workers in South China. *The China Quarterly* 198: 287–303.
Chan, Jenny. 2013. A Suicide Survivor: The Life of a Chinese Worker. *New Technology, Work and Employment* 28 (2): 84–99.
Chan, Jenny, Ngai Pun, and Mark Selden. 2013. The Politics of Global Production: Apple, Foxconn and China's New Working Class. *New Technologies, Work and Employment* 28 (2): 100–115.
Chan, Jenny, and Mark Selden. 2016. The Labour Politics of China's Rural Migrant. *Globalizations* 14 (2): 1–13.
Chan, Kam Wing, and Zhang Li. 1999. The Hukou System and Rural-Urban Migration in China: Processes and Changes. *The China Journal* 160: 818–855.
Chen, Feng. 2000. Subsistence Crises, Managerial Corruption and Labour Protests in China. *The China Journal* 44: 41–63.
Chen, Feng. 2003. Industrial Restructuring and Workers Resistance in China. *Modern China* 29 (2): 237–262.

Chen, Feng. 2006. Privatization and its Discontents in Chinese Factories. *The China Quarterly* 185: 42–60.
Chen, Feng. 2009. Union Power in China Source, Operation, and Constraints. *Modern China* 35: 662–689.
Chen, Feng. 2010. Trade Unions and the Quadripartite Interactions in Strke Settlement in China. *The China Quarterly* 201: 104–124.
Chen, Feng. 2016. China's Road to the Construction of Labour Rights. *Journal of Sociology* 52 (1): 24–38.
Chen, Ke. 2011. *Labour Law in China*. Alphen aan den Rijn, The Netherlands: Kluwer Law International BV.
China Labor Bulletin. 2021. https://maps.clb.org.hk/statistics?i18n_language=en_US&map=1&startDate=2011-01&endDate=2021-01&eventId=&keyword=&addressId=&parentAddressId=&address=&industry=&parentIndustry=&industryName=. Accessed 15 march 2021.
China Statistical Yearbook. 2015. http://www.stats.gov.cn/tjsj/ndsj/2013/indexeh.htm. Accessed 11 August 2016.
Cooke, Fang-Lee., Yuhua Xie, and Huimin Duan. 2016. Workers' Grievances and Resolution Mechanisms in Chinese Manufacturing Firms: Key Characteristics and the Influence of Contextual Factors. *The International Journal of Human Resource Management* 27 (18): 2119–2141.
Cooney, Sean. 2006–2007. Making Chinese Labor Law Work: The Prospects for Regulatiory Innovation in the People's Republic of China. *Fordham International Labour Journal* 30: 1053–1097.
Cooney, Sean, Sarah Biddulph, and Ying Zhu. 2013. *Law and Fair Work in China*. New York: Routledge.
Database. 2011. Main Indicatior of Private Industrial Enterprises (by Region). http://219.235.129.58/reportView.do?Url=/xmlFiles/en/42e506eeaea24621bec9bcb589ec0a4d.xml&id=0dc9400055324e318b7cf88637af6548&bgqDm=20110000&i18nLang=en_AU. Accessed 31 January 2013.
Dean, Mitchell. 1994. *Critical and Effective Histories: Foucault's Methods and Historical Sociology*. London: Routledge.
Dean, Mitchell. 2010. *Governmentality: Power and Rule in Modern Society*. Los Angeles: Sage.
Deng, Yunhua, and Jonathan Benney. 2017. Selective Use of Political Opportunity: A Case of Environmental Protest in Rural China. *Journal of Chinese Governance* 2 (1): 91–105.
Downing, Lisa. 2008. *The Cambridge Introduction to Michel Foucault*. Cambridge: Cambridge University Press.
Estlund, Cynthia. 2017. *A New Deal for China's Workers?* Massachusetts: Harvard University Press.

Fan, Cindy. 2003. Rural-Urban Migration and Gender Division of Labor in Transitional China. *International JOurnal of Urban and Regional Research* 27 (1): 24–47.

Fan, Cindy. 2004. The State, the Migrant Labor Regime, and Maiden Workers in China. *Political Geography* 23: 283–305.

Foucault, Michel. 1980. *Power/Knowledge: Selected Interviews and Other Writings 1972–1977*. New York: Vintage Books.

Foucault, Michel. 1980. *Truth and Subjectivity Howison Lectures*. Berkeley: University of California.

Foucault, Michel. 1982. The Subject and Power. In *Michel Foucault: Beyond Structuralism and Hermeneutics*, ed. Hubert Dreyfus and Paul Rabinow. Chicago: University of Chicago Press.

Foucault, Michel. 1997. *Ethics, Subjectivity and Truth: The Essential Works of Foucault 1954–1984*. New York: The New Press.

Foucault, Michel. 2001. *Madness and Civilization: A History of Insanity in the Age of Reason*. New York: Vintage Books.

Foucault, Michel. 2006. *History of Madness*. New York: Routledge.

Foucault, Michel, and Lawrence Kritzman. 1988. *Politics, Philosophy, Culture : Interviews and Other writings, 1977–1984*. New York: Routledge.

Foucault, Michel, and Paul Rabinow. 1991. *The Foucault Reader: An Introduction to Foucault's Thought*. Harmondsworth: Penguin.

Franceschini, Ivan, Kaxton Siu, and Anita Chan. 2016. The "Rights Awakening" of Chinese Migrant Workers: Beyond the Generational Perspective. *Critical Asian Studies* 48 (3): 422–442.

Friedman, Eli, and Ching Kwan Lee. 2010. Remaking the World of Chinese Labour: A 30-Year Retrospective. *British Journal of Industrial Relations* 48 (3): 507–533.

Fujita, Masahisa, and Dapeng Hu. 2001. Regional Disparity in China 1985–1994: The Effects of Globalization and Economic Liber. *The Annals of Regional Science* 35: 3–37.

Gallagher, Mary. 2005. "Use the Law as Your Weapon!": institutional Change and Legal Mobilization in China. In *Engaging the Law in China: State, Society, and Possibilities for Justice*, ed. Neil Diamant Staanley Lubman and Kelvin O'Brien. Stanford: Stanford University Press.

Gallagher, Mary. 2006. Mobilizing the Law in China: "Informed Disenchantment" and the Development of Legal Consciousness. *Law & Society Review* 40 (4): 783–816.

Gallagher, Mary. 2007. *Contagious Capitalism: Globalization and the Politics of Labor in China*. New Jersey: Princeton University Press.

Gallagher, Mary, John Giles, Albert Park, and Meiyan Wang. 2013. China's 2008 Labor Contract Law: Implementation and Implications for China's Workers: The World Bank.

Gold, Thomas. 1989. Guerrilla Interviewing Among the Getihu. In *Unofficial China: Popular Culture and Thought in the People's Republic*, ed. Perry Link Richard Madsen and Paul Pickowicz. London: Westview Press.

Goldman, Merle. 2000. The Potential for Instability Among Intellectuals and Students in Post-Mao China. In *Is China Unstable?: Assessing the Factors: Assessing the Factors*, ed. David Shambaugh. New York: M.E. Sharpe Inc.

Gramsci, Antonio. 1988/2000. *The Gramsci Reader: Selected Writings, 1916–1935*. New York: New York University Press.

Grasso, June, Jay Corrin, and Michael Kort. 2009. *Modernization and Revolution: From the Opium Wars to the Olympics*. New York: M.E. Sharpe Inc.

Gray, Kevin, and Youngseok Jang. 2015. Labour Unrest in the Global Political Economy: The Case of China's 2010 Strike Wave. *New Political Economy* 20 (4): 594–613.

Harvey, David. 2005. *A Brief History of Neoliberalism*. New York: Oxford University Press.

Hassard, John, Jackie Sheehan, Meixiang Zhou, Jane Terpstra-Tong, and Jonathan Morris. 2007. *China's State Enterprise Reform: From Marx to the Market*. New York: Routledge.

Haugaard, Mark. 1997. *The Constitution of Power: A Theoretical Analysis of Power, Knowledge and Structure, Manchester*. Manchester: Manchester University Press.

Hess, Steve. 2013. *Authoritarian Landscapes: Popular Mobilization and the Institutional Sources of Resilience in Nondemocracies*. New York: Sprinkler.

Ho, Peter. 2007. Embedded Activism and Political Change in a Semiauthoritarian Context. *China Information* 21 (2): 187–209.

Howell, Jude. 2008. All-China Federation of Trades Unions Beyond Reform? The Slow March of Direct Elections. *The China Quarterly* 196: 845–863.

Howell, Judy. 1998. An Unholy Trinity? Civil Society, Economic Liberalization and Democratization in Post-Mao China. *Government and Opposition* 33 (1): 56–80.

Huan, Guocang. 1986. China's Open Door Policy, 1978–1984. *China in Transition* 39 (2): 1–18.

Hui, Elaine. 2020. Labor-Related Civil Society Actors in China: A Gramscian Analysis. *Theory and Society* 49: 49–74.

Hunter, Christopher, Louisa Lam, and Ketong Lin. 2008. *Employment Law in China*. Hong Kong: CCH Hong Kong Limited.

Hurst, William. 2008. Mass Frames and Worker Protest. In *Popular Protest in China*, ed. Kevin O'Brien. Cambridge, MA: Harvard University Press.

Hurst, William, and Kelvin O'Brien. 2002. China's Contentious Pensioners. *The China Quarterly* 170: 345–360.

ITUC. 2010. Internationally Recognised Core Labour Standards in the People's Republic of China: Report for teh WTO General Council Review of the Trade Policies of the People's Republic of China. http://www.ituc-csi.org/IMG/pdf/Chinal_Final-2.pdf. Accessed 2 November 2012.

Jantz, Jilka. 2010. Soft Approaches to Social and Labor Standards in Adverse Environments: The Case of Sector Wide Self Regulation in the post-ATC Textile and Clothing Industry: University of Potsdam.

Keith, Ronald, and Zhiqui Lin. 2003. The "Falun Gong Problem": Politics and the Struggle for the Rule of Law in China. *The China Quarterly* 175: 623–642.

Kent, Ann. 2007. *Beyond Compliance: China, International Prganizations, and Global Security*. Standford, CA: Standford University Press.

Koo, Hagen. 2001. *Korean Workers: The Culture and Politics of Class Formation*. London: Cornell University Press.

Korsch, Karl. 1938/2016. *Karl Marx*. Boston: Brill.

Lai, Hongyi. 2010. *The Domestic Sources of China's Foreign Policy: Regimes Leadership, Priorities and Process*. New York: Routledge.

Lee, Ching Kwan. 1999. From Organized Dependence to Disorganized Despotism: Changing Labour Regimes in Chinese Factories. *The China Quarterly* 45: 44–71.

Lee, Ching Kwan. 2000a. Pathways of Labour Insurgency. In *Chinese Society, 2nd Edition: Change, Conflict and Resistance*, ed. Elizabeth Perry and Mark Selden. New York: Routledge.

Lee, Ching Kwan. 2000. The "Revenge of History": Collective Memories and Labor Protests in North-Eastern China. *Ethnography* 1 (2): 217–237.

Lee, Ching Kwan. 2002. From the Specter of Mao to the Spirit of the Law: Labor Insurgency in China. *Theory and Society* 31: 189–228.

Lee, Ching Kwan. 2002. Revisiting the South China Miracle. *Lador Studies Journal* 27 (2): 61–64.

Lee, Ching Kwan. 2007. *Against the Law: Labor Protests in China's Rustbelt and Sunbelt*. Berkeley: University of California Press.

Lehman. 2008. Labour Contract Law of the People's Republic of China. http://www.lehmanlaw.com/fileadmin/lehmanlaw_com/laws___regulations/Labor_Contract_Law_of_the_PRC__LLX__06292007_.pdf. Accessed 12 October 2010.

Lenin, Vladimir. 1918/1992. *The State and Revolution*. London: Penguin Books.

Leung, Elly, and Donella Caspersz. 2016. Exploring Worker Consciousness in China. *Labour & Industry: A Journal of the Social and Economic Relations of Work* 26 (3): 237–250.

Leung, Paknang, and Ngai Pun. 2009. The Radicalisation of the New Chinese Working Class: A Case Study of Collective Action in the Gemstone Industry. *Third World Quarterly* 30 (3): 551–565.

Li, Lianjiang, and Kevin O'Brien. 1996. Villagers and Popular Resistance in Contemporary China. *Modern China* 22 (1): 28–61.

Li, Sheng. 2006. Low Wage and Low Labor Standards in China: A Substitute Explanation of 'The Race-to-the-Bottom'. In *The Chinese Economy after WTO Accession*, ed. Shuming Bao Changwen Zhao and Shuanglin Lin. Hampshire: Ashgate Publishing Limited.

Li, Xiaobing. 2012. *China at War: An Encyclopedia*. Santa Barbara, CA: ABC-CLIO, LLC.

Lin, Jake. 2017. Do More Strikes Mean a Stronger Working Class's Agency: A Comparative Study in Post-Socialist China. *Journal of Labor and Society* 20: 85–106.

Lin, Jake. 2019. Chinese Politics and Labor Movements.

Lin, Kelvin. 2015. Recomposing Chinese Migrant and State-Sector Workers. In *Chinese Workers in Comparative Perspective*, ed. Anita Chan. Ithaca: Cornell University Press.

Lorimer, Doug. 2004. *The Class Nature of the People's Republic of China*. Newtown: Resistance Books.

Lu, Yiyi. 2009. *Non-Governmental Organizations in China: The Rise of Dependent Autonomy*. New York: Routledge.

Lukacs, Georg. 1968. *History and Class Consciousness: Studies in Marxist Dialectics*. Massachusetts: The MIT Press.

Mallee, Hein. 2000. Migration, Hukou, Resistance in Reform China. In *Chinese Society, 2nd Edition: Change, Conflict and Resistance*, ed. Elizabeth Perry and Mark Selden. New York: Routledge.

Marx, Karl. 1844/2007. *Economic and Philosophic Manuscripts of 1844*. New York: Dover Publications.

Marx, Karl. 1894/1992. *Capital*. London: Penguin Books.

Merchant, Toby. 2004. Recognizing ILO Rights to Organize and Bargain Collectively; Grease in China's Transition to a Socialist Market Economy. *Case Western Reserve Journal of International Law* 36 (223): 223–253.

Munck, Ronaldo. 2004. Introduction: Globalisation and Labour Transnationalism. In *Labour and Globalisation: Results and Prospects*, ed. Ronaldo Munck. Liverpool: Liverpool University Press.

O'Brien, Kevin. 1996. Rightful Resistance. *World Politics* 49: 31–55.

Perry, Elizabeth. 1993. *Shanghai on Strike: The Politics of Chinese Labor*. California: Standford University Press.

Perry, Elizabeth. 1996. Introduction: Putting Class in its Place: Bases of Worker Identity. In *Putting Class in its Place: Worker Identities in East Asia*, ed. Elizabeth Perry. Los Angeles, CA: University of California.

Perry, Elizabeth. 2009. A New Rights Consciouness? *Journal of Democracy* 20 (3): 17–20.

Potter, Pitman. 2001. *The Chinese Legal System: Globalization and Local Legal Culture*. New York: Routledge.

Pringle, Tim. 2011. *Trade Unions in China: The Challenge of Labour Unrest*. New York: Routledge.

Pringle, Tim, and Simon Clarke. 2011. *The Challenge of Transition: Trade Unions in Russia, China and Vietnam*. New York: Palgrave Macmillan.

Pun, Ngai. 2005. *Made in China: Women Factory Workers in a Global Workplace*. Durham: Duke University Press.

Pun, Ngai. 2007. Gendering the Dormitory Labor System: Production, Reproduction, and Migrant Labor in South China. *Feminist Economics* 13 (3–4): 239–258.

Pun, Ngai. 2019. The New Chinese Working Class in Struggle. *Dialectical Anthropology* 44: 319–329.

Pun, Ngai, Chris Chan, and Jenny Chan. 2009. The Role of the State, Labour Policy and Migrant Workers Struggles in Globalized China. *Global Labour Journal* 1 (1): 132–151.

Pun, Ngai, and Jenny Chan. 2012. Global Capital, the State, and Chinese Workers: The Foxconn Experience. *Modern China* 38 (4): 383–410.

Pun, Ngai, and Huilin Lu. 2010. A Culture of Violence: The Labor Subcontracting System and Collective Action by Construction Workers in Post-Socialist China. *The China Journal* 64: 143–158.

Pun, Ngai, and Huilin Lu. 2010. Unfinished Proletarianization: Self, Anger, and Class Action among the Second Generation of Peasant-Workers in Present-Day China. *Modern China* 36 (5): 493–519.

Pun, Ngai, Yuan Shen, Yuhua Guo, Huilin Lu, Jenny Chan, and Mark Selden. 2016. Apple, Foxconn, and Chinese Workers Struggles from a Global Labor Perspective. *Inter-Asia Cultural Studies* 17 (2): 166–185.

Qi, Dangtao. 2010. Chinese Working Class and Trade Unions in the Post-Mao Era: Progress and Predicament. *International Journal of China Studies* 1 (2): 413–433.

Shepley, Nick. 2013. *Russia's Struggle With Modernity 1815–1929*. Bedfordshire: Andrews UK Limited.

Silver, Beverly, and Zhang, Lu. 2009. China as an Emerging Epicenter of World Labor Unrest. In *China and the Transformation of Global Capitalism*, ed. Ho-fung Hung. Baltimore, MD: The Johns Hopkins University Press.

Skålén, Per, Martin Fougère, and Markus Fellesson. 2008. *Marketing Discourse: A Critical Perspective*. New York: Routledge.

Smart, Barry. 1985. *Michel Foucault*. London: Tavistock Publications Limited.

Smith, Chris, and Jenny Chan. 2015. Working for Two Bosses: Student Interns as Constrained Labour in China. *Journal of Human Relations* 68 (2): 305–326.

Smith, Chris, and Ngai Pun. 2006. The Dormitory Labour Regime in China as a Site for Control and Resistance. *The International Journal of Human Resource Management* 17 (8): 1456–1470.

Solinger, Dorothy. 2002. Labour Market Reform and the Plight of the Laid-off Proletariat. *The China Quarterly* (170): 304–326.

Solinger, Dorothy. 2006. Interviewing Chinese People: From High-Level Officials to the Unemployed. In *Doing Fieldwork in China*, ed. Maria Heimer and Stig Thogersen. Honolulu: University of Hawai'i Press.

Solinger, Dorothy. 2012. The New Urban Underclass and its Consciousness: Is it a Class? *Journal of Contemporary China* 21 (78): 1011–1028.

Su, Yang, and Xin He. 2010. Street as Courtroom: State Accomodation of Labor Protest in South China. *Law & Society Review* 44 (1): 157–184.

The Washington Post. 1989. https://www.washingtonpost.com/archive/opinions/1989/08/06/kissingers-kowtow/c23ac659-2da5-449c-bc31-e43628d3f005/. Accessed 11 August 2020.

The World Bank. 2019. www.worldbank.org/en/country/china/overview. Accessed 10 October 2019.

Thogersen, Sig, and Heimer, Maria. 2006. Introduction. In *Doing Fieldwork in China*, ed. Maria Heimer and Stig Thogersen. Hawaii: NIAS Press.

Thompson, E.P. 1966. *The Making of the English Working Class*. New York: Vintage Books.

Thompson, E.P. 1978. Eighteenth-Century English Society: Class Struggle without Class? *Social History* 3 (2): 133–165.

Tong, Yanqi, and Shaohua Lei. 2010. Large-Scale Mass Incidents and Government Responses in China. *International Journal of China Studies* 1 (2): 487–508.

UNHCR. 1989. Law of the People's Republic of China on Assemblies, Processions and Demonstrations. http://www.unhcr.org/refworld/docid/3ae6b592e.html. Accessed 22 October 2012.

UNHRC. 1997. Criminal Law of the People's Republic of China. http://www.unhcr.org/cgi-bin/texis/vtx/refworld/rwmain?docid=3ae6b5cd2&page=search. Accessed 31 October 2012.

Wagner, Donald. 1998. *A Classical Chinese Reader: The Han Shu biography of Huo Guang*. New York: Routledge.

Walder, Andrew. 1991. Workers, Managers and the State: The Reform Era and the Political Crisis of 1989. *The China Quarterly* 127: 467–492.

Walder, Andrew, and Xiaoxia Gong. 1993. Workers in the Tiananmen Protests: The Politics of the Beijing Workers' Autonomous. *The Australian Journal of Chinese Affairs* 29: 1–29.

Wang, Tianyu, and Fang-Lee Cooke. 2016. Striking the balance in industrial relations in China? An analysis of court decisions of 897 strike cases (2008–2015). *Journal of Industral Relations* 59 (1): 22–43.

Warner, Malcolm. 1991. Labour-Management Relations in the People's Republic of China: The Role of the Trade Unions. *The International Journal of Human Resource Management* 2 (2): 205–220.

Wong, Linda. 2011. Chinese Migrant Workers: Rights Attainment Deficits, Rights Consciousness and Personal Strategies. *The China Quarterly* 208: 870–892.

Wu, Chongqing. 2016. Introduction. In *Mapping China: Peasants, Migrant Workers and Informal Labor*, ed. Chongqing Wu. Leiden, The Netherlands: Koninklijke Brill.

Yi, Xu. 2013. Labor Non-Governmental Organizations in China: Mobilizing Rural Migrant Workers. *Journal of Industral Relations* 55 (2): 243–259.

Zhang, Qizhi. 2015. *An Introduction to Chinese History and Culture*. New York: Springer.

CHAPTER 2

The (Re-) Making of a Docile Working Class in China

> I have tried to get out from the philosophy of the subject through a genealogy of this subject, by studying the constitution of the subject across history which has led us up to the modern concept of the self. This has not always been an easy task, since most historians prefer a history of social processes (where society plays the role of the subject) and most philosophers prefer a subject without history.
>
> (Foucault, 1997b: 176)

This chapter applies Foucault and Rabinow (1991) genealogical (or historicalization) methods to analyze the historical events that (re-) shaped worker consciousness and working-class politics in today's China.

As noted previously, Foucault and Rabinow (1991: 95) historical studies illustrate the effects of power-knowledge relations in conditioning individuals into certain kinds of thinking. Contrary to the traditional conceptualization of a knowing consciousness, Foucault argues that individuals' consciousness is historically constituted through forms of constructed knowledge (truth or discourse). His analysis of madness (2006), imprisonment (1977), and sexuality (1976) has each demonstrated that these discourses are historically established to inform individuals' experiences in their social interactions. In *The History of Sexuality* (1976, 1986, 1990), for example, Foucault analyzes how individuals'

E. Leung, *The (Re)Making of the Chinese Working Class*, Palgrave Debates in Business History,
https://doi.org/10.1007/978-3-030-83313-8_2

experiences were objectified by the "medical knowledge" of 'homosexuality' since the nineteenth century. 'Homosexuality' was a historical discourse constructed by "sexual scientists" to refer, not to the natural kinds of practices, but to 'abnormal' sexual practices in Western societies. Practices thus represented social reality that further constituted categories of people—for example, 'heterosexuals'/ 'homosexuals'—who behaved and acted according to that "scientific knowledge". These kinds of "truths" subsequently worked to influence the ways people managed themselves, lived their lives, and related to themselves and others (or governmentality) in particular ways. These looping effects of the (re-) production of subjects (or individuals) through the relations of power established over the accepted forms of knowledge (or power-knowledge relations) are the focus of analysis in Foucault's works.

In challenging against the power-knowledge that exercises over our lives, Foucault (1971/1977) develops a genealogical method to produce a *history of the present* (counter-history or effective history). This method requires a thorough study of history through detailed documentation of historical events and facts to investigate the inevitable character of "problematic" forms of practices that are 'brought into play' in the present. History, by definition, is about the past. However, Foucault's historical analysis begins with his perception that something is problematic in the present. In so doing, Foucault engages with the 'past' (or history) to demonstrate that certain problems of current social circumstances, such as 'sexuality', are linked to that past. For instance, Foucault was directly involved in political campaigns for the reformation of the prisons in France in his day (1977). To inquire about the status of French prisons, his text *Discipline and Punish* (1977) showed how the punishment systems were problematized in the past and how the imprisonment practices of 'the present' were related to those previous problems. The characterization of *Discipline and Punish* as a 'history of the present' considers the history of a problem in relation to how that problem is now seen in the present.

This chapter argues that the (re-) creation of a docile working class is a central component for the Chinese Communist Party (CCP) to monopolize its political power in its thought management system. To substantiate this argument, I begin the chapter by summarizing Foucault's works that rest on his interrelated themes surrounding the concepts of power/knowledge, governmentality, and ethics (or care of the self). I then discuss Foucault's geneaological method that he uses to diagnose the problematic forms of our thoughts and practices in the present. Finally, I apply Foucault's method to investigate the ways CCP exercised its power to develop Chinese governmentality among workers by analyzing key historical events.

Power/Knowledge and Governmentality

Under the rubric of genealogy, Michel Foucault (1980a; b) proposes the concept of governmentality to investigate the technologies (techniques or strategies) of power exercised to govern individuals.

Foucault's genealogical work of governmentality explores how certain knowledge emerges as a social "truth" to shape thoughts and behaviors among individuals in particular society (1980b, 1982). Much like sexuality, our scientific understanding of ourselves as maleness or femaleness leads us to think "we know ourselves". Our knowing of our true sexual identities is revealed by Foucault as effective functioning of the discourses in constituting us as "normal" men and women. To be "normal" in our stable gender categories, we thereby uphold our "proper" gender behavior and desire for the opposite sex in our social relations. For instance, what makes us perceive someone as sexually sick or a pervert emerges because of the power relations that confirmed this as 'knowledge' (or objectify) in webs of beliefs (Foucault and Rabinow 1991, 2001). Knowledge, therefore, worked to internalize disciplinary power (or "microphysics of power" or "biopower") by the individuals themselves to self-govern their (and others') thoughts and behaviors in their power-knowledge relations (1977: 26).

Unlike the juridical view that power is exercised by the State and its apparatuses (see Giddens and Dallmayr 1982; Crowther and Green 2004; Musto 2012; Noon et al. 2013), Foucault and Rabinow focuses on the capillary nature and the dispersed character of micro-power that is exercised through the networks of productive, individual relations. Their engagement in co-constructing the realities according to the given discourses, such as 'criminals' and 'madmen', has worked to shape and correct their minds and behaviors in their power networks (1991). This view of power is elaborated in Foucault's understanding of Jeremy Bentham's (1843: 39) nineteenth-century interior design of the Panopticon (or prison). The Panopticon consists of a circular structure with an inspection house at the center of the tower. The concept of this design is to guide the prisoners to believe the watchmen in the tower are observing them as they cannot see into the tower, and hence they self-regulate their behaviors as if they are being watched. This form of self-government (or self-regulation) creates a 'new mode of obtaining power of mind over mind [governmentality or "conduct of conduct" in Foucault's terminology], in a quantity…' (Bentham 1843: 39) to effectively control and reform the criminals (Magill 1997; Oksala 2007: 57). This is because the truth of *being watched* under constant surveillance in the panoptic system facilitates the automatic functioning of a disciplinary power within the minds and bodies of the criminals without external authority being imposed (Ransom 1997).

Using the metaphor of the Panopticon, Foucault (1977) notes that a disciplinary power is embedded in all levels of social relations in smaller elements like the hospitals, the schools, the factories, the prisons and even in individuals' families. Together these social relations exercise a *regime* of a disciplinary power among the masses of people to produce a norm (truth or rule) of behaviors, all the while ensuring that deviant behaviors from this norm are identified as needing to be corrected according to their identities such as 'homosexuals' or even 'criminals'. For example, schools and families constitute minute social 'observatories' and surveillance systems to train and correct children's behavior—their piety and morals—toward their teachers and parents (Foucault 1977). Foucault (1977) suggests that these domains subsequently resemble a carceral (or prison) system that creates a dominant class of manageable, controllable useful bodies who serve as the judges of normality in society—the teacher-judge, the doctor-judge, and the social worker-judge—to ensure everyone acts to the discourses of truth that are embedded in a particular society (Foucault 1980a, b; Foucault and Rabinow 1991).

The extension of the panoptical power exercised in various social settings has made individuals subject their bodies, soul, and practices to the given "truth" of their society. Foucault (1980a, b) argues that a disciplinary society emerges, not by the making of laws, but by the internalization of norms that have conjoined the mind, body, and movement of individuals. This effect is referred to as governmentality (or conduct of conduct) that guides the individuals to self-regulate their own (and others') behavior, to achieve the status of truths (or norms) of their society within their power-knowledge network of their culture without engaging in critical thinking (Foucault 1980b). Foucault thus describes the outcome of this government of mentalities as the effective operations of both direct (the State or institutions per se) and indirect (the social network) forms of disciplinary power in guiding people's behaviors to the *desired end* of others (2008).

For Foucault (1982), the intertwined relations of the discourses and governmentality are problematic to individuals in the processes of subjectivation[1] (or the self). His work on, for instance, 'madness' and 'criminals', illustrates the nature of selfhood within the forms of discourses that have worked to constitute individuals as specific kinds of subjects in self-governing and self-regulating their thoughts and behaviors in particular ways (Davidson 2003). It is in such a way that self-formation is repressed by truths from outside the self in its own history. That is, the force of a carceral system is to repress any other thought about how else "we can think about what we come to know as being true".

In *The History of Sexuality* (1978), for example, Foucault draws on a long history of Christian confession. In this work, he analyzed the Western values of sex since the seventeenth century to reveal how sexual knowledge such as "sex with boys" was constructed as evil and sin. This discourse had ultimately tied individuals into that given "truth" about sex and turn themselves into silent subjects. Just like the truth of "sex with boys is evil" in Christianity, our self-formation in the processes of becoming "who we are and so what we do" is grounded in the moral majority (Besley and Peters 2007: 41) about what is regarded as 'truth' (Richardson and Woolfolk 2013: 11) in the specific social relations. It is within these relationships that the conduct (or behavior) of the subject (or the self) has become governed by others while at the same time become the governor of the self (or the government of the self) in the given power-knowledge networks (Dean 2010).

The government of the self is crucial in Foucault's (1987) analysis of the power resistance against the specific normalizing disciplinary practices in particular culture(s). For example, cultural representations of the body and its sex are constructed as natural for gender identification. This knowledge forces individuals into two opposite gender categories that (re-) produced normative practices based on the social expectations of what it means by "normal" (Oksala 2005). Taking the homosexuals as an example, Foucault argues that those engaged in sadomasochistic (or SM) activities had organized themselves as alternative communities. Doing so

[1] Subjectivation is a process of self-formation in which individuals construct identities for themselves throughout the process. See Clifford, Michael (2001) *Political Genealogy After Foucault: Savage Identities*, New York: Routledge.

enabled them to escape aping heterosexuality and culturally approved coupledom around their own principles of 'pleasures and bodies' (1997a). The notion of 'bodies and pleasures' thus becomes an important element for resistance. For instance, performing gay SM sexual activities for bodily pleasures, such as binding the penis, through sex desires or fantasies, challenged the normative queer idea that the gay identity must perform certain acts (Downing 2008). Using this examples, Foucault wishes to show that the refusal of the gay SM to act in accordance with what queer identification is habitually put is a form of reversal power that presents a possibility for subverting normalization or normative practices of the 'true' identity categories.

Thus, while forms of subjectivity correspond to the discourses of truths, Foucault (1997a) argues that re-subjectivation (or alternative self-reformation) can be achieved through ethical practices (or aesthetics of existence). In an interview in 1984, Foucault (1997a) emphasizes that the discourse of truth is an *ascetic* practice of self-reformation. *Ascetic*, as Foucault defines, is an "exercise of self upon the self by which one attempts to develop and transform oneself, and to attain a certain mode of being" (1997a: 282). This task is focused on practices related to taking care of one's soul in order to make one's life into an art of existence:

> When you take care of the body, you do not take care of the self. The self is not clothing, tools or possessions; it is to be found in the principle that uses these tools, a principle not of the body but of the soul. You have to worry about your soul – that is the principal activity of caring for yourself. The care of the self is the care of the activity and not the care of the soul-as-substance.
>
> (Foucault 1997a: 230)

Foucault (1997a) perceives taking care of the self-as-soul as a form of knowing the self (*gnothi seauton*), which enables one to relate the self and its life, not as something simply given, but as a thing that can be transformed in the direction of freedom. Foucault's genealogical study of his unfinished project of the *Care of the Self* (1986) illustrates how the Greek monastics transformed themselves by adjusting the codes of sexual conduct within Christian discourses:

> each of the three great arts of self-conduct, the three major techniques of the self, that were developed in Greek thought – dietetics, economics and erotics – proposed, if not a particular sexual ethic, then at least a singular modulation of sexual conduct. In this elaboration of the demands

> of austerity, not only did the Greeks not seek to define a code of conduct binding everyone, neither did they seek to organize sexual behaviour as a domain governed in all its aspects by one and the same set of principles.
> (Foucault 1990: 251)

Foucault's (1997a) study of the Greeks and their corresponding conception of the self demonstrates that there is no true self that can be emancipated from the forms of discourses. The example of Greeks demonstrates that even their sexual behavior was still referenced to a code of conduct, their counter-conduct was guided by their own definitions of the use of pleasure for the selves. Like the gay SM, Foucault understands the Greeks' self-care sexual practices as resistant activities to normalizing power by liberating the selves to experience pleasures with others in their relationships. The important legacy of Foucault's thought about resistance is that self-control is embodied in the nature of selfhood among others while re-subjectivation is a conscious process of opening up spaces of freedom to make a different way of life possible in the power-knowledge relations (1997a). Thus, self-care practices are ethical substances as they emphasize one's relationships and duties toward others, such as family members and other people in society:

> Care for self is ethical in itself, but implies complex relations with others, in the measure that this ethos of freedom is also a way of caring for others… ethos implies also a relation with others to the extent that care for self renders one competent to occupy a place in the city, in the community or in interindividual relationships… And the care for self implies also a relationship to the other to the extent that, in order to really care for self, one must listen to the teachings of a master …the problem of relationship with others is present all along this development of care for self.
> (Foucault 1987: 118)

By making reference to the close relationship between care of the self and care for others, Foucault's notion of individuals' self-care practices is bounded by a system of reciprocal obligations (Smart 1998). In other words, responsibility for others is fundamental to the care of the self and care for others. Henceforth, in the process of making something different in the self, one is obligated to control the self's conduct because the *ethos* (or action) of freedom is an ethical act that deals with (and impacts upon) a surrounding community (of family, friends, and others) (Oksala 2005). The self is subsequently never isolated from, but always linked to, proper practice in society and relationship with others throughout their power-knowledge relations.

In summary, resistance as characterized in Foucault's (1987) philosophy is developed from the notion of the art of life that is associated with the principle of the 'caring for the self' to resist normalizing practices. For Foucault, self-care practices are forms of knowing the self which enable one to consciously adjust the codes for one's conduct and to question the subtle forms of domination that have constructed individuals as different types of subjects—such as homosexuals, madmen, as normal and healthy, and as workers (1980a, 1997a). Thus, Foucault's work on power-knowledge relations is never about total domination or manipulation, but rather in those who are ruled sharing the acceptance discourse—a discourse that masks the reality of power imbalances and inequality—wherein they always present a possibility of resistance[2] in irregular fashion.

Genealogy and the Resistance

Toward the end of his life, Foucault (1980a, 1997a) describes his interests of exploring the 'genealogy of how the subject constituted itself as subject' (1988: 4) in his own works as part of an aesthetic self-reformation project that strives to resist against governmentality.

Insofar as noted in this chapter, the critique of the problem of knowledge which reinforced the effects of governmentality in Foucault's work is historical. This is because Foucault perceives our accepted accounts of "history" as an endlessly repeated play of dominations over the reproduction of certain "true" values, rules and rituals. As such, Foucault's (1971/1977: 150) accounts of what is accepted as historically "true" have not so much a history, as a "genealogy", a process in which certain groups and individuals construct a "history" that is popularly held to be true. For example, his analysis of historical knowledge about 'sexuality' (1976) and 'madness' (2006) has each showed us how these discourses were (and are)

[2] Foucault argues that "there are no power relations without resistances", for example: slavery is not a power relationship when men are in chains. See Foucault, Michel (1980a) *Power/Knowledge: Selected Interviews and Other Writings 1972–1977*, New York: Vintage Books, Foucault, Michel (1982) The Subject and Power. in Hubert Dreyfus and Paul Rabinow (eds.) *Michel Foucault: Beyond structuralism and hermeneutics*. Chicago: University of Chicago Press.

accumulated and internalized by individuals themselves that they imposed the rules for themselves to guide their ways of living their lives based on that *given* "truths" in Western culture. Thus, "history" is socially constructed, a superior form of discourse; a discourse whose "genealogy" cannot only be traced and understood but also combated, resisted, and overturned in the present.

One of the essential characteristics of Foucault's genealogical approach is his rejection of the notion of continuity that underpins much in traditional's historiography (O'Farrell 1989, 2005; Gutting 2003). While history, by definition, is about the past, Foucault perceives it as a form of knowledge and at the same time a form of power that constitutes the "truth" about "how things are" in establishing the basis for modern *episteme* (or knowledge) (Poster 1982) to form the foundations of human perceptions and ways of thinking (O'Farrell 1989). In this respect, Foucault's (2002) critique of knowledge (or episteme) is that traditional historians' efforts to write history in a way that maintains and reinforces a continuous status of knowledge, such as "sexuality" and "madness", to reflect 'where we are', 'who we are' and 'what we do' is inevitably resulting from cumulative knowledge of causes and effects (Gutting 2003; Hook 2005).

Foucault (1976, 1977, 2006) calls for a suspension on the notion of continuous progression of thought by dismantling the way we think about supposedly universal truths. Foucault urges us to instead unravel how fragmented and incoherent events (as opposed to sequence of events) that emerged from the historical knowledge have continued to influence individuals' thoughts and practices (or lived experience). In this context, Foucault's genealogical works have demonstrated to us how we can rethink an 'event' by searching the multiplicity of causes and conditions through a precise study of history and a detailed documentation of historical facts to analyze the governmental discourses, such as 'sexuality' and 'madness', which constituted *that* event or a problem (Foucault and Rabinow 1991). Henceforth, while recognizing the deficiency in traditional, historical writing, Foucault does not advocate abandoning knowledge and investigation of the past (Thacker 1997). Rather, he suggests that the quest for a more authentic knowledge is to think and identify contingencies between historical events and to then reinterpret earlier interpretations of the intellectual works to make sense of the past (Thacker 1997). It is through our effort to discontinue the intellectual landscapes of necessary forms of thinking to instead develop a genealogical study (effective history or history of the present) by focusing upon the fragmentary nature of histories (or events) (Nicholls 2009) that we can free our thoughts 'from what it silently thinks, and enable it to think differently' in our present day (Foucault 1990: 9).

Confucian (*Li*) Rules: A Genealogy of the Chinese Workers

Following the lead of Foucault, this section charts the historical development and the conceptual underpinnings of social practices and knowledge that have subtly directed workers to think and behave themselves as *workers* (see also Chapters 3 and 4) in today's China. In so doing, I do not aim to reconstruct the past, but to locate 'traces of the present in the past' (Burrell 1988: 225) of how the class consciousness and a *class-for-itself* development is constraining by an 'older rules consciousness' (see Chapter 1) through the re-interpretation of the key events in Chinese histories.

The selected historical events are arguably produced important—but hidden—*li* 禮 (proprieties)—rules—to continuously constitute filial practices to maintain docility among workers and the hierarchical power of rulers since the Imperial periods through to the present-day China. Noted by many (Goldman 1975; Tsou 1986; Mathur 1987), the Imperial order associated with the *li* (and later Confucian) values were substituted by orthodox Marxism since the founding of the People's Republic of China (PRC or China) in 1949. However, I argue that the concept of "Chinese Marxism" consisted of different governmental discourses that were frequently, albeit selective, referenced to the Confucian past. It is the internalization of these centuries-long discourses among the Chinese workers that influenced the ways they think and act as *workers* in today's China.

Originating in the pre-Confucian primitive society as early as 2070 B.C.E., *li* 禮 rules were predominately associated with the "truth" about *tian*天 (heaven) and *di* 地 (earth) (Zhou 1930: 168). The acceptance of this "truth" had made it mandatory for the Chinese on earth (the low) to "naturally" worship the spirits of the heaven (the high) (Zhang 2014). Based on this utmost filial practice toward the spirits, *li* rules were transformed into mandatory rules of conduct by various emperors to standardize Chinese thinking and behaviors to maintain the monarchical power of the rulers from the Zhou dynasty (13th B.C.E.) onwards. Zhou Gong (922 B.C.E.–900 B.C.E.), the sixth king of the Western Zhou dynasty (1040 B.C.E.–771 B.C.E.) (Melton 2014), modified *li* rules to differentiate the social ranks of the noble (the high) and the peasants (the low) in a feudalistic social system (Zhou 1930). To fortify the dominant position of the royal ruling classes and maintain the status quo, *li* rules were subsequently linked to a code of capital punishment (or death penalties—*sihsing* 死刑) under the laws of the ancient Zhou:

> Death to anyone who disturb[s] the government by initiating reforms… death to anyone who rebell[s] against authority…
>
> (Zhou 1930: 172)

The criminal code enacted by the Zhou dynasty exemplified *li* rules that focused on the "true" values of filial piety (*xiao* 孝) was used to regulate the conduct of individuals toward their authority figures within a social hierarchy. The violations of the stated prohibitions and restrictions were subject to forms of torturous capital punishments. Methods of torture and execution ranged from being boiled in oil or water; to being stoned or crushed; and to 'death by a thousand cuts' (or *Lingchi* 凌遲 in Qing criminal code) by slicing the body of a confessed criminal with a maximum of 3,600 cuts, in a public space (Miethe and Lu 2005; Brook et al. 2008). By producing pains in the bodies of the convicted criminals for all to see, the mechanism of public torture and punishment was a visible form of truth-power relation to suppress the thoughts and actions of the masses to ensure the hegemony of the ruling class in its social relations (Lu 1998).

Using Zhou *li* as a template, Confucius (2003) legitimized dynastic *li* rules by rectifying social ranks and names to establish an orderly set of social relations of the high and low positions, such as the father and the son, the older and the younger brother, and the husband and the wife, under a truth of the 'Mandate of Heaven' (*tianming* 天命). In the Confucius discourse (2003), the 'Mandate of Heaven' defined the individuals' true positions to then identify their life tasks and responsibilities in their *ming* 命 (fate or destiny). These were articulated as something that was predetermined by *tian* 天 (or heaven) from birth:

> The relation between superiors and inferiors is like that between the wind and the grass. When the wind blows across it, the grass must bend.
>
> (Confucius 2010: 111)

The Confucian *li* (2003) under the truth of the 'Mandate of Heaven' emphasized the need to accept and obey the "natural" ruling order and the power of superiors imposed on *ming* by *tian*. Superiors, such as the emperors were regarded by Confucius as the 'Sons of Heaven' (*tianzi* 天子), with divine mandates to rule and control the lower classes (or inferiors) (Confucius 2003; Grasso et al. 2009). A challenge to the 'Mandate of Heaven' of the ruling classes (or superiors) by inferiors was to disobey or deviate from the *li* codes of conduct (Confucius 2003). These codes of proper conduct of filial piety and obedience to superiors were central to Confucius's thought to regulate the social behaviors of the inferiors, such as son, wife, and pupil, by reaffirming their given status imposed by their *ming* (Confucius 2003).

By connecting the truth of *ming* with individuals' status (or positions), the followers of Confucius (or the Confucians) sought to inculcate a morality of obedience (or a mentality of respect for authority) into their mindsets in order to create an orderly society (Rojek 1989; Fouts and Chan 1995). In this context, the Confucian *li* rules prioritized the moral teaching of proper conduct from the moment of birth (Fouts and Chan 1995). One example was the teaching of filial piety to children (Rojek 1989), which contributed to influencing and correcting individuals' actions by their given status in broader contexts, such as community schools and extended family networks. By socializing an individual in the practices of education and culture, one's behaviors became observable to others. In this way, individuals' behaviors became increasingly regulated by others based on a collective moral judgment (of others) and the self. The creation and maintenance of the culture of obedience had thus enabled the royal ruling classes to continue to produce docile bodies and minds to serve their interests until the Qing dynasty—the last Imperial dynasty—in China (Rojek 1989; Grasso et al. 2009).

Toward the final years of the Qing dynasty, Western moral values that challenged the Confucian tradition were introduced into China (Dreyer 1993; Chen 2002). The inability of the Qing emperors to stop the imposition of Western influences through foreign trade relations, diplomatic missions, and ideas of democracy made it difficult for the Chinese State to exert the control they would have liked over people's lives (Whyte 1988b). Social conflicts, such as the Boxer Rebellion by peasants to oppose the European and Japanese power in 1900, and particularly after the fall of the Qing dynasty in 1911, became apparent as the nation came to be characterized by cultural diversity (Grasso et al. 2009). In the period after 1919 (the 'May Fourth Movement[3]'), Chinese pro-Western intellectuals asserted that the 'backwardness' of Confucian culture was the cause of individual passivity and it accounted for the restriction of individual freedoms (Mao 1986). Subsequently, new Western cultural and political values, ranging from socialism to liberalism (Mao 1966), were advocated as alternative moral frameworks to guide Chinese society.

The "Demise" of Confucianism Under Mao Zedong

With the formal establishment of the PRC following the victory over the anti-Japanese War (1937–1945) and Kuomintang (KMT or the Nationalist) Party in the Chinese Civil War (1946–1949) (MacFarquhar 1997), the CCP—as a product of the 'May Fourth Movement' between 1915 and 1922—deplored the "intolerable elements" of Confucian values, exalting instead the socialist ideology (or Stalinism) of the Union of Soviet Socialist Republics (USSR or Soviet Union) (Whyte 1988a; Leung 2016).

These founding principles of the socialist Chinese State were spelled out by the CCP Chairman Mao Zedong (1949–1976)—who was perceived as the charismatic leader with the prolonged character of his revolutionary struggle for the "New Democratic China"—with a speech that was subsequently published *On the People's Democratic Dictatorship*. In this speech, Mao (1949/2013: 4) defined the "people" as "the workers, the peasants, the urban petty bourgeoisie and the national bourgeoisie". By categorizing "the people" into different classes, Mao further declared that "the people" were "led" by the "working class"—an alliance of workers and peasants (proletariats or masses)—and the CCP.

From these principles, Mao proclaimed his theory of "New Democracy" as the basis of the CCP policies, a form of "democracy" that associated communism with the direct and active role of "the people" in Chinese politics to resist the class domination characteristic of 'imperialism, feudalism and bureaucratic capitalism' (Mao 1949/2013: 5–7).

[3] The May Fourth Movement (1915–1922) was brought about by the complete rejection of Confucian values by advocating a substitution of Western values, such as democracy, egalitarianism, republicanism and Marxism. See Grasso, June, Corrin, Jay and Kort, Michael (2009) *Modernization and Revolution: From the Opium Wars to the Olympics*, New York: M.E. Sharpe, Inc.

Thus, as a supposedly socialist society, Mao embraced Stalinism as a base and subsequently developed Marxism-Leninism (see Chapter 1) into the *Thought of Mao Zedong* (or Maoism) to impose revolutionary ideologies, that is, to destroy the system of private property ownership, for Chinese model of socialism.

However, the post-1949 Chinese society was characterized by a relatively small middle-class population dominating a much larger urban proletariat in the cities. Despite this, Chinese society was also characterized by a relatively small number of landowners dominating a greater number of peasants in rural areas (Chen 2013). Over eighty percent of the entire Chinese population resided in the rural areas, while less than twenty percent resided in the cities (Chen 2013). For this reason, Mao emphasized the important role of peasants, rather than the proletariat as identified by Marx and Lenin, in the success of the Chinese revolution (1966). Mao contended that the virtues of the peasants, such as purity and simplicity, were the strengths of the Chinese people because they could be taught, educated, indoctrinated, and 'proletarianized' by the CCP to transform society (1966).

The Making of a Chinese Working Class

Thus, while denouncing a range of Confucian values, Mao initiated the Confucian-inspired thought reform program *zhengfeng* 整風 (or 'Rectification Campaign') (Mao 1966: 2) to impose his revolutionary ideologies on the Chinese masses in the already poor China (Chen 2013).

In contrast to the models of Marx and Lenin, who believed a revolutionary consciousness was derived from one's economic and class conditions, Mao insisted that reforming one's consciousness to alter norms and behaviors was a more effective way to accomplish a socialist society (1966). To achieve this purpose, Mao sought to revolutionize the peasants to get them to adhere to the truth of Maoism (Guo 2013). In this context, the Confucian inner-control technique was once again manipulated to define the destiny (*ming*) of the Chinese inferior masses by facilitating their internalization of the correct Maoist truth (Rojek 1989; Pye 1999).

Manipulating the Chinese *ming* was exercised through Confucian thought control methods by turning the masses into a total obedient instrument of Mao (Schram 1969; Pye 1986; Teiwes 2000; Landsberger 2002). To begin with, the CCP sought to align the correctness of Mao's ultimate truth and leadership with Marx and Lenin to legitimize his hierarchically superior position:

> In our Party, there are no special privileges for individuals; any leadership which is not exercised in the name of the organization cannot be tolerated... We obey the Party, we obey the Central Committee, we obey the truth; we do not obey individuals. No individual merits our obedience. Marx, Lenin and Mao [Zedong] have done their work well; they represent the truth, and it is only for this reason that we obey them...
>
> (Mao 2013: 154–155)

The validity of the new 'mandate' of Mao's ruling legacy was further reinforced through all possible means of propaganda, including newspapers and public broadcasts, to transmit principles of obedience to his sole authority (Weatherley 2006). This Confucian-inspired thought control method was adopted to persuade prospective supporters to form the Red Army (or the People's Liberation Army) to combat the Nationalists in the civil war in the late 1920s (Lu 2004). While discrediting the Confucian culture, a large-scale thought reform program, Rectification (*zhengfeng*) campaign commenced in the early 1940s to control the behaviors of the CCP members (Mao 1966). This was extended further after 1949 to control non-party members by eradicating negative thoughts about Maoism (Lu 2004; Grasso et al. 2009). A more personalized method of compulsory study groups (Mao 1966), conducted by CCP authority figures, was also used to inculcate correct thought into the masses. Either willingly or under duress, the masses had to self-criticize and confess any incorrect personal thoughts that ran counter to Maoism (Mao 1966). Party cadres had to report the political thought of the masses to the CCP leaders (Dittmer 1973). These strategies enabled the CCP leaders to evaluate the thoughts of the masses and then implement the most appropriate techniques to continuously cultivate docile bodies and minds to Mao.

To demonstrate a high level of loyalty to Mao, the docile bodies had to translate their political ideas into revolutionary practices (Schram 1969; Barlow 1981). In 1951, Mao initiated two "Antis-" (*fan* 反)

campaigns[4] in the urban centers that "taught" the masses of class identification with "correct" actions toward their class enemies. Declaring that 'corruption and waste are the capitalist practices of the KMT' and that 'bureaucratism is the basis for corruption and waste' (*People's Daily* 人民日报 21 November, 1951), the "Three Antis-" (*sanfan* 三反) movement (1951) was launched to demand the masses exposed and denounced the government officials—mainly non-CCP members—who were accused of committing "three evils" (*sanhai* 三害) criminal activities—corruption, waste, and bureaucratism[5]—*with* their KMT-linked bourgeoisie (Mao 1977: 73). By attributing the "three evils" influence to the bourgeoisie as a class, Mao subsequently merged the "Three-Antis" into the "Five-Antis" (*wufan* 五反) campaign in 1952 to explicitly attack the businessmen for allegedly engaging in "five poisons" (*wudu* 五毒) activities—bribery, tax evasion, fraud, theft of State assets, and leakage of State economic secrets—to undermine the "people's democracy" by corrupting the targets of the "Three-Antis" with "illegal profits" in socialist economy. Under the rubric of "people's democracy", the masses were invited to humiliate, accuse, condemn, punish, and attack the "offenders", causing

[4] The "Antis-" (*fan* 反) campaigns were launched shortly after the patriotic movement of "Resist America, Aid Korea" following China's entry into the Korean War (1950–1953) with its Communist coalition—the USSR and North Korean—to struggle against the "American imperialism" in Communist world. See (1952) People's Daily 人民日报, http://www.nlc.cn/dsb_zt/xzzt/ghgdsj/1952/event1/, accessed 20 May 2020. The objective of the "Anti-American imperialism" campaign was implemented that directed the masses to participate in supporting activities such as collecting funds for the soldiers and signing "patriotic pacts" for cutting ties between the Chinese Christian churches and their American or Western counterparts as a means of applauding China's war effort. See (1950) People's Daily 人民日报, http://www.nlc.cn/dsb_zt/xzzt/ghgdsj/1950/event12/, accessed 12 April 2020.

[5] 'Corruption, waste, and bureaucratism' was broadly interpreted to include a wide range of governmental "malpractices" in the "Three Antis" campaign. For example, nonessential expenses irrelevant to the State production were defined as wasteful. Mismanagement and inefficiency were considered corruption and bureaucratism. See (13 February, 1952) People's Daily 人民日报, http://www.nlc.cn/dsb_zt/xzzt/ghgdsj/1951/event7/, accessed 14 March 2020. Other offences ranging from not attending the CCP meetings; spending on entertainment including the use of drugs and prostitution services or luxurious home furnishings to "damaging people's democracy" through bribery or misappropriating government funds was conceived as evidence of corruption. See (16 December, 1951) People's Daily 人民日报, http://www.nlc.cn/dsb_zt/xzzt/ghgdsj/1951/event7/, accessed 14 March 2020.

approximately 800,000 people to die in these campaigns (Stavis 1978: 29).

The war against the bourgeoisie class was further expanded to the countryside as Mao launched nationwide land reform campaigns aimed at transferring land ownership (Chen and Goodman 2013) from 'feudal' landlords to the peasantry in rural areas (Mao 1966). Following Mao's order of '*criticizing the seizure of land*' in a series of 'mini-revolutions', peasants denounced their 'feudal' landlords under the slogan '*spitting bitter water*' (*tukushui* 吐苦水) (Lu 2004). This provocative slogan aimed to raise the revolutionary consciousness of the peasantry such that they were reminded of the suffering caused by landlord exploitation over the centuries (Weatherley 2006). Many landlords were forced to publicly confess their own so-called crimes, while others—approximately 15 million 'feudal exploiters'—were executed or stoned to death (Lu 2004; Grasso et al. 2009: 139). In proclaiming themselves the advocates of social justice, the CCP had consequently dismantled the traditional hierarchical landlord-tenant relationship in the rural areas (Lu 2004; Grasso et al. 2009). While transferring land ownership to the peasantry, rural poverty continued and was exacerbated by a rapidly expanding population and a scarcity of farmland, which led to the next stage of agricultural development—the collectivization of farmland (Mao 1986).

The assault on the disobedient 'feudal exploiters' had subsequently pushed the rural masses to engage in Mao's (1986) program of collectivization of farmland (Weatherley 2006). In this program, Mao sought to reshape public life through the creation of a collective economy by introducing work units (*danwei* 單位)[6] in urban areas and the Chinese commune in rural areas within the State-owned enterprises (SOEs) (Mao 1986). The establishment of the latter was by forcing the rural masses to participate in agricultural cooperative planting and harvesting through the scheme of agricultural producers' cooperatives (APCs) (Dikotter 2010).

[6] The significance of the work units (*danwei* 單位) was that, beginning from 1951, all SOE workers were guaranteed pensions of approximately 80 to 90% of their salaries at the retirement age of 55 (women) and 60 (men) Hurst, William and O'Brien, Kelvin (2002) 'China's Contentious Pensioners', *The China Quarterly* 170: 345–360.. This was followed in 1952 by the release of the important document '*Decisions on the Problems of Employment*', the effect of which was to guarantee job security and welfare benefits, known as the *iron rice bowl* (*tie fanwan* 鐵飯碗), and which secured the livelihood of the SOE workers Fung, Ho-lup (2001) 'The Making and Melting of the "Iron Rice Bowl" in China 1949 to 1995', *Social Policy & Administration* 35(3): 258–273.

Under this arrangement, approximately 20 to 40 peasant households (Lin et al. 1996: 56) were formed into production teams by consolidating their farmland into collective agricultural units (Mao 1986). To coerce peasant families to join APCs, the CCP made it illegal to sell or purchase anything not produced through the APCs in the countryside (Grasso et al. 2009). While unwilling, peasants who wanted to survive were forced to join the APCs in order to participate in agricultural development in the rural areas (Dikotter 2010).

Although it was assumed that the APCs would enable the peasants to farm more efficiently by achieving economies of scale, the APC collectivization experiment resulted in poor harvests in both 1953 and 1954 (Grasso et al. 2009: 148). Food shortages occurred because of poor weather conditions and inadequate agricultural production outputs combined with stable consumption and a rapidly growing population (Breslin 2014). Yet rather than denouncing the collectivization project, Mao attempted to reinvigorate the APC structures by transforming them into People's Communes for agriculture and steel productions (Mao 1986). This decision was part of a more far-reaching program called the Great Leap Forward (1958—1961) (Mao 1986) for China's industrialization.

Despite food shortages, the deterioration of USSR-Sino-relations[7] that was due to different interpretation of Marxism as well as the anti-communist movements[8] arose around the world after 1956 was another

[7] Stalin had by this time died, and his successor Kruschev denounced Stalin's regime, accusing Stalin of a 'grave abuse of power' in a secret speech at the 20th Congress of the Soviet Union. In the wake of the speech by Kruschev, relations deteriorated between the USSR and PRC bureaucracies, before Kruschev finally withdrew aid from China in August 1960. See Teiwes, F 1997, 'The Establishment and Consolidation of the New Regime, 1949–57', in *The Politics of China: The Eras of Mao and Deng*, 2nd edn, ed. R MacFarquhar, Cambridge University Press, Cambridge, pp. 5–86, Mitter, R 2004, *A Bitter Revolution: China's Struggle with the Modern World*, Oxford University Press, New York.

[8] During the Cold War period in the mid-1950s, anti-communism arose among the major countries such as the United Kingdom (U.K.) and the United States (U.S.) to support political democracy and economic freedom. In 1957, the U.S. imposed trade embargos on China, North Korea and North Vietnam under the Trading with the Enemy Act of 1917. See Mitter, R 2004, *A Bitter Revolution: China's Struggle with the Modern World*, Oxford University Press, New York, Oi, J 1995, 'The Role of the Local State in China's Transitional Economy', *The China Quarterly*, no. 144, pp. 1132–1149, Weatherley, R 2006, *Politics in China since 1949: Legitimizing Authoritarian Rule*, Routledge, New York.

element causing Mao to launch the Great Leap Forward programs to generate self-sufficiency for Chinese socialism (Oi 1995; Teiwes 1997; Fund 2001). In 1958, Mao mobilized the masses to transform China into an industrialized, socialist country under the Great Leap slogan of 'overtaking Britain's steel production in less than 15 years' (Breslin 2014: 5). To accelerate industrial productivity, the masses were forced to labor in both the agricultural and industrial sectors on collective farms (Withington 2008). In this program, Mao converted the APCs into large-scale labor armies by combining 750,000 collective farmlands, containing over 500 million people, into 26,000 small People's Communes (Ahn 1975: 632). Each 'small' commune contained small-scale manufacturing facilities (or backyard steel furnaces), and individuals were forced to labor day and night to achieve Mao's daily production quotas and targets to surpass Britain's steel industry (Grasso et al. 2009; Breslin 2014). They were later forced to melt personal items such as cooking pots and pans to achieve Mao's objective of the Great Leap Forward (Li and Yang 2005; Weatherley 2006). This policy led to the reduction of peasants harvesting the fields and caused the subsequent nationwide famine in 1959 and 1960 (Grasso et al. 2009).

During the great famine of 1959 and 1960, Mao further tightened the *hukou* 戶口 (or household registration) system to restrict peasant mobility (Wu and Treiman 2004). In 1955, the *hukou* system was introduced to register all households and categorize them as either agricultural or non-agricultural (Mao 1986: 752). In the early period, Chinese people were guaranteed the right to move into and out of urban cities and throughout the countryside in China (Chan and Li 1999). Between 1953 and 1957, millions of rural peasants sought employment in exchange for the guaranteed job security and welfare benefits of *iron rice bowl* (*tie fanwan* 鐵飯碗) within SOEs in the urban cities (Chan and Li 1999). Yet in the aftermath of the Great Leap Forward, there were an additional 25 million rural peasants flooded into the cities in serach of work (Fund 2001, p. 261). The demands that were placed on the State by this rapid shift triggered an "overheating" of the *iron rice bowl* program and economic disaster, as the Chinese State struggled to meet the demands of the populace (Fund 2001).

The State's response was to force the return of thousands of former SOE *danwei* workers to their original rural villages with only minimal resources to help their survival. This confinement of the greater portion of population to the rural environment was reinforced by introducing the household registration or *hukou* system, which regulated rural–urban migration (Mallee 2000). Those who secured an urban *hukou* were entitled to food, housing, education, work, and other social services, whereas those tied to a rural *hukou* had to fend for themselves (Cheung and Selden 1994; Fan 2004). Through this system, Mao secured a permanent supply of low-cost agricultural products, because thousands of workers were confined to rural areas (Fan 2004), while State-enforced policies demanded that these rural cadres continue to supply grain to the State, even though they had minimal or no grain for their consumption which caused 30 million Chinese to die of starvation between 1958 and 1961 (Mitter 2004: 3–6). Yet in the aftermath of the Great Leap Forward, the *hukou* system was further used to restrict rural–urban migration more stringently, and to effectively remove approximately 18 million peasant workers from the urban cities (Chan and Li 1999). As a result, the restriction of peasant mobility in the wake of the famine conditions contributed to another 45 million deaths in the rural areas (Dikotter 2010).

Concern about the Maoist policies that had led to these effects triggered a revolutionary movement within the CCP itself. The CCP Vice Chairman Liu Shaoqi (1961–1968), who until then had been publicly acknowledged as Mao's successor and had supported the Great Leap Forward (Dittmer 1981), voiced concerns about the deleterious effects of Mao's policies, and along with others such as Deng Xiaoping, who became the leader of the CCP following Mao's death in 1976, introduced a system of contract employment and other economic reforms to address the effects of the Great Leap Forward (Fund 2001). With Liu and Deng's post-Great Leap success, Mao was pushed to the CCP sidelines. In order to retain his mandate to rule the CCP and the country, Mao sought to regain political power by removing his CCP opponents, particularly Liu and Deng, through a program of mass criticism (later the Cultural Revolution) to '*criticize bourgeois reactionary thinking*' in 1965 (Tsou 1969; McCormick 2010: 3–16).

To gain support for the Cultural Revolution, Mao exploited the fear that he had created in the populace against those who became known as "capitalist roaders" (*zouzipai* 走資派) (Dittmer 1981) by asserting that their initiatives would see the return of capitalism to China. In this context, Mao sought to legitimize his Cultural Revolution by mobilizing the masses against, not only his CCP opponents, but also those people from what was called "Five Black Categories" (*hewulei* 黑五類) family class backgrounds—rich farmers, landlords, counter-revolutionaries, rightists, and bad elements (*huaifenzi* 壞份子) of Confucian sympathizers such as those labelled as "reactionary educators" (intellectuals or teachers)—who were said to be "enthusiastic" in their support of capitalism (Tsou 1969; McCormick 2010). Although the "traditional class enemies" were predominately annihilated in the past campaigns, Mao (2013) argued that the "reactionary" educators, intellectuals, writers, and artists alongside the family members of the "class enemies" in the "Five Black Categories" perpetuated the "Confucian standards" that inherently harbored the economic values of the dominant capitalist class that were established in traditional China (Mao 2013). It is in this context Mao contended that while the capitalist means of production had largely been removed, a dominant, proletarian culture of the peasantry was still unrealized in socialist China (Grasso et al. 2009). He insisted that China's socialist revolution could be realized only if the feudalistic (or capitalistic) consciousness deeply rooted in Confucian culture was destroyed and replaced by his own idea of working-class values to establish a proletarian culture in China (2013). Mao thus sought to mobilize the masses through a Cultural Revolution, which he hoped would defeat his free market opponents (MacFarquhar and Schoenhals 2006).

Immediately before the Cultural Revolution, Mao's followers (the Maoists) promoted Mao's personality cult and the knowledge of *Mao's Thought* to new heights (Tsou 1969). From 1964, the song '*The East is Red*' (*Dongfang Hong* 東方紅) that extolled Mao as the "sun" and "savior" was frequently played, on the radio, television, and public address (PA) systems (He 2010), as national anthem to indoctrinate the masses that the position of Mao was equivalent to the Emperor in New China. The efforts of mass indoctrination were further expanded by the Maoist Lin Biao, commander of the People's Liberation Army (PLA), who promoted '*Mao Zedong Thought*' by circulating the publication '*Quotations from Chairman Mao*' (or *Little Red Book*) to every Chinese citizen across the country (Grasso et al. 2009). Later, Lin turned '*Mao's Quotations*' into PLA policy. He further politicized the PLA through the establishment of several compulsory political classes for soldiers (Weatherley 2006). The purpose of repositioning Mao as a 'supreme leader' was to enable him to gain a new sense of legitimacy and correctness. Through this newfound legitimacy, the disobedient CCP leaders, such as Deng and Liu, who turned against Mao, were subject to criticism (Tsou 1969).

To ensure that the inferior masses were thinking and feeling what he wanted them to think and feel, the apotheosis of Mao and his Cultural Revolution was promoted through art and literature in China's cultural sphere (Grasso et al. 2009). Jiang Qing, Mao's wife and a former actress, and later a member of the Gang of Four,[9] was appointed to take charge of China's cultural and artistic affairs (Weatherley 2006). Subsequently, Jiang and her allies began to establish Mao's values about revolution and the working class in the Beijing opera (Weatherley 2006; Grasso et al. 2009). In this context, traditional performances of 'Confucian-feudal style' plays, which featured characters such as emperors and princes, were outlawed (Grasso et al. 2009). Writers, directors, and performers were forced to write and act scenes that portrayed the masses as destined to 'master the country' (Tsou 1969; Lippit 1982). This revolutionary type of theatrical production was further extended to schools, factories, and neighborhoods to mobilize young people throughout the country to join the Red Guards (*hongweibing* 紅衛兵) (Mao 1966) in order to 'save China' (Grasso et al. 2009). Bewitched by the Maoist propaganda that was pushed by PLA commander Lin and Jiang's committees, millions of Chinese joined the ranks to participate in the Cultural Revolution (Grasso et al. 2009).

In 1966, the Red Guards and the PLA were ordered to repudiate the traditional Confucian culture of feudalism and capitalism under the slogan '*eliminate the Four Olds: old ideas, old culture, old customs and old habits*' (Weatherley 2006; Grasso et al. 2009). As well as destroying items of traditional Chinese culture, including books and paintings, the masses were instructed to capture and seizure control of labor organizations, including the Ministry of Labor and All-China Federation of Trade Unions (ACFTU), as bases to promote the socialist vision of Mao (Bridgham 1968). This involved further brutal attacks on members of the Chinese populace. Approximately 142,000 teachers, 53,000 scientists, and 2,600 writers and artists, who had been identified as members of "Black Five Categories", were assaulted, tortured, murdered, or executed (Gao and Yan 1986) while the disobedient CCP "capitalist roaders" Liu was repeatedly beaten to dead by Mao's supporters, wherein Deng was

[9] Gang of Four was coined by Mao to describe Jiang Qing and her allies Wang Hongwen, Zhang Chunqiao and Yao Wenyaun, who supported the Cultural Revolution. See Grasso, June, Corrin, Jay and Kort, Michael (2009) *Modernization and Revolution: From the Opium Wars to the Olympics*, New York: M.E. Sharpe, Inc.

imprisoned in solitary confinement when the revolution was abandoned by 1969 (Weatherley 2006; Grasso et al. 2009; Dillon 2015).

In summary, the turmoil of the Cultural Revolution alongside a series of mass campaigns revealed that the Maoists were concerned with generating loyalty of the Chinese masses to Mao being a legitimate ruler. The use of the old social system to complement and bolster the "new Chinese Marxism" to build a fierce repudiation of the old feudal order was designed to reinforce the Confucian concept of "mandate" to the "virtuous" Mao and the pro-Mao CCP leaders. While Mao's discourse "mass participation in Chinese politics" appeared to show a "genuine concern" for the needs of the masses, the genealogical analysis in this section has illustrated that "mass politics" were linked with the "truth" of Maoism. In other words, "mass participation" was intended as a series of thought reform programs to reshape the consciousness of those labelled as a class of workers (or proletariats) to legitimize Mao's hierarchically superior position. This point was reflected in the active participation of the docile working class in what Mao defined as "anti-capitalist movements" under the 'class' discourse. Rather than bringing benefits to the masses by "liberalizing" China, the success of the Maoist thought control programs had created a working class of hundreds of millions of docile bodies and minds to automatically respond to Mao's revolutionary ideologies and practices in deteriorating the already poor country into chaos.

The Chinese History of the Present

These historical events that indelibly created the Chinese docile minds and bodies to the rulers are fundamental to the success of the post-Mao leaders' goal of transforming China from a rural, agrarian economy into a modern, urbanized, and industrialized 'socialist market economy' (see Chapter 1) following the death of Mao in 1976.

This decision is spurred on by decades of political instability and a stagnating economy with massive unemployment characterized by the succession of the past events in Mao's period. Hence, the immediate post-Mao CCP leader Deng Xiaoping (1977–1997)[10] initiates economic

[10] In 1978, Deng Xiaoping consolidated his return to power by imprisoning Mao's allies—the Gang of Four—for life, and replaced the practice and ideology of *Mao Zedong Thought* with the *Deng Xiaoping Theory* of economic reforms and modernisation See Girdner, Eddie (2004) 'China as a Capitalist State: From "Primitive Socialist Accumulation" to Neoliberal Capitalism', *The Turkish Yearbook* XXXV: 121–144, Harvey, David

modernization programs to shift China's development strategy from one based on "class struggles" to one that focuses on "economic productivity" by actively engaging in global markets. In reconciling the "Chinese Marxism" with this economic initiative, Deng at the Third Plenum of the Eleventh Central Committee declares that a socialist market economy is the correct path for China's development[11] as Mao's revolutionary practices were:

> [being] too rigid and bureaucratic, constraining the flexibility of the economy, perpetuating poor labor production, and retarding technical changes. Changes were necessary... to increase the flexibility of movement of labor work-force, give management more power over their work-force labor, and to break the iron rice bowl of the state workers. Specifically... the degree of direct administrative control over urban labor has been excessive, rendering the economic actors themselves – both managers and workers – inert
>
> (White 1989: 155)

To improve the economic performance of the Chinese socialist market system, an 'Open Door' policy (see Chapter 1) is adopted as an essential component of modernization programs to create a cheap and docile labor force for export-led industrialization.

Post-Mao China's creation of a cheap and docile labor force begins with cutting back social welfare and loosening regulations by opening Special Economic Zones (SEZs) in the coastal areas, such as Shenzhen, Zhuhai, and Shantou cities, to attract foreign investment (Wei 2001; Harvey 2005). Flexible labor markets are also introduced, both by dismantling the SOEs through the approach of '*releasing the small and grasping the large*'[12] (Harvey 2005: 129; Liew 2005: 336). The diversification of SOE ownership through corporatization thus enables foreign

(2005) *A Brief History of Neoliberalism*, New York: Oxford University Press, Weatherley, Robert (2006) *Politics in China since 1949: Legitimizing Authoritarian Rule*, New York: Routledge.

[11] China's GDP was recorded at 364.52 billion yuan, while the value of the GNP slumped from 12% in 1978 to 7% in 1979 and 5.5% in 1980. See Dittmer, Lowell (1981) 'China in 1980: Modernization and its Discontents', *Asian Survey* 21(1): 31–50.

[12] Under a policy described as '*releasing the small*', small SOEs were either privatised or permitted to go bankrupt whereas the approach '*grasping the large*' referred to the conversion of medium and large SOEs into shareholding enterprises. See Harvey, David (2005) *A Brief History of Neoliberalism*, New York: Oxford University Press, Liew, Leong

investors to exercise their own organizational practices to manage the SOE workers in order to maximize profits in the State sector.

Under this arrangement, SOE managers are granted increased operational autonomy to restructure their workforces in accordance with production needs in order to improve profitability. For instance, from 1982, SOE managers have introduced base wage system with bonus payments based on the work performances of individual workers (Walder 1991). SOE managers also introduce a labor contract system as a means of converting permanent SOE workers into contract workers in order to recruit temporary contract workers and to fire surplus workers, as well as those perceived as 'disobedient'[13] workers (Leung 1988; Lee 1999: 60). The adoption of these flexible measures thus signals a dismantling of the Maoist iron rice bowl lifetime employment system, under which all SOE workers are faced with fewer work benefits and lower incomes, as well as job insecurity in post-Mao period (Yip 2006; Chen and Goodman 2012). It is reported that, between 1987 and 1999, about 8.05 million SOE workers were converted into contract workers, with about 7 million workers being laid off annually, while more than 50 million workers were made redundant by the State sector between 1987 and 2004 (Fund 2001: 113; Yueh 2011).

As well as massive job losses in the State sector, underemployment is also a crucial issue for rural peasants. This is due to the People's communes being either privatized or destroyed while over 60% of private enterprises have been established in the fast-growing regions in the coastal areas (Mallee 2000). The trend of coastal-inland (or urban–rural) inequality and the wide income gaps led to the relaxation of the *hukou* (or household registration) system that is established to restrict rural peasants from migrating to the cities in Mao's period (Walder 1991; Bao et al. 2002). Based on the Maoist urban–rural principle, the Chinese State introduces temporary residence permits to enable rural peasants (or peasant workers) *only* to work in the cities (Mallee 2000). The dream of better job opportunities and wages offers by the private enterprises has attracted a flood of peasants to relocate from the inland regions to the cities (Bao et al. 2002; Fan 2004). Thus local governments begin

(2005) 'China's Engagement with Neo-liberalism: Path Dependency, Geography and Party Self-Reinvention', *The Journal of Development Studies* 41(2): 331–352.

[13] The term 'disobedient workers' is used to describe those who fail to behave 'properly' in relation to their immediate superiors at work.

to commodify the urban *hukou* system in the increasingly decentralized market (Fan 2003). Although selling urban *hukou* is forbidden by the Chinese state, central control of its commodification is gradually relaxed due to the increased demand for rural peasants in the cities (Fan 2004). By 1994, approximately three million urban *hukou* books had been sold to peasants across the nation (Chan and Li 1999). The legalization of this wholesale urban *hukou* has not only become an income source to raise revenue for the local authorities, but has also become one of the means to push peasants to engage in the labor force.

Competition between localities for foreign investments to sustain a profitable economic environment has further permitted private investors to establish their own organizational and labor practices to manage peasant workers. While China adopts more than 160 regulations concerning wages, social insurance, and welfare, as well as safety and hygiene among workers at their workplaces since 1979, none of the policies have been officially enforced by the central government (Ngok 2008). This gives the enterprises flexibility to adjust and recreate regulations in accordance with their interests to attract investments across localities (Orts 2001). From the 1980s onwards, employers in the private sector subsequently combine the idea of the *hukou* system with their factory policies by paying the cost of the temporary residence permits on behalf of the peasant workers and then deducting a sum from their monthly wages (Chan 2000). The effect is to force peasant workers to enter into a bonded relationship with the enterprises, because a portion of their wages is being withheld. Within this forced and bonded labor system, peasant workers faced abuses such as being paid irregularly, being forced to work long hours, having restricted toilet breaks, being limited to a certain number of times they could drink water, and being physically punished by their employers (Chan 2001).

In the State sector, similar conditions have also been experienced by millions of workers under the new contract system. Moreover, the new system has created a sense of insecurity because workers could suddenly find themselves unemployed. Large-scale redundancies, for example, endangered the livelihoods of millions of laid-off SOE workers. To redress this situation, the off-duty (or *xiagang* 下崗) policy is endorsed in 1995 at the central level to provide basic livelihood protection for those being laid off (Fund 2001; Hurst and O'Brien 2002). Under the *xiagang* scheme, those workers who have been made redundant or considered as inefficient, unnecessary, or unaffordable are categorized as off-duty (Hurst

2009: 67). Thus, while off-duty workers are no longer employed in the SOEs and consequently are not entitled to wages and other benefits, they are still part of the work units and remained attached to the SOEs (So 2003). Within the *xiagang* policy framework, funding for off-duty workers was to be provided under a *san-san* 三三 (three-thirds or 3:3:3) arrangement. That is, one-third of the funding comes from SOEs, one-third from local governments, and one-third from the central government budget (Hurst 2009: 68). These funds are to provide off-duty workers with job training and job placement assistance, while the amounts of basic living allowances[14] (*jiben shenghuo fei* 基本生活費), including housing and medical services, are provided by the work units of the SOEs as well as the local governments, for a maximum of three years (Hurst and O'Brien 2002; So 2003).

Despite the CCP's intention to minimize economic grievances among those laid-off workers through the *xiagang* policy, it is reported that a large number of laid-off workers are either excluded from or received inappropriate *xiagang*-related assistance in their localities (Leung and Xu 2010: 52). A survey by the Chinese Federation of Labor Unions (1996: 52) revealed that only 5% of the laid-off workers received the *xiagang* subsidies, and 11 million (this increased to 30 million in 1999) of dismissed SOE workers received inappropriate amounts or no financial support to maintain a subsistence lifestyle. This situation is caused directly by the shortage of the central (or CCP) budgetary funds allocated to local governments and hence local SOEs under the principle of the local 'State corporatism' (Oi 1995). In these circumstances, many SOEs find it difficult to provide their share of the *xiagang* subsides, given that they have to lay off workers due to their financial difficulties with paying wages in the first place (Lee 2000: 927).

In light of the substantial increase in the number of laid-off workers, a number of SOEs declared bankruptcy to avoid paying their share of the financial burden (Lee 2007). Delayed redundancy and pension payments that were officially reported by the laid-off workers mounted from 10,780

[14] Given the differences in the cost of living in different cities, the CCP did not define an overall financial assistance guideline for the whole country. In general, the assistance line was set below the legal minimum wage and was adjusted by the local authorities based on the financial capacity of the local governments and SOEs. See Leung, Joe and Xu, Andy (2010) The Emergence of Social Assistance in China: Challenges and Issues. in James Midgley and Kwong-Leung Tang (eds.) *Social Policy and Poverty in East Asia: The Role of Social Security*. New York: Routledge.

to 24,214 workers between 1995 and 1996 (Chen 2000), while many faced a decrease or even went without subsistence subsidies (Cai 2006: 26). In 1997, for example, a large number of laid-off workers were reportedly living in debt, while some died of illnesses because they could not afford medical care (Chen 2000). Given the inadequate *xiagang* subsidies, an estimate of 70 to 85 million laid-off workers have to compete with peasant migrants and other *xiagong* workers to find work in the private sector (Chan 2001).

Constructing poor living conditions is thus arguably an essential prerequisite for pushing peasants and surplus laid-off (*xiagang*) SOE workers to participate in low-rate wages and a high rate of capitalist exploitation[15] for their livelihood (Gabriel 2006). Despite poor labor and living conditions had led to their protest involvement in the 1989 Tiananmen movement (see Chapter 1), the need to sustain a livelihood has secured approximately 42.7 million SOE laid-off workers (Pringle 2011: 42) alongside 230 million peasant workers[16] (Chan 2012: 359) to work in appalling conditions, such as 12 hours a day or longer for 7 days a week, in private sector throughout the 2000s (Mah 2011: 30). While the persistence of this particular labor practice created a business-friendly climate that leads to a subsequent coastal boom and accelerated the process of economic modernization, the failure of the CCP to eliminate abuses in its labor force such as unpaid wages has incited workers to increasingly participate in spontaneous labor protests (see Chapter 1).

[15] In 1997, the legal minimum wage was set at 420 yuan (USD 63.27) a month with a 44-hour week for Shenzhen Special Economic Zone (SEZ) which was lower than any ASEAN (Association of Southeast Asian Nations) countries. Workers were reportedly worked 10 to 12 hours a day or longer and received less than 400 yuan (or USD 60) a month throughout the 1990s. See Chan, Anita (2001) *China's Workers Under Assault: The Expoitation of Labour in a Globalizing Economy*, New York: An East Gate Book. See Skeldon, Ronald (1997) Hong Kong and Coastal China Growth Linkages. in Duncan Campbell Asma Lateef Aurelio Parisotto and Anil Verma (eds.) *Regionalization and Labour Market Interdependence in East and Southeast Asia*. London: MacMillan Press.

[16] The number of SOE laid-off workers employed by the private sector rose from 6.7 million in 1990 to 42.7 million in 2003. See Pringle, Tim (2011) *Trade Unions in China: The Challenge of Labour Unrest*, New York: Routledge. The number of peasant workers had soared from 120 million in 2000 to approximately 230 million in 2010 in the private sector. See Chan, Chris (2012) Labour Policies under Hu-Wen's Regime: Transformation and Challenges. in Joseph Cheng (ed.) *China: A New Stage of Development for an Emerging Superpower*. Hong Kong: City University of Hong Kong Press.

The Discourse of Weiwen 維穩*, Xiaokang* 小康 *and Hexie Shehui* 和諧社會

In the Eleventh Five-Year Plan for 2006–2010, the CCP deploys the discourse of maintenance of social stability (*weiwen* 維穩) (中共中央党史研究室 2016: Chapter 11) to highlight its dual concern with the increased protest activities and the need to secure the cheap labor force for China's economic growth (see Chapter 1). *Weiwen*, therefore, indicated not only the shift in emphasis away from coercive administrative measures and control of workers, but also a new strategy of the CCP to "connect to the global track" (Xu 2009: 38).

'Connecting to the global track', according to Feng Xu (2009: 38), is in part of both participating in the global supply chain production and conforming the administrative practices to international norms, including business and labor regulations. Aware that the rights of workers are often violated in the absence of a labor contract, the CCP promulgated the 2008 *Labor Contract Law* (see Chapter 1) to emphasize workers' responsibility of ensuring their employers signing a labor contract with them in order to protect their legal rights (Pringle 2011). Based on the 2009 Migrant Workers Survey in the Pearl River Delta of Guangdong Province and the 2010 China Urban Labor Survey, Mary Gallagher, John Giles, Albert Park, and Meiyan Wang (2013: 15) reveal that workers' awareness of the *Labor Contract Law* has significantly increased the number of contracts signed. The actions of the workers in signing contracts indicated their acceptance of selling their labor in exchange for a wage based on their positions as being *the workers* under the logic of competition in the labor market (Xu 2009). Workers' engagement in this 'market transaction' is one of the elements guiding them to meet the demands of the labor market, and hence guiding them to reinforce the CCP's *weiwen* project for the development of a well-off (*xiaokang* 小康) and harmonious society (*hexie shehui* 和諧社會) (Xu 2009; Brady 2012a; Benney 2016).

Another key component of building a *xiaokang* and harmonious society under *weiwen* discourse is linked with the CCP's "zero target" (Benney and Marolt 2015) project. This project aims to eliminate visible forms of protest actions, through the horizontal coordination with government agencies and private entrepreneurs (Chen 2015; Benney 2016). Since the last decade, private entrepreneurs are encouraged to become members of the People's Political Consultative Conference

(PPCC)[17] to participate in the governing activities at the national and local levels. Minglu Chen (2015: 616–617), for example, notes that the PPCC, along with the CCP, the Chinese People's Government, and the People's Congress, is referred to as '*the four sets of leadership*' (*si tao banzi* 四套班子), which constituted a "multi-party co-operation and political consultation" system. While the latter is the three political organs through which the CCP leaders exercised State power, the PPCC is the institution in bringing together the non-CCP entrepreneurs to support the CCP's rules (Chen 2015).

Under the leadership of the CCP, the PPCC serves as a channel for entrepreneur members to express opinions and thus influences State policies and regulations to protect their particular interests as a group. For example, the concern with the protection of private property rights raised by the members at the PPCC annual meeting in 2001 was passed into the *Property Law* in 2007 (Chen 2015: 627). The privileged status of the PPCC membership further extended to prevent the entrepreneurs from legal responsibilities even their enterprises have violated the provincial laws and regulations (Chen 2015). By turning private entrepreneurs into the State's 'allies' by raising protection for the PPCC members beyond laws and regulations, it is suggested that the CCP leaders seek to 'buy stability' by marginalizing the notions of laws and rights (Benney and Marolt 2015).

'Buying stability' in the context of the 'retreat from law' is thus extended to the social system to facilitate the work of *weiwen* (Benney and Marolt 2015). The establishment of local '*stability maintenance offices*' (*weiwenban* 維穩辦) which draws officials from the legal profession, the police, quasi-government organizations, and local government has been the mechanism to prevent protest and acts of resistance from formalizing (Benney 2013; Benney and Marolt 2015). Despite exercising physical forces on occasional basis, *weiwenban* tends to use informal negotiation and re-negotiation associated with financial compensation or small

[17] The People's Political Consultative Conference (PPCC) is a political consultative body that worked with the People's Congress in the State system. PPCC members' businesses are registered with capital of a minimum of 500,000 yuan and each member is required to donate a certain amount of money in each PPCC activity. For example, on a visiting trip to poor urban households, each entrepreneur member was assigned to donate 50,000 yuan. See Chen, Minglu (2015) 'From Economic Elites to Political Elites: Private Entrepreneurs in the People's Political Consultative Conference', *Journal of Contemporary China* 24(94): 613–627.

'coordination fees' to 'encourage' workers to discontinue their disputes (Benney 2013; Benney and Marolt 2015: 94). As a result, protests by workers are reportedly easily defused by a couple of yuan as compensation (Chen 2016: 4).

The post-Mao's *weiwen* project is originally linked with Deng's (1983, 1994, 2006) stability project, which aimed to maintain political stability and economic growth after the 1989 Tiananmen crisis. Following the crackdown on the Tiananmen protesters, Maoist leftists within the CCP resented Deng's modernization programs on economic reforms because they posed threats to social stability (Dreyer 1993; Dillon 2015). Against the leftists, Deng uses his "supreme status" as 'core leader' of the CCP[18]—a practice that is rooted in Mao's own struggle to legitimize the Cultural Revolution—to dismiss those who opposed economic reforms (Grasso et al. 2009: 244).

Deng asserts that the strategy for China's socialism is grounded on the expansion and development of productive forces by guiding the "proper" behaviors of 'the Chinese', particularly the 'dissident groups', to engage in a market economy (Xu 2009). Drawing on Mao's thought control methods, the post-Mao 'core leaders' from Deng to Xi Jinping[19] seek to revitalize the Confucian ideologies of filial piety and obey the superiors to continue their 'mandate' to rule under the control of the CCP (Dillon 2015). Already in 1982, the Confucian values of filial piety and obey the superiors are indicated in the '*Four Cardinal Principles*', that is, *Marxist-Leninism, Socialism, Party Leadership, and People's Democratic Dictatorship*, to demonstrate the CCP's commitment to Mao's idea of

[18] While Deng had been imprisoned following his opposition against Mao's approaches of revolutionary programmes such as the *Great Leap Forward* and the *Cultural Revolution*, he continued Mao's habits and strategies to remove his opponents to legitimize his 'mandate' to rule the CCP and the country. See MacFarquhar, Roderick (1997) Introduction. in Roderick MacFarquhar (ed.) *The Politics of China: The Eras of Mao and Deng*. Cambridge: Cambridge University Press, Grasso, June, Corrin, Jay and Kort, Michael (2009) *Modernization and Revolution: From the Opium Wars to the Olympics*, New York: M.E. Sharpe, Inc, Dillon, Michael (2015) *Deng Xiaoping: The Man who Made Modern China*, London: I.B. Tauris & Co. Ltd.

[19] Following previous generations led by Mao Zedong, Deng Xiaoping, Jiang Zemin and Hu Jintao, Xi Jinping is the fifth generation from 2012 to present day. See Kuhn, Robert (2011) *How China's Leaders Think: The Inside Story of China's Past, Current and Future Leaders*, Singapore: Wiley.

embracing absolute political control of the masses (Li 2015). This insistence is further announced in the '*Five Nos*' (*wugebugao* 五個不搞) policy for the modernization process:

> We have made a solemn declaration that we will not employ a system of multiple parties holding office in rotation; diversify our guiding thought; separate executive, legislative and judicial powers; use a bicameral or federal system, or carry out privatization.[20]
>
> (Wu 2011a: 9)

Combining with the '*Four Cardinal Principles*', the '*Five Nos*' policy which emphasized Deng's message on economic with limited political reform is circulated to legitimize his absolute power through the CCP's Central Propaganda Department[21] (Weatherley 2006).

Thought Work in Post-Mao Period

As in the Maoist period, the manipulation and utilization of the Propaganda Department have become an important tool to initiate post-Mao thought management system for complementing and supporting the party policies (Brady 2012a; Benney 2013).

With the new laws and legal system development since the 1980s, the CCP idea of using the '*law popularization campaign*' (*pufa yundong* 普法運動) or '*disseminating legal knowledge*' (*pufa changshi* 普法常識) to herald new policies in activating the masses to engage in the State's defined "good socialist behaviors" (Gallagher 2005, 2006) begins to take shape:

> In the interest of developing socialist democracy and improving the socialist legal system, it is necessary to place the law in the hands of the masses of people so that they will know what the law is, abide by the law, acquire

[20] The word 'privatisation' in China was replaced by numerous terms, such as reorganization, cooperatives, incorporation, leasing contract, and shareholding cooperatives. See Guo, Sujian (2013) *Chinese Politics and Government: Power, Ideology and Organization*, New York: Routledge.

[21] The CCP's Central Propaganda Department was given strong supervisory powers over the major government ministries, for example, the Ministries of Education and Publication, and over the entire nexus of mass media. See Weatherley, Robert (2006) *Politics in China since 1949: Legitimizing Authoritarian Rule*, New York: Routledge.

> a sense of legality and learn to use the law as a weapon against all acts committed in violation of the Constitution and the law...
>
> (Thirteen Meeting of the Standing Committee of the Sixth National People's Congress, November 22, 1985)

Rather than focusing on legal resolution of grievances, the dissemination or *pufa* movement enacted in 1991 aims at acquainting the masses with basic knowledge of the laws by inculcating them with a wide variety of State's propaganda or ideologies to shape their legal consciousness (Benney 2013). These legal educational campaigns are implemented by the CCP cadres through workplaces, mass media, and educational systems (Gallagher 2005). For example, the 'thought emancipation movement' (1979–1981) is regularly used to transmit the truth about *Deng Xiaoping Theory* of economic reform and modernization to cultivate them with correct thoughts and practices—filial piety and hard work—through the Chinese media (Jeffreys and Su 2016). Other ideological campaigns '*anti-spiritual pollution*' (1983–1984) and the '*socialist spiritual civilization campaign*' (1987–1998) are launched against the influx of Western democratic values and habits (Leung 2017). These campaigns are eventually a call for CCP members to promote *Deng Xiaoping Theory* of economic reform and modernization in order to command support from the workers over whom they are to rule (Grasso et al. 2009).

As the *pufa* campaign progressed, a wide range of compulsory re-education programs of the 'party rectification campaigns' and 'theoretical study movements' (1989–2000) of *Marxism-Leninism, Mao Zedong Thought,* and *Deng Xiaoping Theory* are implemented to penetrate the socialist ideologies and moralities (Li 2015) into the minds of workers. For instance, at the national conference on the 'party rectification campaigns' and 'theoretical study movements' in 1998, the philosophical absolutism of the CCP in command of the absolute 'truth' and correctness in building a 'socialist market economy' is emphasized:

> Taking the socialist road is the inevitable outcome of Chinese history and the correct choice of the Chinese people... Any attempt to abandon socialism or take the capitalist road is completely wrong and fundamentally infeasible... Our reform is absolutely not to engage in capitalism, but is the self-perfection of the socialist system and the need of consolidating and developing socialism.
>
> (Jiang Zemin cited in Guo 2013: 118)

The above message is transmitted via the implementation of 'scientific development' and 'harmonious society' campaigns (2010) through the national education system, mass media, residential areas, and workplaces. In so doing, these campaigns further highlight Chinese workers as a 'matter of concern for China's destiny' (Brady 2008: 51) in order to mobilize them to work for economic modernization.

Chinese Habits of Making Docile Bodies and Minds Within Social Hierarchy

While dissociating from Mao's revolutionary orthodoxy, the Maoist past "habits" of ideological indoctrination and techniques of propaganda are repeatedly employed to re-constitute docile bodies and minds among workers for sustainable socioeconomic development (***kechixuxing de shehui jingjin fazhan*** 可持續性的社會經濟發展) (Jeffreys and Su 2016).

With rapid economic development associated with the growth of poverty, the third and the fourth generations of the CCP leaders Jiang Zemin and Hu Jintao seek to minimize social discontent and instability by upgrading the control methods (Xu 2009). From 2001 onwards, the Hu administration incorporated new discourses into the Confucian values to promote awareness of 'proper behaviors', such as respect for authorities, between the positions (or status) of workers and work superiors, to meet the needs of economic modernization in a well-off (***xiaokang***) and harmonious society (***hexie shehui***) (Brady 2012b). The new set of values that are guiding the behaviors of workers begin with the creation of numerous identities through the mass media. In this process, the CCP aimed to change social images of both peasant migrant and SOE workers by referring to the latter as ***gongren*** 工人 (SOE workers) (Wagner 1998) and the former as ***nonmingong*** 農民工 (peasant workers), as well as ***mangliu*** 盲流 (blind floats), ***wailaigong*** 外來工 (outside workers), and ***dagong*** 打工 (working for bosses).

Unlike their former status as 'masters of the state' (Warner and Zhu 2010) under Mao's period, workers' new identities were now accorded a subservient status, which was programmed to be at a lower social position. This status degradation, according to Feng Xu (2009), is linked to the new discourse of 'low personal quality' (***suzhi*** 素質 or human capital). This discourse is used to create a self-value among workers for accepting social inequalities in the market economy. This effort is an attempt to mold workers into 'low personal quality' subjects to become active participants in capitalist exploitation in the updated hierarchy of social relationships.

In making China's economy globally competitive, the value of education has become a priority to constitute 'low personal quality' workers to ensure the supply of a mass of cheap labor for production (Wang 2008). This objective is achieved through the rapid expansion of educational opportunities by popularizing secondary and tertiary vocational-technical education that teaches employment skills to enable graduates to work in the cities (Postiglione 2011). The admission criterion is subject to the completion of the nine-year education program under the *Compulsory Education Law* (Wang 2008). While the national population is "guaranteed" a nine-year of compulsory schooling by law, access to education is determined by the *hukou* (or household) status the person held. The difference in the educational arrangements between rural and urban populations is that the latter is entitled to a set of social rights associated with the provision of medical care, housing, childcare, and access to local schools with very low fees (Wang 2008). These basic entitlements are denied to the rural peasants—which accounted for more than half of the national population—both in their village hometowns and the cities (Wu 2011b).

Children of migrant peasants are thus either left behind (*liushou ertong* 留守兒童) with relatives in the villages or brought into the cities for education (Zhang et al. 2015). In the former case, rural children begin a two- to three-year education in the villages when they turn eight years old. This is because rural schools are far from homes and the roads are generally unsafe for small children (Postiglione 2011). In the latter case, migrant children, formally referred to as *jiedu* 借讀 students (students from outside the community that borrowed a place to study), have to pay three types of fees (see Table 2.1) besides the regular fees that all students have to pay in public schools (Wang 2008: 694):

Given the monthly household income of most migrant parents is between 800 and 1500 yuan in the cities, which is around the local poverty line in most localities, a large proportion of the children of migrants are either educated in migrant schools (*minban xuexiao* 民辦學校) in the cities or in rural schools in the villages. Due to financial issues, these schools have low-quality teaching staff and poor facilities (Wang 2008; Postiglione 2011).

The making of a socialist market in the CCP's economic modernization concerns with the ability of the population to pay for a quality education

Table 2.1 Example of Three Types of Fees in Beijing in 2000

Types of fee	*Fee descriptions*	*Fees per terms per head*
jiedu fei	Fee for non-local resident in a public school	480 yuan
ze xiao fei	Fee for selecting the public school	1000 yuan
zan zhu fei	Fee for supporting the public school	Average: 1908 yuan Highest: 20,000–30,000 yuan

Source The Marginality of Migrant Children in the Rural Chinese Educational System (Wang 2008: 695–696)

that might gain them employment (Postiglione 2011). Compared to their urban counterparts, the majority of poor rural households are excluded from the mainstream norm of access to public schools that offered quality education, both in the cities and in their villages (Wang 2008). This deliberate exclusion of the rural groups from access to educational resources and opportunities beyond a limited circle of eligibilities thus leads to high dropout rates from the low-quality, rural, and migrant primary schools:

> dropout rates... were between 3.66% and 54.05% ...beyond food and clothing, dropping out is caused by a lack of confidence and interest in continuing their education, difficult textbooks, a monotonous school life, tense relationships between students and teachers, poor food and lodging, inconvenient transportation and rising costs of school lodgings.
>
> (Postiglione 2011: 90)

By confining rural and migrant populations to the category of low-quality education, the CCP leaders thus implicitly encourage children to discontinue education, through which a minimum of 300 million illiterate and semi-illiterate[22] people have already been created in China (Mao 2004). The intentional education inequality has thus ensured that a large proportion of people could not get a higher education in order to (re-) produce 'low personal quality' workers for the marketplace.

[22] China defines illiterates and semi-illiterates as people who are twelve years of age or older who do not know characters, or know less than 1,500 characters, cannot read popular books and magazines, and cannot write simple words. See Miao, Xiaochun (1992) China. in John Hladczuk and William Eller (eds.) *International Handbook of Reading Education*. London: Greenwood Press.

Images of 'low personal quality' workers are portrayed as a specific segment of the population that prevented China's progress toward civilization (*wenming* 文明) (Gabriel 2006; Xu 2009). In an editorial comment in a prestigious Party newspaper, the 'low-quality' population is described as lacking discipline and modern civility because 'they behav[e] like barbarians [...] forgetting [...] civility demands [...]' (*China Daily* 2014). As a result of widespread indoctrination, this official 'truth' becomes an everyday discourse that appeared in various cultural mechanisms, such as television and magazines. For example, in a national newspaper *Nanfang Zhoumo* 南方週末 (*Southern Weekend*), a reader complained to the editor that 'the low-quality people are the reason for many things not getting done or not getting done well' (Xiaoyong 1999: 11). In his book, *China's Two Pillars in the Twenty-First Century*, Zhou Yi (2001: 748) suggests a more pessimistic view of the large numbers of so-called low-quality citizens by making the point that it is these people that 'made it so difficult to advance our country… We must get rid of the illiterate people… particularly those illiterate young people'. A Chinese reporter in *Philippine World News* comments that 'we have to admit that our quality is low… when compared to those in Western countries' (Xiaogang 2016).

Social recognition of the 'low-quality' population is applied predominantly to workers and is central to the production of 'new city people' (*xin shimin* 新市民) as the subjects of Chinese "development" (Yan 2003; Xu 2009). This 'development' centered on the 'rectification' of population quality, in terms of which workers are identified by the CCP from the 1980s, as the major focus for 'improvement': 'The national strength and the stamina of economic development was highly dependent on the quality of the laborers' (Zeng 1989: 165). Embedded in this invocation of "quality improvement" (or development) has been the CCP's interest to continue poverty by recoding such "problem" as "quality poverty relief" (*suzhi fupin* 素質扶貧) and "cultural poverty relief" (*wenhua fupin* 文化扶貧) in the labor market (Yan 2003). In this context, "poverty-relief" discourses are functioned as a "motivating force" to cultivate a desire within the 'low personal quality' workers to escape from poverty (*tuopin* 脱貧) (Yan 2008). Thus, the introduction of this new discourse by the State marks a shift from projecting workers as being an object to becoming a subject for "poverty-relief" actions. The project of producing these desiring subjects is appositely a subtle task of producing 'new city people' for Chinese 'development' (or improvement).

It is argued that the production of the *desiring* subjects is facilitated through the production of a market consciousness among workers for "development" in the cultural processes. In these processes, images of the outcomes of "poverty-relief" that resulted from 'improvement', for example with the increased affordability of mobile phones and cars, are promoted in the Chinese media. These commercial activities are used to promote the idea that "the future belongs to those who succeed in the capitalist labor power markets" (Gabriel 2006: 58) to turn workers into customers. With a view to inculcating consumerism into the popular consciousness, instruments of mass media are again mobilized as a form of "social education" (*shehui jiaoyu* 社會教育). The benefits of "improvement" are publicized on media to inspire the subjects' "intentionality" toward the "development" of the selves in the labor market. This vision produced a positive demonstration of "poverty-relief" being gifted through the opportunities offered by "development", because 'low quality' workers could 'improve themselves by learning from their "high quality" superiors at work in the cities' (Yan 2008; emphasis added).

By introducing a self-perception of workers as the subjects of "development", the discourse of "quality improvement" further constituted a 'status consciousness' (Koo 2001) or 'older rules consciousness' (Perry 2009) that is connected to an updated Confucian status ideology framework of a "quality hierarchy" within social relationships. This hierarchal relationship is defined in terms of the deterministic identities with which the 'lower-quality' workers are shaped and programmed to see themselves as inferior to their 'higher-quality' superiors in the labor market (Gabriel 2006). The perception of a fundamental difference of "quality" that comprised distinct "races" of human beings is thereby notionally created:

> "white" workers gaining status as a consequence of racism. To the extent that certain workers gain status within the workplace as a consequence of racism, these workers may be willing to work for less material compensation. This is one way in which racism may reduce the value of labor power. It may also do so by creating self-doubt, self-hatred and low self-esteem in those excluded from the transcendental race. The "black"... worker ...for instance, believe[s] herself lucky to have any job and to be worthless...
>
> (Gabriel and Todorova 2003: 34–35)

By substituting "high-quality" for white and "low-quality" for black, the racialized interactions of the perceived inferiority (the low) and the perceived superiority (the high) served to lower the value of workers in a quality hierarchy. Rather than a "quality improvement", the discourse of "development" hence imposed the notion of *ming* (destiny) on inferiority. The functioning of the discourse as a "truth" of the 'low personal quality' workers would then guide them to think of themselves as low within their subjectivities with respect to their given positions in the current labor market system.

The Destiny (Ming 命) of Low-Quality (or Low-Educated) Workers in the Chinese Occupational Hierarchy

The intention of indoctrinating workers to accept their positions as their '*ming*' and the discourse of "quality development" is to subject the perceived inferiors to continual readjustment and retraining (*zhongsheng xuexi* 終生學習) in order to integrate them into the market economy (Yan 2008).

To achieve this goal, the workers are taught to 'love labor' and respect regulations to behave "properly" according to the everyday behavioral norms (*richang xingweu judong* 日常行為舉動) of the workplaces (Efthymiou-Egleton 2016). For example, they are taught to respect authority to ensure the maintenance of social order (Xu 2009). In this context, compliance with the social order is highlighted by the Chinese media as a way for workers to protect their rights. For instance, the Chinese popular press published cautionary tales about workers trying to find work in their own way outside the norms. These narratives typically end either with the victims being cheated by "black" labor market brokers (*hei zhongjie* 黑中介) (Zhengzhou Wǎnbào 2016) or sold into prostitution (Ma 2013).

To reduce social disruptions, services are provided to workers by the 'carceral network' (Foucault 1980a) of governmental and non-governmental organizations, such as job-seeking and educational training regarding laws and regulations in order to highlight the importance of signing labor contracts (Xu 2009). By exposing themselves to these forms of knowledge, the inferior subjects are supposedly guided to "improve" their understanding of labor rights and conditions throughout the process of 'development'. While the 'low-quality' workers are offered new training opportunities for continuous "self-improvement", these 'opportunities' are arguably designed to engage them as potential agents in their own governance (Jeffreys and Sigley 2009).

The goal of this social management is embodied in the knowledge in which an array of CCP's-conceived standards of modernized behaviors is promoted by means of service activities (or programs) (Cartier 2016). Cooperating with the CCP's interest in developing "population quality" (*renkou suzhi* 人口素質) in the discourse of modernization, social programs run by the everyday 'carceral network' focus on the Chinese cultural economy and industry and standards for social conduct (National Civilised City Evaluation System 2011). These cultural standards are evident in large-format advertising slogans, including "*Be a Civilized Person, Build a Civilized City* (*Zheng zuo wenming ren, gong chuang wenming cheng* 爭做文明人共創文明城)" and "*Speak Civilly, Act Civilly*" (*Shuo wenming hua, ban wenming shi*…說文明話辦文明事) (Cartier 2016). These civilizing perspectives are extensively reinforced by "quality training" (*suzhi peixun* 素質培训) and "quality programmes" (*suzhi jiemu* 素質節目) throughout cultural institutions, such as the mass media, within schools and on the streets (Cartier 2016), and are printed in the form of self-help manuals to encourage workers to act according to sanctioned behavioral standards.

In one 'self-help' manual (MDGIF 2011), for example, 'low quality' workers are encouraged to be satisfied with their low-wage employments, and relinquish excessive consumption behavior, obey traffic lights and adopt good hygiene habits to exhibit 'proper' manners. Constructing these official and standardized "civilized behaviors" (or cultural norms) highlights the CCP's desire to improve self-constraint and self-control (or self-governance) among workers to ensure that they constitute appropriate subjects in the context of "development" programs.

In this manner, the discourse of "quality" under the label "development" is arguably used to confine the 'low-quality' population to a specific status. The knowledge about "development" is aimed at conditioning the self-attitude and conduct of the workers so that they will behave (Davidson 2003) in accordance with cultural norms and the "quality-based" occupational hierarchy in China. It is this knowledge about being *the workers* that has been facilitated by and circulated through the everyday 'carceral network' to continuously inculcate forms of discourses of *truth* in the minds of workers to direct them to think and act toward these normative cultural behaviors. This then enables the ongoing (re-) production of docile minds and bodies to serve the will of the CCP within the power-knowledge networks in China.

Concluding Remarks

Foucault's genealogical method has been used to explore the development of workers' consciousness throughout the various historical periods of Chinese civilization.

The analysis illustrates how *li* (later Confucian) rules had been evolved from direct and brutal forms of physical punishment to internalized social norms to create the Chinese docile bodies and minds among 'the Chinese' to uphold their social behaviors since the Zhou dynasty (13th B.C.E.) through to Mao's period. Based on historical cycles, the post-Mao leaders consolidate their 'mandate' to rule by continuing the production and reproduction of docile bodies and minds among Chinese workers through the internalization of the Confucian concept of social status. This status is further reinforced by the "quality" discourse to guide the 'low personal quality' to think of themselves as destined for marginal positions (or governmentality) throughout their lived experiences in the thought management system.

The next two chapters explore how the experiences of living and working in post-Mao China have shaped the consciousness of everyday Chinese workers, and how this consciousness affects their activism, as well as their ability to develop themselves into organized labor movement to improve their living and working conditions for themselves and others.

Bibliography

Ahn, Byung-Joon. 1975. The Political Economy of the People's Commune in China: Changes and Continuities. *The Journal of Asian Studies* 34 (3): 631–658.

Bao, Shuming, Gene Hsin Chang, Jeffrey Sachs, and Wing Thye Woo. 2002. Geographic Factors and China's Regional Development under Market Reforms, 1978–1998. *China Eocnomic Review* 13: 89–111.

Barlow, John. 1981. Mass Line Leadership and Thought Reform in China. *American Psychologist* 36 (3): 300–309.

Benney, Jonathan. 2013. *Defending Rights in Contemporary China: Reserving the Right*. New York: Routledge.

Benney, Jonathan. 2016. Weiwen at the Grassroots: China's Stability Maintenance Apparatus as a Means of Conflict Resolution. *Journal of Contemporary China* 25 (99): 389–405.

Benney, Jonathan, and Peter Marolt. 2015. Modes of Activism and Engagement in the Chinese Public Sphere. *Asian Studies Review* 39 (1): 88–89.

Bentham, Jeremy. 1843. *The Works of Jeremy Bentham*. Edinburgh: William Tait.

Besley, Tina, and Michael A. Peters. 2007. *Subjectivity & Truth: Foucault, Education, and the Culture of Self*. New York: Peter Lang.

Brady, Anne-Marie. 2008. *Marketing Dictatorship: Propaganda and Thought Work in Contemporary China*. Lanham, MD: Rowman & Littlefield Publishers.

Brady, Anne-Marie. 2012a. Introduction: Market-Friendly, Scientific, High Tech, And Politics-lite: China's New Approach to Propoganda. *China's Thought Management*, ed. Anne-Marie Brady. New York: Routledge.

Brady, Anne-Marie. 2012b. State Confucianism, Chineseness, and tradition in CCP Propaganda. *China's Thought Management*, ed. Anne-Marie Brady. New York: Routledge.

Breslin, Shaun. 2014. *Mao: Profiles in Power*. New York: Routledge.

Bridgham, Philip. 1968. Mao's Cultural Revolution in 1967: The Struggle to Seize Power. *The China Quarterly* 34: 6–37.

Brook, Timothy, Jérôme. Bourgon, and Gregory Blue. 2008. *Death by a Thousand Cuts*. London: Harvard University Press.

Burrell, Gibson. 1988. Modernism, Post Modernism and Organizational Analysis 2: The Contribtion of Michel Foucault. *Organization Studies* 9 (2): 221–235.

Cai, Yongshun. 2006. *State and Laid-off Workers in Reform China: The Silence and Collective Action of the Retrenched*. New York: Routledge.

Cartier, Carolyn. 2016. Governmentality and the Urban Economy: Consumption, Excess, and the 'Civilised City' in China. In *New Mentalities of Government in China*, ed. David Bray and Elaine Jeffreys. New York: Routledge.

Chan, Anita. 2000. Globalization, China's Free (Read Bonded) Labour Market, and the Chinese Trade Unions. *Asia Pacific Business Review* 6 (3–4): 260–281.

Chan, Anita. 2001. *China's Workers Under Assault: The Expoitation of Labour in a Globalizing Economy*. New York: An East Gate Book.

Chan, Chris. 2012. Labour Policies under Hu-Wen's Regime: Transformation and Challenges. In *China: A New Stage of Development for an Emerging Superpower*, ed. Joseph Cheng. Hong Kong: City University of Hong Kong Press.

Chan, Kam Wing, and Zhang Li. 1999. The Hukou System and Rural-Urban Migration in China: Processes and Changes. *The China Journal* 160: 818–855.

Chen, Feng. 2000. Subsistence Crises, Managerial Corruption and Labour Protests in China. *The China Journal* 44: 41–63.

Chen, Jie. 2013. *A Middle Class without Democracy: Economic Growth and the Prospects for Democratization in China*. Oxford: Oxford University Press.

Chen, Minglu. 2015. From Economic Elites to Political Elites: Private Entrepreneurs in the People's Political Consultative Conference. *Journal of Contemporary China* 24 (94): 613–627.

Chen, Minglu, and Goodman, David. 2012. The Asia Pacific, Regionalism and the Global System. In *The Asia-Pacific, Regionalism and the Global System*, ed. Christopher Dent and Jörn Dosch. Northampton, MA: Edward Elgar Publishing Limited.

Chen, Minglu, and Goodman, David. 2013. Introduction: Middle Class China - Discourse, Structure and Practice. In *Middle Class China: Identity and Behaviour*, ed. Minglu Chen and David Goodman. Cheltenham: Edward Elgar.

Chen, Xi. 2016. Elitism and Exclusion in Mass Protest: Privatization, Resistance, and State Domination in China. *Comparative Political Studies* 50 (7): 1–27.

Chen, Xiaoming. 2002. Social Control in China: Applications of the Labeling Theory and the Reintegrative Shaming Theory. *International Journal of Offender Therapy and Comparative Criminology* 46 (45): 45–62.

Cheung, Tiejun, and Selden, Mark. 1994. The Origins and Social Consequences of China's Hukou System. *The China Quarterly* (139): 644–668.

Clifford, Michael. 2001. *Political Genealogy After Foucault: Savage Identities*. New York: Routledge.

Confucius. 2003. *The Analects of Confucius*. Beijing, China: Beijing Book Co.

Confucius. 2010. *The Analects of Confucius*. Auckland: The Floating Press.

Crowther, David, and Miriam Green. 2004. *Organisational Theory*. London: Chartered Institute of Personnel and Development.

Daily, China. 2014. Editorial: Tourists, Behave Yourselves, December 15.

Davidson, Arnold. 2003. Ethics as Ascetics: Foucault, the History of Ethics, and Ancient Thought. In *The Cambridge Companion to Foucault*, ed. Gary Gutting. New York: Cambridge University Press.

Dean, Mitchell. 2010. *Governmentality: Power and Rule in Modern Society*. Los Angeles: Sage.

Deng, Xiaoping. 1983/1994/2006. *Selected Works of Deng Xiaoping (邓小平文选)*. Beijing: 人民出版社 (People's Publishing House).

Dikotter, Frank. 2010. *Mao's Great Famine: The History of China's Most Devasting Catastrophe, 1958–1962*. New York: Walker Publishing Company.

Dillon, Michael. 2015. *Deng Xiaoping: The Man who Made Modern China*. London: I.B. Tauris.

Dittmer, Lowell. 1973. Mass Line and "Mass Criticism" in China: An analysis of the Fall of Liu Shao-Ch'i. *Asian Survey* 13 (8): 772–792.

Dittmer, Lowell. 1981. China in 1980: Modernization and its Discontents. *Asian Survey* 21 (1): 31–50.
Downing, Lisa. 2008. *The Cambridge Introduction to Michel Foucault*. Cambridge: Cambridge University Press.
Dreyer, June. 1993. *China's Political System: Modernization and Tradition*. New York: Paragon House Publishers.
Efthymiou-Egleton, Iris. 2016. *Do We Really Know China?: An Outsiders View*. Bloomington: Xlibris Corporation.
Fan, Cindy. 2003. Rural-Urban Migration and Gender Division of Labor in Transitional China. *International JOurnal of Urban and Regional Research* 27 (1): 24–47.
Fan, Cindy. 2004. The State, the Migrant Labor Regime, and Maiden Workers in China. *Political Geography* 23: 283–305.
Foucault, Michel. 1971/1977. Nietzsche, Genealogy, History. In *Language, Counter-Memory, Practice: Selected Essays and Interviews*, ed. D Bouchard. Ithaca: Cornell University Press.
Foucault, Michel. 1976. *The History of Sexuality*. New York: Penguin Books.
Foucault, Michel. 1977. *Discipline and Punish: The Birth of the Prison*. New York: Vintage Books.
Foucault, Michel. 1978. *The History of Sexuality, Volume 1: An Introduction*. New York: Pantheon Books.
Foucault, Michel. 1980a. *Power/Knowledge: Selected Interviews and Other Writings 1972–1977*. New York: Vintage Books.
Foucault, Michel. 1980b. *Truth and Subjectivity Howison Lectures*. Berkeley: University of California.
Foucault, Michel. 1982. The Subject and Power. In *Michel Foucault: Beyond Structuralism and Hermeneutics*, ed. Hubert Dreyfus and Paul Rabinow. Chicago: University of Chicago Press.
Foucault, Michel. 1986. *The Care of the Self*. New York: Pantheon Books.
Foucault, Michel. 1987. The Ethic of Care for the Self as a Practice of Freedom: An Interview with Michel Foucault on January 20, 1984. *Philosophy & Social Critisim* 12: 112–131.
Foucault, Michel. 1990. *The Use of Pleasure*. New York: Vintage Books.
Foucault, Michel. 1997. *Ethics, Subjectivity and Truth: The Essential Works of Foucault 1954–1984*. New York: The New Press.
Foucault, Michel. 1997b. *The Politics of Truth*. New York: Semiotext(e).
Foucault, Michel. 2001. *Power: The Essential Works of Foucault 1954–1984*. London: Penguin Books.
Foucault, Michel. 2002. *The Order of Things: An Archaeology of the Human Sciences*. New York: Routledge.
Foucault, Michel. 2006. *History of Madness*. New York: Routledge.

Foucault, Michel. 2008. *The Birth of Biopolitics: Lectures at the Collège de France, 1978–1979*. New York: Palgrave Macmillan.

Foucault, Michel, Luther Martin, Huck Gutman, and Patrick Hutton. 1988. *Technologies of the Self: A Seminar with Michel Foucault*. Amherst, MA: University of Massachusetts Press.

Foucault, Michel, and Paul Rabinow. 1991. *The Foucault Reader: An Introduction to Foucault's Thought*. Harmondsworth: Penguin.

Fouts, Jeffrey, and Jack Chan. 1995. Confucius, Mao and Modernization: Social Studies Education in the People's Republic of China. *Journal of Curriculum Studies* 27 (5): 523–543.

Fund, Ho.-lup. 2001. The Making and Melting of the "Iron Rice Bowl" in China 1949 to 1995. *Social Policy & Administration* 35 (3): 258–273.

Gabriel, Satyananda. 2006. *Chinese Capitalism and the Modernist Vision*. New York: Routledge.

Gabriel, Satyananda, and Evgenia Todorova. 2003. Racism and Capitalist Accumulation: An Overdetermined Nexus. *Critical Sociology* 29: 29–46.

Gallagher, Mary. 2005. "Use the Law as Your Weapon!": Institutional Change and Legal Mobilization in China. In *Engaging the Law in China: State, Society, and Possibilities for Justice*, ed. Neil Diamant Staanley Lubman and Kelvin O'Brien. Stanford: Stanford University Press.

Gallagher, Mary. 2006. Mobilizing the Law in China: "Informed Disenchantment" and the Development of Legal Consciousness. *Law & Society Review* 40 (4): 783–816.

Gallagher, Mary, John Giles, Albert Park, and Meiyan Wang. 2013. China's 2008 Labor Contract Law: Implementation and Implications for China's Workers: The World Bank.

Gao, Gao, and Jiaqi Yan. 1986. *Ten Years of the Cultural Revolution: 1966–1976 文化大革命十年史: 1966–1976*. Tianjin, China: Tianjin People's Publishing House.

Giddens, Anthony, and Fred Dallmayr. 1982. *Profiles and Critiques in Social Theory*. Los Angeles: University of California Press.

Girdner, Eddie. 2004. China as a Capitalist State: From "Primitive Socialist Accumulation" to Neoliberal Capitalism. *The Turkish Yearbook* XXXV: 121–144.

Goldman, Merle. 1975. China's Anti-Confucian Campaign, 1973–74. *The China Quarterly* 63: 435–462.

Grasso, June, Jay Corrin, and Michael Kort. 2009. *Modernization and Revolution: From the Opium Wars to the Olympics*. New York: M.E. Sharpe Inc.

Guo, Sujian. 2013. *Chinese Politics and Government: Power Ideology and Organization*. New York: Routledge.

Gutting, Gary. 2003. Michel Foucault: A User's Manual. In *The Cambridge Companion*, ed. Gary Gutting. Cambridge: Cambridge University Press.

Harvey, David. 2005. *A Brief History of Neoliberalism*. New York: Oxford University Press.
He, Shu. 2010. Music Schedule during the Cultural Revolution 文革中的歌曲时间, http://www.aisixiang.com/data/37170.html. Accessed 16 May 2020.
Hook, Derek. 2005. Genealogy, Discourse, 'Effective History': Foucault and the Work of Critique. *Qualitative Research in Psychology* 2 (1): 3–31.
Hurst, William. 2009. *The Chinese Worker After Socialism*. Cambridge: Cambridge University Press.
Hurst, William, and Kelvin O'Brien. 2002. China's Contentious Pensioners. *The China Quarterly* 170: 345–360.
Jeffreys, Elaine, and Sigley, Gary. 2009. Governmentality, Governance and China. In *China's Governmentalities: Governing Change, Changing Government*, ed. Elaine Jeffreys. New York: Routledge.
Jeffreys, Elaine, and Xuezhong Su. 2016. Governing Through Lei Feng: A Mao-era Role Model in Reform-era China. In *New Mentalities of Government in China*, ed. David Bray and Elaine Jeffreys. New York: Routledge.
Koo, Hagen. 2001. *Korean Workers: The Culture and Politics of Class Formation*. London: Cornell University Press.
Kuhn, Robert. 2011. *How China's Leaders Think: The Inside Story of China's Past, Current and Future Leaders*. Singapore: Wiley.
Landsberger, Stefan. 2002. The Deification of Mao: Religious Imagery and Practices during the Cultural Revolution and Beyond. In Woei Lien Chong (ed.) *China's Great Proletarian Cultural Revolution*. Oxford: Rowman & Littlefield Publishers.
Lee, Ching Kwan. 1999. From Organized Dependence to Disorganized Despotism: Changing Labour Regimes in Chinese Factories. *The China Quarterly* 45: 44–71.
Lee, Ching Kwan. 2007. *Against the Law: Labor Protests in China's Rustbelt and Sunbelt*. Berkeley: University of California Press.
Lee, Hong-Yung. 2000. Xiagang, the Chinese Style of Laying Off Workers. *Asian Survey* 40 (6): 914–937.
Leung, Elly. 2016. Docile Bodies and Minds: A Genealogy of Chinese Workers in China. In *TASA 2016 Conference*, ed. Mark Chou. The Australian Catholic University, Fitzroy, Melbourne.
Leung, Joe, and Xu, Andy. 2010. The Emergence of Social Assistance in China: Challenges and Issues. In *Social Policy and Poverty in East Asia: The Role of Social Security*, ed. James Midgley and Kwong-Leung Tang. New York: Routledge.
Leung, Laifong. 2017. *Contemporary Chinese Fiction Writers: Biography, Bibliography, and Critical Assessment*. New York: Routledge.
Leung, Wing-Yue. 1988. *Smashing the Iron Rice Pot: Workers and Unions in China's Market Socialism*. Hong Kong: Asia Labour Monitor.

Li, He. 2015. *Political Thought and China's Transformation: Ideas Shaping Reform in Post-Mao China*. London: Palgrave Macmillan.

Li, Wei, and Dennis Tao Yang. 2005. The Great Leap Forward: Anatomy of a Central Planning Disaster. *Journal of Political Economy* 113 (4): 840–877.

Liew, Leong. 2005. China's Engagement with Neo-liberalism: Path Dependency, Geography and Party Self-Reinvention. *The Journal of Development Studies* 41 (2): 331–352.

Lin, Justin, Fang Cai, and Zhou Li. 1996. *The China Miracle: Development Strategy and Economic Reform*. Hong Kong: The Chinese University of Hong Kong.

Lippit, Victor. 1982. China's Socialist Development. In *The Transition to Socialism in China*, ed. Mark Selden and Victor Lippit. New York: M.E. Sharpe

Lu, Xing. 1998. *Rhetoric in Ancient China, Fifth to Third Century B.C.E.: A Comparison with Classical Greek Rhetoric*. Columbia, SC: University of South Carolina Press.

Lu, Xing. 2004. *Rhetoric of the Chinese Cultural Revolution: The Impact on Chinese Thought, Culture, and Communication*. Columbia: University of South Carolina Press.

Ma, Xīnbīn. 2013. 14 Suì Shàonǚ Zhǎo Gōngzuò Shàngdàng Bèi Bī Màiyín 20 tiān jiēkè 200 Cì (14-year-old Girl Forced into Prostitution), September 27.

MacFarquhar, Roderick. 1997. Introduction. In *The Politics of China: The Eras of Mao and Deng*, ed. Roderick MacFarquhar. Cambridge: Cambridge University Press.

MacFarquhar, Roderick, and Michael Schoenhals. 2006. *Mao's Last Revolution*. Cambridge: Harvard University Press.

Magill, Kevin. 1997. Surveillance-Free-Subjects. In *The Impact of Michel Foucault on the Social Sciences and Humanities*, ed. Moya Lloyd and Andrew Thacker. London: Macmillan Press Ltd.

Mah, Ben. 2011. *China and the World: Global Crisis of Capitalism*. Bloomington: iUniverse.

Mallee, Hein. 2000. Migration, Hukou, Resistance in Reform China. In *Chinese Society, 2nd Edition: Change, Conflict and Resistance*, ed. Elizabeth Perry and Mark Selden. New York: Routledge.

Mao, Xin. 2004. China: Views of a Medical Geneticist. In *Genetics and Ethics in Global Perspective*, ed. Dorothy Wertz and John Fletcher. London: Kluwer Academic Publishers.

Mao, Zedong. 1949/2013. *On the People's Democratic Dictatorship*. Hunan, China: Green Apple Data Center.

Mao, Zedong. 1966. *Mao Zedong Thought*. Beijing, China: People's Publishing House.

Mao, Zedong. 1977. *Selected Works of Mao Zedong 毛泽东选集*. Beijing, China: People's Publishing House.
Mao, Zedong. 1986. *The Writings of Mao Zedong: 1949–1976*. New York: M.E. Sharpe.
Mao, Zedong. 2013. *Quatations from Chairman Mao Tse-Tung*. Beijing: Read Books Ltd.
Mathur, Poonam. 1987. The Chinese Enlightenment Movement. *China Report* 23 (4): 457–463.
McCormick, John. 2010. *Comparative Politics in Transition*. Boston: Cengage Learning.
MDGIF. 2011. *Shenghuo Jineng Shouce (Life Skill Manual)*: MDG Acheivement Fund in China.
Melton, Gordon. 2014. *Faiths Across Time: 5,000 Years of Religious History*. Oxford: ABC-CLIO.
Miao, Xiaochun. 1992. China. In *International Handbook of Reading Education*, ed. John Hladczuk and William Eller. London: Greenwood Press.
Miethe, Terance D., and Hong Lu. 2005. *Punishment: A Comparative Historical Perspective*. Cambridge: Cambridge University Press.
Mitter, Rana. 2004. *A Bitter Revolution: China's Struggle with the Modern World*. New York: Oxford University Press.
Musto, Marcello. 2012. Revisiting Marx's Concept of Alienation. In *Marx for Today*, ed. Marcello Musto. New York: Routledge.
Ngok, Kinglun. 2008. The Changes of Chinese Labor Policy and Labor Legislation in the Context of Market Transition. *International Labor and Working-Class History* (73): 45–64.
Nicholls, David. 2009. Putting Foucault to Work: An Approach to the Practical Application of Foucault's Methodological Imperatives. *Aporia* 1 (1): 30–40.
Noon, Mike, Paul Blyton, and Kevin Morrell. 2013. *The Realies of Work: Experiencing Work and Employment in Contemporary Society*. New York: Palgrave Macmillian.
O'Farrell, Clare. 1989. *Foucault: Historian or Philosopher?* London: The MacMillan Press Ltd.
O'Farrell, Clare. 2005. *Michel Foucault*. Berkeley, CA: Sage.
Oi, Jean. 1995. The Role of the Local State in China's Transitional Economy. *The China Quarterly* (144): 1132–1149.
Oksala, Johanna. 2005. *Foucault on Freedom*. Cambridge: Cambridge University Press.
Oksala, Johanna. 2007. *How to Read Foucault*. London: Granta Books.
Orts, Eric. 2001. The Rule of Law in China. *Vanderbilt Journal of Transnational Law* 34 (43): 43–115.
People's Daily. 1950. 人民日报. http://www.nlc.cn/dsb_zt/xzzt/ghgdsj/1950/event12/. Accessed 12 April 2020.

People's Daily. 1951. 人民日报, December 16. http://www.nlc.cn/dsb_zt/xzzt/ghgdsj/1951/event7/. Accessed 14 March 2020.
People's Daily. 1952a. 人民日报, February 13. http://www.nlc.cn/dsb_zt/xzzt/ghgdsj/1951/event7/. Accessed 14 March 2020.
People's Daily. 1952b. 人民日报. http://www.nlc.cn/dsb_zt/xzzt/ghgdsj/1952/event1/. Accessed 20 May 2020.
Perry, Elizabeth. 2009. A New Rights Consciouness? *Journal of Democracy* 20 (3): 17–20.
Poster, Mark. 1982. Foucault and History. *Social Research* 49 (1): 116–142.
Postiglione, Gerard. 2011. Education. In *Understanding Chinese Society*, ed. Xiaowei Zang. New York: Routledge.
Pringle, Tim. 2011. *Trade Unions in China: The Challenge of Labour Unrest*. New York: Routledge.
Pye, Lucian. 1986. Reassessing the Cultural Revolution. *The China Quarterly* 108: 597–612.
Pye, Lucian. 1999. An Overview of 50 Years of the People's Republic of China: Some Progress, but Big Problems Remain. *The China Quarterly* 159: 569–579.
Ransom, John. 1997. *Foucault's Discipline*. London: Duke University Press.
Richardson, Frank, and Robert Woolfolk. 2013. Subjectivity and Strong Relationality. In *Subjectivity in the Twenty-First Century*, ed. Romin Tafarodi. New York: Cambridge University Press.
Rojek, Dean. 1989. Social Control in the People's Republic of China. *Criminal Justice Review* 14: 141–153.
Schram, Stuart. 1969. The Party in Chinese Communist Ideology. *The China Quarterly* 38: 1–28.
Skeldon, Ronald. 1997. Hong Kong and Coastal China Growth Linkages. In *Regionalization and Labour Market Interdependence in East and Southeast Asia*, ed. Duncan Campbell Asma Lateef Aurelio Parisotto, and Anil Verma. London: Macmillan Press.
Smart, Barry. 1998. Foucault, Levinas and the Subject of Responsibility. In *The Later Foucault: Politics and Philosophy*, ed. Jeremy Moss. Berkeley, CA: Sage.
So, Alvin. 2003. The Changing Pattern of Classes and Class Conflict in China. *Journal of Contemporary Asia* 33 (3): 363–376.
Stavis, Benedict. 1978. *The Politics of Agricultural Mechanization in China*. New York: Cornell University Press.
System. 2011. Quanguo Wenming Chengshi Ceping Tixi (Spiritual Civilisation Commission): National Civilised City Evaluation System.
Teiwes, Frederick. 1997. The Establishment and Consolidation of the New Regime. In *The Politics of China: The Eras of Mao and Deng*, ed. Roderick MacFarquhar, 1949–1957. Cambridge: Cambridge University Press.

Teiwes, Frederick. 2000. The Chinese State during the Maoist Era. In *The Modern Chinese State*, ed. David Shambaugh. Cambridge: Cambridge University Press.
Thacker, Andrew. 1997. Foucault and the Writing of History. In *Michel Foucault on the Social Siences and Humanities*, ed. Moya Lloyd and Andrew Thacker. London: Macmillan Press Ltd.
Tsou, Tang. 1969. The Cultural Revolution and the Chinese Political System. *The China Quarterly* 38: 63–91.
Tsou, Tang. 1986. *The Cultural Revolution and Post-Mao Reforms: A Historical Perspective*. Chicago: The University of Chicago Press.
Wagner, Donald. 1998. *A Classical Chinese Reader: The Han Shu biography of Huo Guang*. New York: Routledge.
Walder, Andrew. 1991. Workers, Managers and the State: The Reform Era and the Political Crisis of 1989. *The China Quarterly* 127: 467–492.
Wǎnbào. 2016. Bèi Piàn 8000 Yuán Nóngmíngōng Shàngdiào Zìshā (8000 Yuan Cheated, Migrant Workers Hanged Himself), Feburary 3.
Wang, Lu. 2008. The Marginality of Migrant Children in the Urban Chinese Educational System. *British Journal of Socialogy of Education* 29 (6): 691–703.
Warner, Malcolm, and Ying Zhu. 2010. Labour and Management in the People's Republic of China: Seeking the 'Harmonious Society. *Asia Pacific Business Review* 16 (3): 285–298.
Weatherley, Robert. 2006. *Politics in China since 1949: Legitimizing Authoritarian Rule*. New York: Routledge.
Wei, Yehua Dennis. 2001. Decentralization, Marketization, and Globalization: The Triple Processes Underlying Regional Development in China. *Asian Geographer* 20 (1–2): 7–23.
White, Gordon. 1989. Restructuring the Working Class: Labor Reform in Post Mao China. In *Marxism and the Chinese Experience: Issues in Contemporary Chinese Socialism*, ed. Arif Dirlik and Maurice Meisner. New York: M.E. Sharpe.
Whyte, Martin. 1988a. Evolutionary Changes in Chinese Culture. *Transformations: Comparative Study of Social Transformations* 14: 1–22.
Whyte, Martin. 1988b. Evolutionary Changes in Chinese Culture. *Transformations: Comparative Study of Social Transformations*: 1–22.
Withington, John. 2008. *A Disastrous History of the World: Chronicles of War, Earthquake, Plague and Famine*. London: Hachette Digital.
Wu, Bangguo. 2011a. Improving Socialist Legal System with Chinese Characteristics on a New Starting Point. Beijing The People's Congress Journal.
Wu, Xiaogang. 2011b. The Household Registration System and Rural-Urban Education Inequality in Contemporary China: Population Studies Center, University of Michigan.

Wu, Xiaogang, and Donald Treiman. 2004. The Household Registration System and Social Stratification in China: 1955–1996. *Demography* 41 (2): 363–384.

Xiaogang. 2016. It's a Worry: Chinese Doesn't Read, March 18.

Xiaoyong. 1999. Burang Tigao Suzhi (Not Allowing to Improve Quality).

Xu, Feng. 2009. Governing China's Peasant Migrants: Building Xiaokang Socialism and Harmonious Society. In *China's Governmentalities: Governing Change, Changing Government*, ed. Elaine Jeffreys. New York: Routledge.

Yan, Hairong. 2003. Neoliberal Governmentality and Neohumanism: Organizing Suzhi/Value Flow through Labor Recruitment Networks. *Cultural Anthropology* 18 (4): 493–523.

Yan, Hairong. 2008. *New Masters, New Servants: Migration, Development, and Women Workers in China*. London: Duke University Press.

Yip, Bennis. 2006. Privatisation. In *Critical Issues in Contemporary China*, ed. Czeslaw Tubilewicz. New York: Routledge.

Yueh, Linda. 2011. *Enterprising China: Business, Economic, and Legal Developments Since 1979*. Oxford: Oxford University Press.

Zeng, Min. 1989. Guangxi Renkou De Wenhua Suzhi Yu Shangpin Shengchan De Guanxi [The Relationship between the Cultural Quality of Guangxi's Population and Commodity Production]. In *Zhongguo Xinnanbu Renkou Xianzhuan Yanjiu (Studies of the Present Situation of China's Southwestern Population)*, ed. Yunnan Provincial Census Office and Yunnan Provincial Research Centre for Population Development Strategies. Kunming: Yunnan Renmin Chubanshe.

Zhang, Dandan, Xin Li, and Jinjun Xue. 2015. Education Inequality between Rural and Urban Areas of the People's Republic of China, Migrants Children Education, and Some Implications. *Asian Development Review* 32 (1): 196–224.

Zhang, Jinfan. 2014. *The Tradition and Modern Transition of Chinese Law*. Berlin: Springer.

Zhongguo zhigong zhangkuang diaocha (China personnel executive survey). 1996. Beijing: Xiyuan Chuanshe.

Zhou, Gong. 1930. Zhou Li Compilation. In *Zhou Li Compilation*, vol. 108–114, ed. Zhonglun Li. Harvard: Harvard University.

Zhou, Yi. 2001. *21 Shìjì zhōngguó liǎng dà zhīzhù: Kējì jiàoyù huà yǔ jiàoyù kējì huà (China's Two Pillars in the Twenty-First Century : Science and Technological Education)*, Fuzhou: Fújiàn jiàoyù chūbǎn shè (Fujian Education Press).

中共中央党史研究室. 2016. *Ninety Years of the Chinese Communist Party (中国共产党的九十年)*. Beijing, China: Chinese Communist Party History Publishing House.

CHAPTER 3

Automatic Docility in Market Socialism

> It is one of my targets to show people that a lot of things that are part of their landscape – that people think are universal – are the results of some very precise historical changes. All my analyses are against the idea of universal necessities in human existence. They show the arbitrariness of institutions and show which space of freedom we can still enjoy and how many changes can still be made.
>
> (Foucault et al. 1988: 11)

In this chapter, I discuss the two phases of original field data gathered from 52 everyday workers in Group One—*who had never engaged in any protest activities*—across a range of industries and occupations at multiple locations between 2011 and 2014 in China.

In many interviews and conversations with everyday workers, contradictory statement such as 'I work because I want to improve my conditions… I can barely live with my little earnings…' (Yaxing, IT Worker, Shenzhen, 2011) was regularly used by workers to describe their ongoing struggle with poverty and the high cost of living. Contrary to the nineteenth-century English workers' revolt against their poor conditions that pushed for the enactments of the *Great Reform Act* (1832) to change the electoral system and the *Factory Act* (1833) to regulate working conditions during the Industrial Revolution, workers in this

E. Leung, *The (Re)Making of the Chinese Working Class*, Palgrave Debates in Business History,
https://doi.org/10.1007/978-3-030-83313-8_3

group appeared to have submitted themselves "voluntarily" both to their work superiors and exploitative conditions.

From Foucault's viewpoint, this particular behavior is an effect of particular types of knowledge (or "truth") that reflects an effective operation of disciplinary power within the workers in their social relations. Foucault (1977) notes that these relations are reinforced through the carceral network (see Chapter 2) such as schools and workplaces which teaches the individuals to act in accordance with the truth of the normality of their given positions (or identities). For example, soldiers are trained to use the rifles in particular ways whereas school children are taught to hold a pen and sit at their school desks correctly in the public institutions (O'Farrell 2005). The new mass forms of these panoptic mechanisms aim at turning different 'classes' of people into units of automatic docility to think and behave in adherence with what is defined as normality for their given positions in their social spaces (Foucault 1977). Thus, it is the visibility of these public spaces that subtly alters individuals' consciousness through their internalization of the thought of the constant watchful gaze that guides them to self-regulate their own behaviors and that of others (or governmentality) in accordance with their social truth.

This chapter examines how the truth discourses have continued to retain an 'older rule consciousness', that is, the status consciousness among the workers interviewed in this study and their behaviors. In so doing, the chapter begins with the narratives of workers' desires to escape poverty (*tuopin* 脱貧), which were influenced by the quality discourses (see Chapter 2), before exploring how they marginalized themselves in the low-wage sectors within their social relationships. It shows that their sense of 'self-marginalization' was linked to the Confucian 'truth' of 'destiny' and their responsibility for others (see Chapter 2). This turned them to voluntarily submit themselves to their work supervisors and to any given conditions. It is subsequently argued that through their continuous submission to an imaginary 'truth' they became—consciously or subconsciously—the agents in constituting themselves as docile bodies and minds to serve the interests of their work supervisors, and ultimately the will of the Chinese Communist Party (CCP) leaders in China's market socialism. However, I conclude that workers' self-care practices toward the matters that affected their lives (and families') opened up the possibilities for them to resist against their given conditions.

The Desire to Escape Poverty (*Tuopin* 脫貧)

> I'm not happy with my living conditions... I'm so poor... I'm only allowed to think about ways to subsist in our society.
>
> (Huage, Security Officer, Shenzhen, 2011)

Huage's perception of his life reflected the views of many everyday workers interviewed across different industrial sectors in multiple locations in China.

I met Huage in October 2011 during the first week of my field trip nearby the 'community area' (*shequ* 社區) I resided in Shenzhen's *Longhua* industrial district. This industrial district was encompassed by numerous factories including the world's largest electronics manufacturer—Hon Hai Precision Industry Company (known as Foxconn)—and mixed with countless rental lodgings in many small community areas that had housed thousands of low-income workers outside their workplaces.

Generally speaking, the external appearances had shared many characteristics with their internal living conditions. The rooms of the lodgings were small; old; filthy; smelly, dark, and filled with mosquitoes and cockroaches. Windows were pasted with yellowing newspapers; window frames were rusty and covered with spiderwebs as well as thick layers of dust. Walls were broken or sagging; the bed frames were snapped or cracked; power went off regularly, and puddles of yellow tap water remained in the shower tubs while there were no flush toilets in the stinky washrooms. I randomly rented one of these rooms as the living conditions of the lodges I viewed were, more or less—the same.

Externally, it was surrounded by the murky and smelly rivers of sewage; the streets were filled with piles of garbage alongside cockroaches and rats, and the foul air was also coated with thick yellow or brown dust. The streets were always crowded with workers. They all wore their work uniforms in a sloppy way with an unbearable smell of sweat, like they have never showered and never enjoyed the air-conditioning. Their hair always looked greasy and messy. They all looked angry; they never smiled. I usually carried out the interviews in the evenings or at nights, hoping that they were in a better mood to speak to me as they looked less angry.

Huage was then 30 years old, short, thin, and dark skinned, with greasy and messy hair. Like many other workers on the streets (see Fig. 3.1) of

Fig. 3.1 Everyday workers in China (*Source* Photo by author)

Shenzhen, he wore a dirty, blue uniform with a red security badge on his left arm.

He was a security officer who worked alone on the sidewalk, either standing or sitting in the middle of the walkway outside the massage center he worked for—which was next to a small eatery I often passed by, or ate at. One afternoon Huage greeted me when I walked out of the eatery. We made small talk about the weather and where each of us came from. Then he told his story:

> I am from a… poor village in Hunan Province… Our conditions were not good – our lives were very bitter… we didn't have money; we barely had enough food in our bellies. I didn't like to live in the village and so when I grew up I [decided] to work in the city…
>
> (Huage, Security Officer, Shenzhen, 2011)

His choice to leave village life was not uncommon for local and migrant peasant workers. For instance, Xiaofong, a 20-year-old waitress, revealed that 'I originally had two sisters [in the village in Guangxi Province], but my grandma gave one away because we were too poor… we had no money to raise her' (2011, Shenzhen). Daqing, a 19-year-old food processing worker, said that 'we were one of the poorest families in our village [in Sichuan Province…] we didn't have meat [to eat…] meat was very expensive… since I was young, I wanted to… work in the cities' (2013, Foshan). Similarly, Yaxing, a 26-year-old IT (or information technology) worker added that 'in our village [in Hubei Province], the first thing that came to mind was to go out to the cities… this was the only choice we had… to make a bit of money to live' (2011, Shenzhen).

These narratives illustrate how precarious peasant life was. The desire to improve their living conditions by escaping poverty (*tuopin* 脫貧) (see Chapter 2) has driven approximately 253 million peasants to work in the cities in 2014 alone (National Bureau of Statistics of China 2015). This phenomenon is one of the dominant themes in Chinese labor as discussed in Chapter 1, which demonstrated that the prolonged exploitative working conditions in the cities as experienced by millions of migrant workers has been a striking feature in fostering workers' class consciousness and action against their conditions of exploitation. Guided by this theme, working conditions were the focus of many of my discussions with Group One workers.

Despite their working lives, I was constantly told during the interviews of their hardships and struggle to access the necessities for daily life, and their dreams of entering the Chinese middle-class by escaping poverty. While their capacity to pursue those dreams were predominately 'empowered' by household (*hukou* 戶口) registration mobility—the freedom to reside, visit and work in any area—under the discourse "to get rich is glorious"—since the 1980s (Mallee 2000; see Chapter 2), all the interviewees said that their employment opportunities were rather limited in the cities:

> I don't have choices… it's impossible for me to get a better job. We work because we have to live, and there's no point thinking about whether we like our conditions or not … everywhere is the same for us [workers]. Even if I don't like my job… I have to do put up with it… uneducated people live like this…
>
> (Bu, SOE Ready-Mix Concrete Worker, Hefei, 2011)

A Sense of Self-Marginalization

As a result of their lack of education (see Chapter 2) as perceived by the workers themselves, they consequently marginalized themselves within the low-wage industries by consciously making 'necessary' adjustments and adaptations to any given conditions to maintain their basic livelihoods in the marketplace.

Rather than being concerned about an improvement in their treatment and conditions at work, workers' self-perception of the 'lack' in themselves encourages a strong sense of fatalism:

> My weekly roster is like nine hours work per day for two days, then one 24-hour shift followed by one day-off… I do 24-hour shifts seven times each month… Literate *gao sizhi* 高素質 ['high-quality'] people are always the leaders above everyone… illiterate *di suzhi* 低素質 ['low-quality'] people are just like mud sitting on the ground for leaders to step on.
>
> (Bing, Hotel Cleaner, Hangzhou, 2011)

Their 'self-knowledge' (Foucault 1966/2005; see Chapter 2) of the 'heaven-and-earth' difference between 'educated' and 'uneducated' classes of people that instilled in their mindset constituted a status consciousness (see Chapters 1 and 2) among these workers. This status consciousness was arguably the main determinant of disguising them to submit themselves to their poor treatment and working conditions. The qualifying statement that "illiterate *di suzhi* 低素質 ['low-quality'] people… are just like mud sitting on the ground for leaders to step on" indicated a self-recognition of a subservient status that was linked to their educational deficits:

> I know my future – I'll be poor for the rest of my life. Once we're poor, we are always poor. Illiterate people like me… didn't even complete primary school… can only get low-wage jobs. Just like any other *dagong* [打工 work for the bosses] or *gongren* [工人 SOE worker])… we have to suffer because we have no 'culture' in us… that's why we do whatever our leaders want.
>
> (Huage, Security Officer, Shenzhen, 2011)

While education is a primary criterion of stratification in capitalist societies generally, workers' understanding of the 'value' of education implies a strong sense of the Confucian doctrine of a 'Mandate of Heaven' (*tianming* 天命) (see Chapter 2) by equating their low societal positions with the 'truth' of their 'low personal quality' within the high-low status hierarchy.

Thus, workers' negative self-image about their 'low quality' had become one of the factors that steered them to obey the natural rule of their work leaders in the Chinese occupational hierarchy.

The Practice of 'Voluntary' Submission

As a result of their hierarchical mindset, most of the interviewees submitted themselves 'voluntarily' to their work leaders by working in 'sweatshop-like conditions'.

Despite the Chinese labor laws (1995 and 2008) stipulating an eight-hour workday, six days a week, and only 36 hours overtime per month, working hours among the interviewed workers varied between eight and 13 hours per day without a fixed rest day:

> We basically work 13 hours a day and we must work overtime every night. Our overtime hour finishes at 9.30 pm – some of us may finish our tasks before 9.30 pm – but we must complete the required overtime hours and leave together.
>
> (Qingjie, Garment Factory Worker, Hangzhou, 2011)

The phrase 'we must complete the required overtime hours' used in the above description was one of many examples that exposed a hidden form of forced labor across all types of ownerships in China. Rather than criticizing this situation as forms of social injustice or rights violations, interviewees regarded their long hours of exhausting work as 'normal' conditions for 'low-quality' workers to ensure their (and that of their family's) basic sustenance:

> ...workers are just workers – we don't have any rights – because power and rights all belong to the leaders... very normal... we *dagong* are so illiterate... we cannot do anything... 'low-quality' people are like that... don't know a thing ... but to obey our leaders and do whatever we are told – so that we can get our wages and keep our 'rice bowl' [paid work] to live... this is what our destiny [*ming* 命] is.
>
> (Bing, Hotel Cleaner, Hangzhou, 2011)

As well as the internalization of the negative self-images and consequences of being 'low quality' by workers themselves, the findings suggest that their predefined 'destiny' (or *ming* 命) (see Chapter 2) that was aligned with their low societal status was further constructed by employers' capacity to exercise flexible wage (or floating wage) systems (Hsing 1998) across various industrial sectors in China.

Forced Labor, Wage Flexibility, and Overtime Work

Since the 1980s, 'flexible wage adjustments' were advocated by Deng Xiaoping under his market principle of "distribution according to labor (*anlao fenpei* 按勞分配) is socialist and not capitalist", as a way to 'reward' workers' 'merits and contributions' (Wilson 2009: 129).

Hence, to increase workers' output and performance, wage flexibility was based either on a component of basic wages with piece rates (sometimes hourly rates), subsidies, bonuses, and overtime rates, or on subsidies and longer hours with positional wages, as a share of the total wage bill (Hsing 1998). These forms of wage practices give enterprises the capacity to set low base wages or positional wages to *make* workers work faster over longer hours:

> I work about 15 hours a day from 7am to 11pm – I work from 7am to 11pm, I want to work long hours... so I can produce more and also to get overtime payment... I don't know how I could live on my basic wage.
> (Yue, Electronics factory worker, Hangzhou, 2011)

While overtime for most workers exceeded 120 hours per month as a result of wage flexibility, nearly none of the interviewees received adequate overtime payment in line with the legal rates[1]:

> We have to work at least 12 hours a day... our overtime hours start after eight hours of work... we're all on piece rates during the regular working hours and then we'll be on time rate during the overtime hours. Our earnings are all dependent on the complexity of the styles... we earn from \$2 to \$8 for an item of clothing... but when the style is too complex or I have made it wrongly and I have to remove the stitches to then sew it back, then I might not even be able to make any money for the hour. Sunday overtime work is not compulsory, but I'd better do it... and eight

[1] The legal overtime wage rate was set to be no less than 150% of the regular rates, while holiday overtime was set at no less than 200% of the regular rates. Hsing, You-tien (1998) *Making Capitalism in China: The Taiwan Connection*, Oxford: Oxford University Press.

hours of work is a must if we work on Sunday so that we can get $20 for our work.

(Yejie, Garment Factory Worker, Shenzhen, 2012)

Despite the ***pufa*** 普法 and ***weiquan*** 維權 campaigns (Benney 2013; see Chapters 1 and 2) had said to exercise to propagate labor laws and legal knowledge to increase the legal rights consciousness (***falu wequan yishi*** 法律維權意識) (Gallagher 2005, 2006; see Chapter 2) among the workers, all interviewees seemed to have little sense about their legal entitlement.

In this context, all the interviewed workers appeared to have crafted an internal acceptance of the abusive labor practices from their work superiors and authority figures, that was seemingly guiding by a status consciousness among themselves, as in the Imperial and Mao's period (see Chapter 2):

Education is the only thing that can change our destiny. *Dagong* always have a tough life… all I learnt throughout my work experience was to obey the leaders so I can earn enough to subsist. The life (or destiny) of 'low-quality' people like me is very bitter (***mingku***).

(Fang, Garment Factory Worker, Hangzhou, 2011)

The Destiny of 'Low-Quality' Workers

The word ***mingku*** 命苦 (or bitter destiny) associated with the phrase '…all I learnt is to obey the leaders so I can earn enough to subsist…' indicates their frustration and everyday struggle over their lives under a 'common sense' notion of inferiority in 'low-quality' workers.

However, their acceptance of this prearranged inferior destiny since the Imperial China was generated by the workers' self-degradation, which led them to behave 'properly' toward their work superiors by accepting any work conditions in the post-Mao period (see Chapter 2):

I work 12 hours a day from 8am to 8pm… I don't have a day-off… and I could earn up to $1,300 a month[2]… not quite enough live on, but I only have to do the cleaning work and do whatever my boss wants me to and

[2] Legal Minimum Wage was set at 1,310 Yuan a month in Hangzhou in 2011.

> that's all… for someone who is so uneducated to have a job like this I feel very lucky.
>
> (Yang, Motel Cleaner, Hangzhou, 2011)

Given the prevailing mentality regarding a status order of 'educated (high) – uneducated (low)' (see Chapter 2), social relations were perceived either as superordinated or subordinated to the extent to which the 'low quality' of workers themselves was the key factor confining them to think that only certain types of jobs were available to them (Leung and Caspersz 2016).

This mentality guided workers to subject themselves to any given conditions in an occupational hierarchy:

> I know all of us have to sign a contract… so our work leaders got us to sign on a piece of paper that we were not allowed to read. When our work leaders were not looking at us then some of us looked at the contract but there was nothing written on the paper. We signed the paper anyway… we didn't have to know what we'd signed because we must do what our leaders want anyway.
>
> (Shao, Garment Factory Worker, Hangzhou, 2011)

It is argued that workers' awareness of their submission to the 'rights' or the 'mandate' of those higher than them has further induced enterprises to continue to exercise exploitative and illegal labor practices as Chapters 1 and 2 have illustrated:

> when we renewed our contracts, we had to sign an additional clause in the 'mistake' section to indicate that we agreed to have our wages deducted when one or more team members was injured or contracted occupational diseases, because these sorts of abnormal things only occur when someone makes mistakes. We all understood that we had to make no mistakes at work.
>
> (Qing, SOE Car Factory Worker, Hefei, 2011)

Besides occupational injuries and illnesses, the findings suggest other types of mistakes, ranging from refusing to work overtime to improper work postures, which were also defined as abnormal behavior (Foucault 2006) across numerous workplaces.

In this context, all the respondents mentioned that they had to 'train' their bodily movements to fit into the prescribed destiny (*ming*) to perform 'normal' work behavior (see Chapters 2) in order to avoid potential wage cuts:

> My task is to wipe the screens of the mobile phones... I must follow our normal procedures... I must ensure that I only wipe once – horizontally from the left to the right of the screen – and the screen has to be clean. If I wipe it twice or do it vertically then it's a mistake and I would get a work fine because I wiped the wrong way and slowed down the production.
>
> (Yanam, Foxconn Worker, Shenzhen, 2011)

Coupled with disciplinary wage cuts, humiliating measures were also used to control the behavior of workers in order to maximize their efficiency at work:

> Apart from paying our fines, we are also required to stand at the door and read out the company's rules and policies, such as the types of mistakes we shouldn't make at work, in front of the other workers.
>
> (Ge, SOE Car Factory Worker, Hefei, 2011)

As a result of the disciplinary practices, all the interviewed workers reported that they had to perform their work tasks according to the 'prescribed' normal routines by moving in conformity to the correct, mechanized manners (Smart 1985).

Despite the potential punishments, the findings suggest that their guilt feelings strongly directed their commitment toward the work routines:

> I got a 100 yuan fine just a few days ago... I ordered the wrong materials... and our production was disrupted for half a day because of my mistake. We all have to bear the economic responsibility of the mistakes we make, because making mistakes means a profit loss for our company and so we should cover any financial loss we caused... I personally feel guilty when I make mistakes.
>
> (Bu, SOE Ready-Mix Concrete Worker, Hefei, 2011)

Rather than complaining about their work penalties, the workers' discourses indicated that their guilt feelings evolved from their failure to meet the 'prescribed' routines that *made* them accept the punishments 'voluntarily' and to maintain the 'mandate' of the work leaders to rule them in the occupational hierarchy (see Chapter 2).

It is suggested that the ways in which workers' thought and felt about their 'wrongdoings' were generated by their concern over the fact that their behavior deviated from the normal practices of their positioning—both self-positioning and being positioned:

> if we put the wrong accessories into the trolley then the production workers won't be able to find the correct items to build the cars. Last time I made such a mistake, causing a seven-minute disruption on the production line. Our company rule is that if any of the line is stopped for over 3.5 minutes then we'll get a penalty of $20 for each minute. It's not the penalty that bothered me... I felt really bad about disrupting the entire production by making such a stupid mistake... so I stood up and apologized to everyone and the leaders for my disobedient act.
>
> (Ge, SOE Car Factory Worker, Hefei, 2011)

Such self-directed confessional acts (Foucault 1978; see Chapter 2) by workers demonstrate a high level of obedience (or docility) arising out of their truth (or knowledge) about the expected performance of their particular positions. This truth can occur only in conjunction with the social structures and norms through the internal relationships that the workers engage in (Evasdottir 2004; McKinlay and Taylor 2014).

As a result of these social relationships, the workers became cultivated bodily and spiritually as a self-directed means of alteration and betterment in upholding their shared normal standards of behavior (Faison 2007) under the doctrine of similarity to judge and correct their actions and others' (see Chapter 2) within their given positions.

'Positive' Punishments and Doctrine of Similarity

The findings support the discussion in Chapter 2 in illustrating that the notion of similarity among the workers in all the workplaces has effectively softened their negative view of the disciplinary and punitive measures.

A Foxconn worker, for example, shared his thought about being forced to write confession letters concerning the mistake he made at work:

> I once dropped a cloth on the floor and my work leader made me write 'I'll never drop the cloth again' fifty times. It's in this way I will not – at least I'll try not – to make the same mistake again. This made me always remember not to make mistakes again.
>
> (Yanam, Foxconn Worker, Shenzhen, 2011)

Similarly, workers in other enterprises also expressed a positive perception of the disciplinary measures, even when their work leaders abused them:

> In most factories, workers are not allowed to chit-chat with one another… we should not chat anyway because we are there to work to earn more money… anyone of us who are slow on the production line deserve to be punished and yelled at because being slow is affecting our entire workflow.
>
> (Xun, Lift Manufacturing Worker, Hangzhou, 2011)

While oppressive, the findings demonstrate that the workplace disciplinary systems functioned as a positive technique of normalization (Foucault 1977; see Chapter 2) that socialized the workers from within.

The Disciplinary Techniques of Normalization

The disciplinary techniques of normalization operated as a specific apparatus of knowledge (Foucault 1977; see Chapter 2) within the mindset of the workers thereby enabled them to examine and judge the immoral behavior of themselves and others:

> it's teamwork; so if anyone of us is injured because of someone else's careless mistakes, then all of us in the team will get a wage deduction. We have to make sure no mistakes are made at work. Also, all of us in the team must be healthy and must contract no occupational diseases, like skin or eye problems, because these sorts of mistakes will also incur a penalty on all of us.
>
> (Qing, SOE Car Factory Worker, Hefei, 2011)

The natural consequence of the normalizing judgment thus provided a necessary condition that 'prohibited' workers from complaining about their work-related issues:

> I used to operate a machine to cut short the edge of the snack food bag and then seal it. That day, a bag was dangling on the machine and so I grabbed the bag – it's at that moment the machine squashed two of my fingers… you know we are all uneducated and we don't know a thing… so occupational injuries are a very normal thing that happens to us when we made mistakes.
>
> (Daqing, Food Processing Worker, Foshan, 2013)

Their self-knowledge about themselves as uneducated, unknowing, and mindless had profoundly stabilized the normative function of constituting a normal experience (Foucault 1977; see Chapter 2) and destiny (or *ming*) for themselves as 'low-quality' workers in their social relationships:

> My working environment was very smelly and dusty… sometimes the dust was yellow, sometimes it was grey, but most times it was black… A few workers at work were sick and then they never come back to work. I never wear a face mask… no one is wearing one at work and I don't want to look odd. Getting sick from work is a normal thing for most of us… our *ming* is bitter, isn't it?
>
> (Rong, Tyre manufacturing worker, Hefei, 2011)

While recognizing that their lives and health were potentially endangered by their working environments, most of the workers demonstrated an internal acceptance of these threatening conditions as part of their normal destiny (or *ming*).

Hence, despite it being their rights to enroll themselves in the social insurance scheme for medical needs and to refuse to work in the unsafe conditions under the Labor Laws (1995 & 2008), most of the interviewees felt that these rights were not relevant to them:

> those are rubbish… how could I not work in unsafe working environments? All working environments are dirty and unsafe for 'low-quality' people… what do you think we are? You think we can choose where we want to work and can refuse to work in dirty, dangerous areas? All of us working here don't have social insurance… we only earn $70 a day and we have to budget our daily expenses… why would we want to pay for that insurance? Low-quality is low quality – low-quality people live like this.
>
> (Ding, SOE Ready-mix Concrete Worker, Hefei, 2011)

Given their perception of their low societal status, the thought of themselves as 'low quality' had become a foundational reason for all the interviewed workers to continue to behave properly to fit into their given positions.

Thus, most appeared to be willing to abandon any sense of reclaiming their legal rights with regard to matters such as long working hours, forced overtime, deductions from their subsistence wages, and even occupational health and safety:

> ...compared to others – mine was just a very small matter... it's not like I was dying or anything... some workers lost their whole arms or all their fingers at work, but I lost only two fingers so I was quite lucky. Imagine if I had lost my whole arm or leg. I wouldn't even have been able to find a job to earn a living. I feel that occupational accidents and illnesses are just some kinds of normal things that are destined to happen to the low-quality people... it's just a matter of when.
>
> (Daqing, Food Processing Worker, Foshan, 2013)

'Normalizing' the 'True-Selves'

By accepting the above conception of 'truth' about themselves, the thought of quality had become an essential construct in determining not only the identities (or positions) of the workers, but also in creating and manufacturing their 'true-selves' through their destiny.

This was in turn associated with a view of socially accepted normal behavior among those considered as 'low quality'. These elements worked to shape workers' desires, health, lives, habits, and moral worth to then guide them to move toward the norm:

> I don't want a contract because I don't understand the content of the contract... I don't know what should be listed in the contract... just in case I am signing something that is harmful to me. You know, illiterate 'low-quality' people don't know anything, so most of us don't care about things like contracts... we have no rights anyway.
>
> (Min, Springs Manufacturing Worker, Hangzhou, 2011)

Rather than being forced or threatened into compliance with external (or capitalist) demands, the 'moral sense' of the workers as a community of 'low-quality' sub-individuals had become a major instrument in steering them to repeatedly perform in the prescribed 'proper' manner (Ransom 1997) within their given positions.

The cumulative effect of their repetitive behavior thus approximated the normative and regulatory ideal among the workers and had essentially subjected them to vulnerable, exploitative, and abusive conditions:

> I didn't sign the contract... the leader promised to pay me 30 yuan for an eight-hour shift each day during the probation period. I worked with another six new workers for two days. On my second day of work yesterday, seven of us were called to get paid in our leader's office. We went in there,

> sitting in his office for about half an hour... we didn't get our pay so I went up to the leader and politely asked him for my wages... He beat me up straightaway and ordered the other security officers to smash me altogether ... and then I was ordered to leave.
>
> (Minge, Security Officer, Hefei, 2011)

Even though he had been denied his wages and even suffered physical abuse, the above respondent, like many other workers, demonstrated his commitment to the standardized conditions in accordance with his given position:

> My boss owed me $60 altogether for my two days of work but I know I can't get it back ...I called the police officers after getting beaten up... they said they couldn't do anything about it but told me to have a medical check-up at my own expense if my wounds were too painful. I only had $500 in my bank and I took $400 for a check-up. When I got to the hospital, I realized it would cost at least $700 to check all my injured areas. I didn't have enough money so I skipped the medical examination of my face, neck, upper and lower back – I only got a check-up for my chest and stomach. I think security officer work isn't for everybody... I'm just an illiterate old man. I don't know a thing... I will try to find some small factory jobs and hopefully I won't have to experience the same thing again.
>
> (Minge, Security Officer, Hefei, 2011)

Given the tremendous harassment, mistreatment, and abuse that the workers experienced routinely in their daily lives, some subsequently adopted an orientation of 'exit', rather than attempting to improve their working conditions:

> I kept quiet while I was waiting and hoping that my boss would give me back the wages, he owed me one day. You know my boss didn't pay me wages for around three months, from August [2011] until now [October]. I didn't say anything about it but just continued to complete my work tasks, because I didn't want to ruin my working relationship with my boss and maybe my leaders – I didn't want to get revenge at work or to lose my job... I decided that if I didn't get paid for a few more months, until no one else wants to lend me money to live, then I will have to quit the job and work somewhere else... we are very flexible... and our jobs are forever temporary; nothing permanent...
>
> (Yaxing, IT Worker, Shenzhen, 2011)

By defining their employment as a temporary phase in their lives resulting from the typical 'exit' orientation, most of them realized there was nothing much better waiting for them when they left their jobs:

> I thought about quitting this job many times... but I have nowhere to go... I worked a few places previously... and to me all jobs are just about the same for any low-quality people like me – the working conditions, treatment and the earnings at all the jobs I could choose were quite similar to one another. Like this young migrant [pointing at a girl] in the sewing line, we didn't even complete junior high school – what sort of better jobs and opportunities do we have? What are our options? We have a huge population in China but the quality of most of us is really low. Low-quality people aren't even worth a cent [no value] and that's why we can't get better jobs with better pay and conditions.
>
> (Qingjie, Garment Factory Worker, Hangzhou, 2011)

The evidence suggests that the self-degradation of the self-value among the 'low-quality' workers undermined their will to attempt to improve their treatment and conditions at work, as well as their positions as workers and their rights as human beings in general. This mindset further strengthened their sense of 'normality' as the workers confirmed their given identities through their 'norm' of performance:

> I have to put up with my own conditions like everybody else... I'll just do whatever my leaders want me to... it's even... say to clean the toilets. Work leaders have every right to ask the *dagong* to do anything because we're getting paid to work. We have to listen and obey our leaders and we also have to show them our ability to complete many tasks, even if those are extra work. You know, one of our co-workers got fired because she told the leader she didn't want to do extra work... who did she think she was? She's just a low-quality *dagong* but being so disobedient she deserved to lose her rice bowl [job].
>
> (Xiaoqin, Cosmetic Sales Assistant, Shenzhen, 2011)

The emphasis of workers' punitive rationality and their conscious rejection of deviation from the 'norm' was attributed to the 'disobedient act' (or direct challenge) to the authority figures by those categorized as 'low quality' within the superior (high)—inferior (low) relationships (see Chapter 2).

This practice thus reflects a successful internalization of the 'inferiority' (or status) consciousness within the workers, leading them to regulate their own behavior and that of others to become the persons they *ought* to be within their social and historical setting. Workers thus became entangled in automated and deindividualized power relations, because their choices of action (or individualization) were "proposed, suggested, imposed upon [them] by their culture, [their] society and [their] social groups" (Foucault 1997: 291).

The 'Selves' and the Everyday 'Carceral Network'

The mental acquiescence of most of the interviewees to their conditions further suggests that their experience and perception of their selves as 'low quality' was maintained through their interaction with people, history, and culture in the social relations in their everyday 'carceral network' (see Chapter 2).

Institutions of normalization are to be found within this 'carceral network', such as schools providing moral education and organizations offering assistance for moral improvement, to discipline the entire social body (Smart 1985):

> We won't discuss our grievances with our work leaders... but Foxconn is very good because we have Wang Mama Hotline and so all of us can speak to the counsellors at the unions about anything we want. I rang up Wang Mama Hotline once because my work leader was either swearing at me or punishing me because I didn't stand or sit properly at work, so I was feeling a bit upset. The counsellor said I was very lucky that Foxconn hired me because my quality is better than most of the Chinese workers. She said that's why I earn a bit more than many other workers and that our leaders were a bit harsh on us because they wanted us to improve to become better workers. She's right because the quality of the leaders is higher than us – that's why they're our leaders ... I felt much better after talking to her.
>
> (Xiaoyuan, Foxconn Worker, Shenzhen, 2011)

Within the everyday 'carceral network', the findings suggest that judgments, assessments, and diagnoses of the Chinese institutions, organizations, and the workers themselves were implicitly made up of the hierarchized 'high-low' quality discourses intended to achieve a restoration of the norm:

> Last time my co-workers found out we earned 200 yuan less than other factory workers, so they went to talk to our trade union officials at work. Our union officials said that it was because the workers of other factories were of a higher quality than us and so they were able to earn a bit more. The officials also said that we could also earn that extra 200 yuan or more if we worked faster to exceed our work quota... They're right about this because this is how the 'low-quality' people earn a living in China – it's just the way it is.
>
> (Ge, SOE Car Factory Worker, Hefei, 2011)

As well as the enterprises and the State-run trade unions in the workplaces, labor NGOs also acted as educators to teach and correct workers' thoughts and behavior to neutralize (or normalize) the technical power of discipline:

> Workers only came to see us for their unpaid wages, and none of them came here to sort out their working conditions... I mean you might think that their conditions were horrible but the workers feel fine about it... we're all in the same boat and we all know that there is no way to improve our conditions for better treatment or better rights at work – we won't get what we want anyway so why would anyone bother to think about all this? We talk to the workers sometimes when they feel upset; you know, sometimes the work leaders are very difficult to please. I just told them to improve themselves to make their lives easier.
>
> (Tai, NGO Worker, Hefei, 2011)

Thus, while labor NGOs played a significant role in filling the missing role of the State-run trade unions in protecting workers' rights as well as nurturing their labor rights' consciousness under ***weiquan*** 維權 discourses (see Chapter 2), daily work issues faced by everyday workers were often ignored by these organizations. This is because most of these organizations relied on international foundations for funding whereby these foundations tended to support the most vulnerable and exploited groups of workers, for example, occupationally injured or diseased workers:

> Our center is sponsored by one American foundation since 2007... they fund our center USD550.00 [approximately 3498 yuan] a month. This money covers the rent and equipment like the computers for the center and our wages. We must run a number of legal seminars each month... and provide legal consultation so we explain to the injured workers how to assess grades of injuries and litigation procedures... Workers have to pay

> the litigation fee for themselves; it's very expensive… from 220 yuan to 3,800 yuan – the more they earn the more they have to pay. We decided to collect as many signatures as possible to try getting the Local People's Congress to cancel the fee. But no one wanted to get into this sort of trouble… I ended up spending a day in jail with another NGO worker… the police officers said that we were intensifying conflicts and disrupting social stability… we were on the news. Our sponsor had since decided to cancel all the projects with us next year [2013]. We may have to close down as we have no money to run the center.
>
> (Mr Zhang, NGO Worker, Shenzhen, 2012)

The withdrawal of the overseas funding from those labor NGOs that had their activities beyond the scope of the CCP rules illustrates that the State had successfully channeled international support for NGOs toward the practices of legal rights protection (*weiquan*) in the form of individual litigation:

> I think we are the only NGO that can represent the workers in court because we're lawyers… but we encouraged the workers to resolve their issues directly with their employers and we taught them the ways to deal with the employers. It is only when that didn't work then we would lodge legal claims… but we have to be very careful and we don't want to represent more than one or two workers who worked in the same company because we don't want to make it a collective case. Last time there were 5 injured workers from the same company – their boss refused to payout the injured compensation and they wanted to take the boss to court. Too many of them from the same company… this is something the government considered as threatening social stability… and so if we helped them, we might be in trouble… and our funder will not collaborate with us.
>
> (Li, Law Professor, Hefei, 2011)

The discourse above has implicitly showed that despite *weiquan*, international funders were primarily committed to the CCP's project of maintenance of social stability (*weiwen* 維穩) according to what they understood as the law-abiding activities in China (see Chapter 2).

This commitment had thus profoundly influenced not only on the NGOs' day-to-day operations, but also on the NGOs' workers' attitudes and behaviors. One result of which had been that they made little or no effort to engage in any activities beyond the norm:

> I don't care about the workers and I'm not interested in knowing how they live – everyone lives this way. It's not my job to think about their conditions or their rights – what sort of rights do the low-quality people expect to have? They have no rights; they won't have anything better unless they improve their quality if they want to make their lives easier – I really don't care. My job is only to provide legal advice to those who come to see us about their issues, such as unpaid wages or occupational injuries; but otherwise, I don't care about their little things.
>
> (Yu, NGO Worker, Hangzhou, 2011)

In line with this view, the interviewees revealed a preoccupation with and conformity to the implicit cultural norm that sought to control the manners of all their 'little things':

> We don't have employment contracts; only the leaders have the contracts – we don't have anything – so our work leaders can fire us anytime they don't want us and the factory doesn't have to pay social insurance for us. I know what they do is illegal and we can lodge a complaint with something like the labor bureau and I also called non-profit organizations, but what's the point when everywhere is like that? Laws are something for rich people, not for poor people. We have to bear with the consequences of going against the leaders – we will lose our jobs and be black-listed forever from the labor market.
>
> (Lei, SOE Ready-mix Concrete Worker, Hefei, 2011)

Self-Control and Others at the Lowest Level

The thoughts and behaviors of the workers about their societal positions represented an accumulation of a vast network of discourses on 'quality' to control themselves and others in a constructed hierarchy (see Chapter 2).

The evidence highlights that this control method had been internalized as general practice among the workers and constructed a status consciousness within themselves at the lowest level of society:

> I think the quality of China's education system might not be so good. That's why some rich parents send their children to somewhere else, like Hong Kong, to study. I don't know about the difference in terms of the quality between China and other countries … I feel that our grades are not equivalent to the effort we put in. It's about the behavior that our teachers wanted to see. If we behaved properly, like respecting the teachers by

> greeting them each time we saw them, then we could get better grades... It's just like the way we have to treat our parents.
>
> (Zhi, Foxconn Worker, Shenzhen, 2011)

While the control methods were seemingly different from the Imperial period (see Chapter 2), their knowledge about themselves had still emphasized on the proper behavior of respect for superior and authority figures in their hierarchized social relations.

Implicit in this practice is the fabrication and production of useful and docile workers through minute forms of correction, training, and retraining the minds of children in their social lives:

> I grew up in a poor family in the village and we had to do farming work to maintain our living – we grew fruits and vegetables – and we had chickens and ducks too but we didn't usually eat them before Chinese New Year, because meat was very precious to us. Sometimes when I tried to avoid working on the farms or contradicted my parents, they would beat me; when I did what they told me then I usually got to go out to play with the other kids and sometimes I got to eat meat. I was so naughty back then; we should always do what our parents want – it's just the rules in our culture that we all followed.
>
> (Tai, NGO Worker, Hefei, 2011)

A prolonged training and retraining of a large group of people to perform various activities in repeated motions and movements in accordance with the particular rules had constituted specific mindsets within the workers:

> It's just a normal practice for us to do whatever our parents want because they're our seniors (superiors)... like I married because my parents had organized this for me – it really didn't matter if I liked it or not because all parents will have to organize marriage for their kids – we just have to obey their decisions. I wanted to divorce my wife because I found out she had an affair with someone else using my money. I told my parents but they didn't allow me to divorce because this is too abnormal for our family.
>
> (Xun, Lift Manufacturing Worker, Hangzhou, 2011)

The hierarchical environment thus created a receptive psyche within family life to implant a sense of fatalism within the workers that was ultimately generated from their loyalty to their families in their original home villages:

> ...we must look after our parents when we grow up because they spent a lot of time and money on us when we were young, so it's our turn now. That's why I had to come to the city to work, and I can send them more money so they can have meat and also fix the roof of our house in the village. It's my turn to look after them and to maintain or, even better, to improve their living conditions... They're getting older and they can't do farm work anymore.
>
> (Yanam, Foxconn Worker, Shenzhen, 2011)

The findings further suggest that commitment to their impoverished families had ensured their submissiveness and filial behavior (Javeline 2006; Faison 2007) in their workplaces:

> I earn 1,450 yuan a month... I only allow myself to keep 200 yuan... I've got two kids in the village... I'm the only one to support my family, my parents... and also the family of my late husband... We *dagong* are like this... we have to look after ourselves and also our families... so most of us tolerate any conditions in the cities... we don't have any other choices.
>
> (Chong, Motel Cleaner, Shenzhen, 2011)

The Other as Self-Responsibility

To support their suffering families, most of them sacrifice themselves by enduring the travails of work in the cities.

The workers' sacrifice for their families thus underpins the link between their rightful positions and unique responsibilities (Foucault 1987, 1997; Smart 1998) in a close relationship that forms part of the condition of their constitution:

> ...my husband and I earn very little... only 2000 to 3000 yuan a month... Very tough ... have to be extra careful when we spend our money... We have to pay tuition fees for our boy and also give money to parents of both families... Altogether they need around 20,000 yuan a year... we need to save up at least 1,500 yuan each month... No choice; taking care of the

family is the normal responsibility for most of us in China … that's why we come out to *dagong*.

(Wang, Motel Cleaner, Shenzhen, 2011)

In order to 'maintain' their responsibility, most of the interviewed workers had become a hostage of their families by subjecting themselves to poor conditions in the cities:

I know this metal-shed dormitory is very small and so we have to keep our suitcases and other belongings on our beds. But we don't have a choice because we are only earning 70 yuan a day and we can't afford to rent a flat for ourselves elsewhere. Living in this dormitory is much cheaper – each of us has to pay only 100 yuan a month and all the utilities are included… although it's extremely dusty we don't have to spend additional money and time to travel to and from work… and we can save much more money for my wife, my kids and parents in my village.

(Cai, SOE Ready-mix Concrete Worker, Hefei, 2011)

Apart from reducing accommodation expenditures, a large proportion of interviewed workers revealed that they had to consume low-quality food to minimize their spending in order to support the financial needs of their families:

"I only have my daily lunch at the canteen when I am at work because their food is too expensive. I earn around 2000 yuan a month and I have to pay 300 yuan to our canteen at work, so that is about 10 yuan each time I eat at the canteen. I can only choose vegetable dishes because meat dishes are way too expensive… I have my dinner elsewhere because we're not allowed to cook in the dormitory… eating out is not cheap. It costs me 6 yuan for a bowl of plain noodles. But only in this way I can save a bit of money for my family – everyone does this in China

(Yanam, Foxconn Worker, Shenzhen, 2011)

All the interviewed workers appeared to maintain themselves by engaging in the socially accepted moral and ethical practices that constituted and were embedded in their social networks (or power-knowledge networks):

Being a worker is not good… we're just a bunch of uneducated people. We can't do any other things apart from working or staying in our dormitory because we don't have spare money. We must put up with whatever

> hardships we have; we don't have time and we don't have energy to think about any other things but our subsistence – this is our only right and our only concern. We only want to make enough to subsist and support our families.
>
> (Yaxing, IT Worker, Shenzhen, 2011)

Their direct encounter with their constructed 'true selves' (or not selves) when they upheld the 'truth' about their status of 'degradation' and continued to take on responsibility for others had ingrained the attitudes of passivity and vulnerability in the core of their subjectivities (Foucault 1977, 1978, 1982).

This subsequently became the 'true' characters and personalities of the workers, who worked to serve the interests of their employers and eventually the will of the Chinese State to maintain a docile labor force within the thought management system in China.

Concluding Remarks

Rather than reflecting the 'universal' view that resistance activity is undoubtedly motivated by their exploitative experience as a class, the workers' discourses reflected that the possibility of class action was undermined by their shared perception that 'subsistence' was all that they were entitled to in their daily lives and lived experiences as 'low-quality' workers.

It is argued that these experiences were culturally constituted by the Confucian 'truth' about their social status through 'quality' discourses regarding the workers place in the hierarchy of relationships. The findings show that their 'low quality' due to their lack of education was their particular 'self-knowledge' that guided them to accept their given conditions. This is because of the lower status that they occupied in the 'quality-based' occupational hierarchy. Their self-governance (or automatic docility) illustrated the effectiveness of the making of docile bodies and minds through their encounter with themselves and others as responsible in a relationship of proximity within the thought management system in China.

While the workers' mentalities and their sense of responsibility for others constrained the workers' perceptions and experiences in this group, Chapter 4 explores how self-care practices (Foucault 1986) by these workers may open up possibilities for them to break out of the totality of their constituted experiences to improve their living and working conditions.

Bibliography

Benney, Jonathan. 2013. *Defending Rights in Contemporary China: Reserving the Right*. New York: Routledge.

Evasdottir, Erika. 2004. *Obedient Autonomy: Chinese Intellectuals and the Achievement of Orderly Life*. Vancouver: The University of British Columbia.

Faison, Elyssa. 2007. *Managing Women: Disciplining Labor in Modern Japan*. Berkeley: University of California Press.

Foucault, Michel. 1966/2005. *The Order of Things: An archaeology of the Human Sciences*. New York: Routledge.

Foucault, Michel. 1977. *Discipline and Punish: The Birth of the Prison*. New York: Vintage Books.

Foucault, Michel. 1978. *The History of Sexuality, Volume 1: An Introduction*. New York: Pantheon Books.

Foucault, Michel. 1982. The Subject and Power. In *Michel Foucault: Beyond Structuralism and Hermeneutics*, ed. Hubert Dreyfus and Paul Rabinow. Chicago: University of Chicago Press.

Foucault, Michel. 1986. *The Care of the Self*. New York: Pantheon Books.

Foucault, Michel. 1987. The Ethic of Care for the Self as a Practice of Freedom: An Interview with Michel Foucault on January 20, 1984. *Philosophy & Social Critisim* 12: 112–131.

Foucault, Michel. 1997. *Ethics, Subjectivity and Truth: The Essential Works of Foucault 1954–1984*. New York: The New Press.

Foucault, Michel. 2006. *History of Madness*. New York: Routledge.

Foucault, Michel, Luther Martin, Huck Gutman, and Patrick Hutton. 1988. *Technologies of the Self: A Seminar with Michel Foucault*. Amherst, MA: University of Massachusetts Press.

Gallagher, Mary. 2005. "Use the Law as Your Weapon!": Institutional Change and Legal Mobilization in China. In *Engaging the Law in China: State, Society, and Possibilities for Justice*, ed. Neil Diamant Staanley Lubman and Kelvin O'Brien. Stanford: Stanford University Press.

Gallagher, Mary. 2006. Mobilizing the Law in China: "Informed Disenchantment" and the Development of Legal Consciousness. *Law & Society Review* 40 (4): 783–816.

Hsing, You-tien. 1998. *Making Capitalism in China: The Taiwan Connection*. Oxford: Oxford University Press.

Javeline, Debra Lynn. 2006. *Protest and the Politics of Blame: The Russian Response to Unpaid Wages*. Ann Arbor: The University of Michigan Press.

Leung, Elly, and Donella Caspersz. 2016. Exploring Worker Consciousness in China. *Labour & Industry: A Journal of the Social and Economic Relations of Work* 26 (3): 237–250.

Mallee, Hein. 2000. Migration, Hukou, Resistance in Reform China. In *Chinese Society, 2nd Edition: Change, Conflict and Resistance*, ed. Elizabeth Perry and Mark Selden. New York: Routledge.

McKinlay, Alan, and Philip Taylor. 2014. *Foucault, Governmentality, and Organization: Inside the Factory of the Future*. New York: Routledge.

NBSC. 2015. Statistical Communiqué of the People's Republic of China on the 2014 National Economic and Social Development. Accessed 15 December 2016.

O'Farrell, Clare. 2005. *Michel Foucault*. Thousand Oaks, CA: Sage.

Ransom, John. 1997. *Foucault's Discipline: The Politics of Subjectivity*. London: Duke University Press.

Smart, Barry. 1985. *Michel Foucault*. London: Tavistock Publications Limited.

Smart, Barry. 1998. Foucault, Levinas and the Subject of Responsibility. In *The Later Foucault: Politics and Philosophy*, ed. Jeremy Moss. Thousand Oaks, CA: Sage.

Wilson, Scott. 2009. *Remade in China: Foreign Investors and Institutional Change in China*. Oxford: Oxford University Press.

CHAPTER 4

"Beyond" the Selves and Reflective Docility

> I don't believe there can be a society without relations of power, if you understand them as means by which individuals try to conduct, to determine the behaviors of others. The problem is not of trying to dissolve them in the Utopia of a perfectly transparent communication, but to give one's self the rules of law, the techniques of management, and also the ethics, the ethos, the practice of self, which would allow these games of power to be played with the minimum of domination.
>
> (Foucault 1987: 18)

The aim of this chapter is to present and discuss the two phases of empirical data elicited from 22 everyday workers in Group Two—*those who had engaged in protest activities*—that was deliberately collected at multiple locations, mainly through contact labor NGOs in Hong Kong and Guangzhou Province in China between 2011 and 2014.

This body of data illustrates that, while protest activities by everyday workers open a space to transform the way they relate to themselves and to each other and to their conditions, these possibilities are conditioned by their cultural knowledge. This is because, according to Foucault (1982), 'being a subject' is possible only within the power-knowledge networks, and thus meaningful and effective resistant actions are always inherent in that particular context of concrete constraints traversing in society. While historically constituted, Foucault insists that the subjects

E. Leung, *The (Re)Making of the Chinese Working Class*,
Palgrave Debates in Business History,
https://doi.org/10.1007/978-3-030-83313-8_4

can deconstruct a part of themselves by actively modifying their manner of action and mode of being through practices of the self (or *care of the self*) (1986, 1987, 1997).

Drawing on 22 interviews from Group Two, the cultural dimension of how 'care' or 'concern for oneself' becomes a particular goal that potentially modifies the behaviors and modes of living among the workers within the thought management system is examined. This chapter begins with a presentation of both the given conditions and oppression that the workers experienced in their daily lives. These experiences were inexorably intertwined subconsciously with the 'quality' discourses that guided workers to perceive themselves as 'low-quality sub-individuals' by accepting any given conditions, as with their Group One colleagues in the occupational hierarchy. The workers' accumulated feelings about their prolonged experiences of low status and poor conditions were a major determinant in shaping their oppositional thoughts toward their superiors and authority figures. These thoughts were further sharpened when the workers articulated their intense feelings about their daily experiences among themselves and they reinterpreted an alternative discourse and 'truth' about themselves through their participation in social and cultural activities.

This chapter demonstrates that their involvement in these activities contributed to implanting a sense of 'togetherness' within them, which then acted to spark spontaneous embryonic trade union consciousness (Chan and Siu 2012) and increased their solidarity to mobilize resistance activities. However, their actions were predominately guided by a status consciousness that was arguably preconditioned by their sense of deservingness with respect to subsistence and sustenance matters for themselves (and their families) within the limits of their perceptions of 'normality' within their given societal positions. Thus, while their emotions had spurred up their oppositional spirit, the effectiveness of their protest actions was undermined by their self-care practices within the 'normative' descriptions in China.

The Tears of *Yayi* 壓抑

One early morning in December 2013, I was invited to interview seven State-employed street cleaners (see Fig. 4.1) at the office of a non-government labor organization (labor NGO) in Foshan, Guangdong Province.

Fig. 4.1 State-employed street cleaners (*Source* Photo by author)

I was told that some of these cleaners had taken a few hours off from work to attend this interview because they were eager to discuss their thoughts about their second attempt to protest against their working conditions. When I arrived at the NGO office and was waiting for the rest of the cleaners, one cleaner with strong body odor suddenly burst into tears while debriefing me about their situation:

> I've been working for this *danwei* 單位 [work unit] for 10 years but the money I earned over those years wasn't even enough to buy a toilet bowl. Everyone who decided to come here today has been trying to spend money carefully because we have no money to waste. I came out to work in the city because I pictured myself being able to save up a bit of money so that I don't have to worry about my living when I get older. This was just a dream – a dream is a dream – it will never happen… because *di zuzhi* 低素質 [low-quality people"] are destined to do low-pay dirty work but we should be allowed to make enough to eat rice [feed themselves]; we feel very *yayi* [repressed 壓抑] deep inside…
>
> (Yao, SOE Street Cleaner, Foshan, 2013)

A recurring theme that emerged when this group explained their motivation for engaging in the resistant activity was their collective concern about their minimal subsistence and sustenance levels (see Chapter 1). Like their colleagues in Group One (see Chapter 3), their self-knowledge about themselves as low-quality (*di zuzhi* 低素質) people was a determining factor in accepting any given work conditions as their destiny (*ming* 命) in exchange for subsistence. Their daily experiences of deep frustration, resentment, anger and sorrow over the continual struggle against the difficulties to maintain their 'right to subsistence' (*shengcun quan* 生存權) (Chen 2000; see Chapter 1)—the only deservingness as being low-quality workers—were described as *yayi* (repressed 壓抑) by all the interviewed workers.

Thus, *yayi* is a concept of long-accumulated emotional feelings of contradictions, involving both their passive acceptance of their given situation as their destiny (*ming*) (see Chapters 2 and 3) and a desire to overcome or to work against that situation.

The mixture of these intense feelings of *yayi* was frequently verbalized by the workers to interpret their anger, frustration, and resentment about their everyday lives. Min, for example, a 36-year-old worker, revealed the treatment he experienced at work: 'I know as a worker I don't have any rights and so it is up to work leaders to muck me around whenever they like. I worked very long hours and they paid me so little that I could barely survive—you know I feel so *yayi* when I go to work and then I have to repeatedly think about my next bills when I am home' (Springs Manufacturing Worker, Hangzhou, 2011). Shen, a 24-year-old worker, spoke about his *yayi* about not having received more education: 'I'm so illiterate that I can't have a better job to marry anyone… my life is already *yayi*… my earnings are so low and it'll be really hard for me to look after a family… I can't even look after myself' (Lighting Factory Worker, Shenzhen, 2011). Xiaoling, a 30-year-old masseuse, interpreted her deeply felt *yayi* that she shared with her fellow workers over the constant deductions from their subsistence wages:

> …our team leaders deduct money from our wages for nearly everything… like when we are doing overtime with the client(s) in the room; or whenever a client puts in a complaint about us; or if we eat the food that the clients offer us. You know each mistake is going to cost us between 300 and 500 yuan – our monthly earnings are already so low – one work fine is equivalent to at least two weeks of our wages! We are so *yayi* when we

have or even don't have clients; we are so *yayi* for trying not to make mistakes; we are so *yayi* when our wages are deducted; we are so *yayi* to earn our living when we actually have a job to do and we worked for so many years!

(Xiaoling, Masseuse, Shenzhen, 2011)

Despite emotional feelings toward the inhuman treatment they faced at work in exchange of minimal subsistence wages for survival, they also used the word *yayi* to describe their non-work personal lives under the weight of their daily hardships.

A 33-year-old jewelry worker who was suffering from leukemia elaborated this:

I was diagnosed with leukemia... not long after our first strike... in 2007. My wife left me as well as our [twin] boys... since then, because she didn't want to waste her time a sick person... My boys live with my parents in the village... I only saw them a few times since they were born... I'm so sick I can't travel a long way to get back home to see them and yet I also can't look after them in the city. I have to go to the hospital nearly every day. The boys are 7-year-old; I could only speak to them on the phone over the past years. I always feel *yayi* when the boys talked to me like they are talking to a stranger rather than to their father, though I also have nothing much to talk to my boys. It feels like I have no family and no one... I feel so *yayi* my life is all about going to work and to the hospital... I feel so *yayi* to live... I sometimes feel like to put an end to it...

(Fa, Jewelry Worker, Haizhu, 2013)

The comments made by the interviewed workers about their frustration and resentment over their work and non-work lives have illustrated how the cultural concept and expression of *yayi* has played a significant role in shaping their daily experiences.

While the concept of *yayi* as expressed by these workers did not indicate an awareness of inequality of their social status (or position) or a realization of their common interest as being the workers, it is a moral language that may work to heighten their sense of injustice as well as their spirit of resistance to the oppression of their work superior and authority figures within the hierarchical occupational structure:

Our work leaders were very mean and nasty – they subcontracted our work to other factories to low down the production cost and keep the excess in

their own pockets. I can give you an example: our factory had to pay us 0.2 yuan for each stone we inserted but the subcontractor charged only 0.15 yuan per stone inserted and so the work leaders saved 0.05 yuan each stone and they kept this money for themselves and yet we didn't have sufficient work to earn enough money. You know working and putting up with our nasty work leaders were already a very *yayi* thing for us; having us working but not letting us to make enough [money] to live had increased [the level of] our *yayi*... even though they were work leaders they shouldn't be so mean and unfair [...] because of this we must get rid of our work leaders.
(Jinhua, Jewelry Worker, Panyu, 2013)

Yayi-Based Protest Actions

Henceforth, beneath the expression of *yayi* lies a perception of egalitarian and spiritual resistance to the hierarchical social order that is disguised by workers' long-suppressed resentment and anger over their work superiors and by their own interpretation of the idea of injustice in their lived experiences:

My life started off here [Hangzhou] by working in a very small factory – my boss was my work leader and I was the only worker he employed. In the beginning I thought he was very nice as he bought me a television, microwave, a pillow and a blanket and he let me live inside the factory – so the machines were operated downstairs and I lived upstairs. But after a few days I found that I had to work at least 10 hours a day and in the peak season I had to work 24 hours a day – I had to bring my blanket and pillow to sleep with the machines... I worked and lived in this way for a long period of time but he didn't even increase my wages. I felt so *yayi* about that so I asked him for a pay-rise, but he yelled at me as usual. I felt more *yayi* as he kept barking [yelling] at me like he has every right to look down on me just because he's a rich man. It's so unfair because I was his tool helping him to make money and he yelled at me but didn't even give me a bit of pay-rise. You know I had to pay for my food and I had to send money home; I was extremely *yayi* so I punched him.
(Min, Spring Manufacturing Worker, Hangzhou, 2011)

Workers' spontaneous, violent reaction toward the constant labor abuses exercised by their work superiors suggest that *yayi* played a crucial role in promoting a growth of consciousness of injustice among the workers.

This consciousness concealed an explosive potential for workers' oppositional and resistant attitudes to flare up as strong feelings of affinity occurred when the deep-seated *yayi* matters had touched the minds of those who shared similar experiences:

> Our strikes occurred all of a sudden usually – no one organized the strikes but we just told each other to stop working when we felt too *yayi* to live and to feed our families as our wages were way too low, so that we couldn't even earn our basic living. We got very angry and *yayi* when our leaders refused to discuss the pay-rise with us; that's why we stopped working.
> (Gong, Batteries Manufacturing Worker, Haizhu, 2013)

Rather than class opposition or antagonism (Walder 1991) as suggested by scholars such as Leung Pak Nang and Pun Ngai (2009) as illustrated in Chapter 1, *yayi*-based protests had insinuated a sense of injustice toward what Feng Chen (2003: 242) has referred to as the 'subsistence crisis'. Thus, it is when the abuses reached an extreme level to the extent that threatened their minimal subsistence level, the accumulated pain and anger of the workers burst into acts of resistant activities in defense of their only deservingness as being the low-quality workers.

Yi, 22-year-old—who was categorized in the group of well-educated second generation of peasant workers in academic literature (see Chapter 1)—revealed how the *yayi* feelings had spontaneously turned workers into a group of emotional protesters to engage in one of the resistant activities that was frequently described as an organized, interest-based action (Chan and Hui 2012, 2016; Gray and Jang 2015) at Honda's transmission and engine parts factory in Foshan:

> I started working at Honda since 2007… it's a very *yayi* thing to work on the production line… We were not allowed to talk; we had to repeat the same task over and over at a fast pace without making mistakes; we earned very little money. We also felt *yayi* even when we were not at work… We stayed in the flat because we didn't have much money to go out… We lived on a tight budget because we had to save money to send home. By 2010, doing a living became impossible because our wages were extremely low and we were unable to catch up with the inflation… I realized that everyone became so grumpy… It's very easy for us being rude to other people – not only because we are low-educated, but also because we cared only about ourselves and so we couldn't be bothered about other people… One day, we started to text each other on our QQ group chat [instant

> messaging application and online forum in China] using our phones when we were having lunch or dinner ... We talked about our income; our money and our family... The more we talked about it, the more *yayi* we felt; and as our *yayi* feeling increased we felt like we were all in the same boat that we had to stick to each other... We decided that we couldn't live any longer with the little money so we turned off [pushed a stop button] the production line and so all of us had to stop working.
>
> (Yi, Honda Worker, Foshan, 2013)

Thus, intensified emotional feelings within the workers had stimulated a rather embryonic trade union consciousness among themselves which laid the foundation for motivating them to struggle against their given conditions.

Their sense of solidarity (or coalescence) appeared to become stronger when their *yayi* feelings of injustice were being translated into emotional words and content in their ordinary conversations:

> We whinged about our *yayi* every time we met each other at work... Can you imagine, I earned only 1,170 yuan each month for three years and our leaders keep deducting money from our already low wages, from 0.01 to $8 yuan, whenever they found rubbish in the areas we handled? We all tried to save our money and we only go to the market to buy the 'ready-to-throw-away' food at night – we never buy meat, we never buy fresh food, because they're all too expensive. We tried so hard to save our money but our leaders just took our money away when they saw a chance. Each time when we talked about this we felt angry... we felt very *yayi* to work and to live... We feel our *yayi* deep inside cannot be *shifang* 释放 (released) so we talked to one another. We know we must stick together and do something about it...
>
> (Ying & Yao, SOE Street Cleaners, Foshan, 2013)

The forms of releasing (*shifang* 释放) *yayi* among the interviewed workers were either symbolically, through conversation or dance, or practically, through actions and/or through a combination of both:

> We stopped working because our leaders deducted another 100 yuan a month from our wages for our meal money at the canteen – but the food was really bad – you know the food we ate for each of our meals had some funny smell. We only had one hour lunch break and it was really far for us to walk to any other eateries outside. We worked very hard and every dollar we earned was through our blood and sweat... but our leaders fed

> us with some pig food and we all felt very *yayi* about this... so we stopped working. I felt that it was fun to stop working because we didn't have to work – we laughed and talked; some slept or danced on the shopfloor – we just did whatever we liked. It felt like we could eventually *shifang* our *yayi*, particularly when we looked at how angry the leaders were.
>
> (Shen, Lighting Factory Worker, Shenzhen, 2011)

Many of the protest actions that accompanied the workers' sit-in demonstrations (or work stoppages) were manifested in forms of *shifang yayi*. Across private as well as State-owned enterprises (SOEs), large and small, some interviewed workers appeared to vent their long-suppressed anger and resentment on their work leaders by 'humiliating' them in the protest actions:

> The days before we stopped working, we had tried to discuss our issues with the leaders so many times but they refused to talk to us. I wrote a list of our issues on a piece of paper and handed to the leader (manager) – I also told him 'we are going to stop working if the leaders are not going to redress our issues'. This leader rang up the higher leader (Chinese director) and told him what was happening but no leaders talked to us; so we stopped working. Then the higher leader came to tell us how wrong we were and that he didn't even know why we'd stopped working. We were so *yayi* when he said that; we were very angry with him; but you know we couldn't do anything too disrespectful to our leaders, so we ignored him – he basically talked and shouted by himself for three hours. I felt my *yayi shifang* a bit when I saw his face turning angry red – it was so funny to look at.
>
> (Feng, Plastic Board Factory Worker, Foshan, 2013)

While the significance of self-directed status oppression (or status consciousness) (see Chapters 2 and 3) was demonstrated in workers' collective responses, their actions indicated that their desire to *shifang* their compressed feelings was their motivating force to spark a *yayi*-based solidarity among those who suffered the same experiences.

Cultural Activities and *Yayi*-Based Solidarity

The evidence suggests that *yayi*-based solidarity sharpens further when workers *shifang* their intense feelings by engaging in cultural activities organized by the non-government labor organizations (or labor NGOs).

While these organizations did not engage in any workers' protest activities, they provided the workers with an interactive platform through learning and entertaining activities, for example, small group discussions (see Fig. 4.2) on labor rights, readings, movie sharing, singing, and dancing, to release their emotional feelings:

Many reported that their initial motivation to participate in these forms of activities was just to have fun, but they slowly established close ties with other fellow workers across enterprises and geographical areas:

> I lived around this area… I was a bit curious about this center as I saw that it organized many different activities. One night I just walked into the center after work. Since then I have come here to 'play' every night. You know we are very *yayi* at work and we all come here to *shifang* ourselves… we work in different factories and places and we all came from different regions. It feels like we are all in a big family… it's a close feeling of being together – we are all together.
>
> (Min, Springs Manufacturing Worker, Hangzhou, 2011)

The feeling of 'togetherness' implanted within the circles of workers thus reflected their 'belongingness' to the NGO cultural center(s). The 'togetherness' and 'belongingness' among the interviewed workers

Fig. 4.2 Small group discussions at the NGO (*Source* Photo by author)

appeared to be deepened by the content of the NGO's cultural activities, which were oriented to forging a more inclusive and positive sense of the workers' positions as well as promoting a critical consciousness among the workers as a class. This intention was expressed in the lyrics of the labor song in a singing session:

> We workers have power
> Hey! We workers have power
> We're busy at work every day
> Hey! We're busy at work every day
> We changed the world
> We built houses
> We built railways
> We turned on the machines,
> to make hammers for farming production;
> to make guns and weapons for our soldiers!
> Our faces glowed
> Our sweats dropped
> Why? We wanted to be released
> Why? We wanted to be released
> We wanted our entire country to be released!

This labor song, titled '*We workers have power*', was produced in 1947 to construct a positive working-class identity in Mao's socialist period. The lyrics of the song were crafted to mobilize workers for physical and manual labor using nationalistic ideology.

In this context, nationalism was combined with military rhetoric, equating industrial workers with soldiers fighting for national defense (Koo 2001). Workers' dedication to China's market economy is now advocated as a patriotic act that a working class should be proud of as in the Mao's period (see Chapter 2) in post-socialist China.

Nationalistic Sentiments and the 'Truth' of *Yayi* Lives

While the nationalistic (or Maoist) rhetoric had little effect on the workers' consciousness, enthusiastic singing of the labor songs had worked to heighten their emotions about their experiences as a class.

A garment factory worker used Maoist language (see Chapter 1) to describe their daily work life:

> Mao Zedong was a great leader – without him there's no China. Back in Mao's time everyone was treated equally – no one was particularly rich or poor. But Deng Xiaoping opened up China for economic development [...] he said some of us must get rich first... we *jiceng* 基層 (grassroots), *dagong* 打工 and *gongren* 工人 worked hard... labored day and night for those leaders to get rich first... but what about us? Why, we can't even earn enough to live... we have to live our *yayi* lives every day for the rich people.
>
> (Shao, Garment Factory Worker, Hangzhou, 2011)

By using nationalistic sentiment to interpret the *yayi* feeling experienced in their daily work lives, some workers began to criticize the social 'truth' (Foucault 1980b; see Chapters 2 and 3) about their conditions within the given occupational status hierarchy:

> I felt like I was a machine myself...
> Like a robot repeating the same tasks and motions...
> Repeating the same tasks and motions was boring and tiring...
> We didn't need brains to do work...
> ...Just like a robot repeating the same things over and over...
> It felt like the Japanese turned us into their machines...
> and made a lot of money by selling a lot of cars we made...
> I was one of their robots... (Di, Honda Worker, Foshan, 2013)

By relating the personal feelings of despair about the alienation and exploitation that caused them to question the status quo, the workers appeared to attain a new level of understanding of themselves.

The consequent revised knowledge (or truth) about themselves (see Chapter 2) created possibilities for reshaping workers' consciousness to one that can encourage them to engage in a sequence of exercises to facilitate self-modification (or re-subjectification of the self) (Foucault 1987, 1997; see Chapter 2).

Counter-Hegemonic Discourse and Alternative 'Truth'

Opportunities for workers' self-modification were presented in the working-class materials produced by the NGOs, such as poems, songs, and short stories, which were assessable in the workers' newspapers, newsletters, and magazines, as well as in the Chinese online forums, such as QQ and Weibo.

These media channels also provided alternative information about current labor protests and informative educational columns on labor laws and workers' rights that were not normally covered in the regular, State-controlled daily newspapers (see Chapter 2). Hence, it is suggested that the objective of the NGOs was to counter the 'official' reality by establishing the counter-hegemony of a Chinese working-class culture.

Given the 'official' cultural environment and material conditions of the everyday workers, new counter-hegemonic discourse (Gramsci 1988, 2000) was an alternative 'truth' (or reverse discourse) (Foucault 1997; see Chapter 2) that worked to empower the workers:

> We *qingjie gongren* 清佞工人 (street cleaners) are human too. We had enough! We must *nao* 鬧 [create trouble] and make it big to get our justice back… we must stick together in our work strike until we get what we want…
>
> (Fang, SOE Street Cleaner, Foshan, 2013)

Their assertive sense of their positions through the revelation of an alternative truth about themselves consequently contributed to turning their normal practices (Foucault 1977; see Chapters 2 and 3) of adaptation or 'exit' orientation to their given conditions into 'voice':

> We must stand up for ourselves and fight for our own things – things that belonged to us. If we don't fight for ourselves… who will? And if we don't fight for ourselves… employers will take advantage of all of us!
>
> (Hung, Jewelry worker, Panyu, 2013)

'Automatic' Self-Devaluation

While the alternative 'truth' was a critical ingredient for increasing their consciousness to one that posed oppositional attitude toward their superiors and authority figures, the findings suggest that workers still devaluated themselves automatically.

This 'automatic' self-devaluation was arguably guided by their status consciousness that had severely prevented them from obtaining a sense of power vis-à-vis their superiors in the resistance activities:

> We… street cleaners (*qingjie gongren*) do not have 'culture' in us – we are extremely illiterate, extremely grassroots, extremely dirty. Our work leaders wouldn't want to talk to us… wouldn't want to look at us. We

> know we shouldn't expect much... because our quality is extremely low. We are always at the bottom of society.
>
> (Yao, SOE Street Cleaner, Foshan, 2013)

The workers' recognition of the truth about their devalued societal status, which was associated with their educational deficiency (see Chapters 2 and 3) that sprang from their cultural reactions and experiences, had played a critical role in defining their 'collective demands':

> We only want to get a raise to earn our basic living – we didn't ask for that much – and that's because we're just a bunch of low-quality people. But even if we're uneducated, illiterate and at the bottom of society, our work leaders should at least allow us to have 'full bellies'.
>
> (Ying, SOE Street Cleaner, Foshan, 2013)

The threats to their entitlement and deservingness of a 'subsistence wage' within their given positions had angered the 'low-quality' workers (see Chapters 2 and 3), which triggered protest actions. The outbursts of these protests were therefore predominantly motivated by a cultural reflection of the workers' desperate economic situations in relation to their everyday sustenance.

Rather than being concerned with a more humane treatment or better conditions at work, the workers' demands were still centered on their immediate economic conditions relating to their moral sense of a right to basic subsistence in the protest activities:

> We're not being greedy – we just want to get a raise so all of us will be able to live. Our leaders are so mean to us... keep deducting our wages... they come to check on us to see if there's any rubbish in the streets. Sometimes when the weather was too hot. I stood there to rest a little bit... the leaders would just come out from nowhere to swear and yell at me. I don't mind the leaders yelling at me or insulting me as long as I can earn enough to live... because they are our work leaders.
>
> (Ying, SOE Street Cleaner, Foshan, 2013)

As with Group One workers, their internal acceptance of the 'rights' or 'mandate' of their work superiors to treat them badly in return for a liveable income. This indicates that the truth about different destinies for the perceived superiority (the high) and the perceived inferiority (the low)—as discussed in Chapters 2 and 3—had been internalized by the workers themselves within their relations of power-knowledge (Foucault 1977, 1980a, b).

It is this status consciousness among the interviewed workers that had become forms of subtle power which exercised by themselves in their daily lives had undermined the potential for effective protest activities.

The Struggle for a United 'Voice'

During their protest actions, all the interviewed workers reported that they were asked by their work leaders to 'voice' their problems (or demands) and their proposed solutions to redress their issues:

> Our strike broke out suddenly... during the work stoppage... we hadn't really thought about what we wanted and no one was able to represent anyone to speak. Our leaders asked many times what we wanted but none of us said anything. The leaders started to get pissed off with us... they slammed the tables and yelled at us... we were feeling very *yayi* as the leaders were angry at us so we started saying different things on our own at the same time for about two hours... We didn't know how much money we needed... we didn't know how much we should say... we only knew we were all very *yayi* about our basic living with our little incomes.
>
> (Yuan, Plastic Board Manufacturing Worker, Foshan, 2013)

The highly spontaneous and defensive *yayi*-based protests illustrate the workers' failure to articulate their needs in their particular situations. The difficulty with such a self-assessment was caused by their silent habits (Foucault 1978; see Chapters 1–3; Cooke et al. 2016) associated with their inferior status and hence their status consciousness:

> On the 2nd or the 3rd day of our strike, our work leaders did ask about our demands. We all had our heads down immediately – we tried not to look at our leaders... we just kept our heads down – didn't say a word – we were too scared to speak to the leaders because they were normally on top of us. And after I don't know how long some workers told the leaders that our wages were extremely low so we didn't have enough to live on. Other than that, none of us dared to speak to our work leaders... we just stood there listening to what our leaders had to say to us with our heads down.
>
> (Di, Honda Worker, Foshan, 2013)

Despite a vague emphasis on a 'subsistence wage', it becomes evident that the workers' demanding attitude was weakened by their self-knowledge (or truth) about themselves as inferior (or low) on normative grounds (see Chapter 2) of their quality-based structure (see Chapter 2).

Without a doubt, being born and shaped in certain ways to interact with the historical mode of 'high-low' hierarchy, their unthinking and uncritical engagement with the norm-based moralities (Chapter 2) had further legitimized the 'prescribed' values of their given positions by themselves:

> We didn't know what we wanted… we wrote 117 items on our demand list but at least 70 of them were repeating each other. It was like we wanted many things to be improved, but we didn't know what exactly needed improving. The only thing we knew was a pay rise […] but we didn't know how much exactly we needed to live on. Honestly, it's very hard for us to tell the leaders what we want… because we're just *dagong*.
>
> (Yi, Honda Worker, Foshan, 2013)

Like their colleagues in Group One, their low level of legal rights consciousness (*falu wequan yishi* 法律維權意識) (Gallagher 2005, 2006; see Chapters 1–3) along with their unchanged perception of themselves as 'unknowing' low-quality subjects together with the sense of inferiority had been a crucial factor to maintain their status consciousness.

It is in such a way that the workers had disempowered themselves and had thus diminished the possibility of mobilizing an effective resistance to improve the working as well as living conditions for themselves and others:

> I had to join the work stoppage anyway… because our production line had stopped already… and I also wanted to get a pay rise. But *dagong* is just *dagong*. We are just some uneducated 'low-quality' people – we know nothing – so we didn't ask for a particular amount because we didn't think and didn't know how much [money] was reasonable to sustain our basic living… some of us wanted (a raise of) 300 yuan; some wanted 500 yuan; some wanted 600 yuan… so on and so forth… it was like a chaotic market… our leaders were so confused and angry as everybody was saying different things at the same time.
>
> (Yuan, Plastic Board Manufacturing Worker, Foshan, 2013)

Thus, despite hovering the main concern on their personal and immediate economic issues as with those in Group One (see Chapter 3), their lack of a united voice was by and large inherent in the absence of any form of leadership in their resistance activities:

> No one organized the work strike... we didn't have a strike leader... but there were two I think so-called leaders who already resigned before the strike and later on I found out they were the ones who pushed the button to stop the production lines and so there was no work to do. We just stopped working all of a sudden... I think all of us supported it because we're very *yayi* at work... we couldn't live any longer with that little money.
>
> (Yi, Honda Worker, Foshan, 2013)

It is even with the Honda strike, which had been articulated by scholars (see Chapter 1) as a breakthrough of class consciousness development among workers, the above discourse illustrates that the workers had no long-term plan or solid core of workers to lead or continue the protest activity.

This spontaneous and unorganized resistant activity, like those preceded it, remained isolated as workers' consciousness had not increased beyond reacting to immediate economic circumstances.

The Attacks on Workers

While spontaneous and unorganized, the workers' actions during most of the protest actions were predominantly developed by seeking the right moment and right excuse to *shifang* (release) their long-suppressed *yayi* feelings:

> Our first strike happened in July (2013) – we picked July because it's school holidays and it's also the hottest month. Can you imagine how much rubbish would be accumulated and how smelly the streets would be when we stopped cleaning for only an hour? We had about 400 to 500 cleaners not cleaning the streets and we were all sitting outside the local government building. We wanted to tell the local government how *yayi* our lives were and how hungry we were – no food, no energy to work.
>
> (Yao and Ying, SOE Street Cleaners, Foshan, 2013)

Despite enjoying a sense of 'freedom' to *shifang yayi* without immediate fear of the consequence of their actions, most of these spontaneous and unorganized protests hardly ever brought any gains for the workers:

> We sat out at the local government building all day from 12pm but no one bothered coming to speak to us… but we wanted to speak to the government – we wanted to get a raise to be able to live. We tried to draw the government's attention by going out onto the main road to block the traffic three times, but the security officers blocked us and they put barriers between the pedestrian path and the main road. They also beat up some of our cleaners. We got called into the leaders' office the day after the strike – we were forced to take a 30-yuan wage increase or resign.
>
> (Ying, SOE Street Cleaners, Foshan, 2013)

Not only had the forms of unorganized protests brought few positive outcomes for the workers, but also led to dismissal for some of those who participated in the strikes:

> The leaders had warned us that if we did not resume work straightaway then we would be dismissed without compensation. We resumed our work along with all the other workers without getting a wage increase. The five of us in the same team were not happy with the outcome so we refused to work overtime… and then we were fired. Our leader told the five of us that, according to the Labor Law – Clause 39, companies can dismiss any disobedient workers without compensation.
>
> (Xiaohuang, Carton Box Manufacturing Worker, Panyu, 2013)

Besides dismissal, enterprises were able to remove 'impure and disobedient elements' by blacklisting the activist workers from gainful employment:

> People like me causing troubles for the companies are all blacklisted by the business council. Joining work stoppages is just like stealing things from the companies, causing financial damage to the enterprises; and so, I am blacklisted by the business council… There's no way for me to get a regular job at a large factory anymore because these factories are members of the business council… I can only do some temporary or casual work in small factories.
>
> (Heng, Jewelry Worker, Panyu, 2013)

While these fierce attacks on resistance activities had forced the majority of workers into silence and submission again, some angry workers took their grievances to the streets:

> Our leaders deducted a large part of our wages anytime they liked… and there was this one time they declined my application for exemption from overtime work… but I really couldn't work that night and so I didn't. The next day they deducted 350 yuan from my earnings because I didn't work overtime. We were very angry that our hard-earned wages got deducted all the time so the six of us stopped working. Our leaders threatened to fire us if we continued to not work… four of them resumed work and two of us were sacked. I was very *yayi* and upset… so I went out onto the street and handed out some flyers to tell people what happened to me at work. I wrote on the flyers: 'My leaders are thieves – they took away my money'.
> (Qiang, Jewelry Worker, Panyu, 2013)

Externalizing the Worker Struggle in the 'Carceral Network'

Some of these street demonstrations were significant for developing closer interconnections between the labor NGOs and activist workers who were unwilling to bear the consequences of joining the work strikes:

> On the third day of handing out flyers on the street… three NGO workers came and talked to me… I couldn't stop telling them how *yayi* I was as the leaders fired me without giving me compensation… because I joined the strike to try to get back my hard-earned money. I was invited to meet with some workers of other firms and also to have a discussion with other NGO workers in their office to work out a better solution.
> (Qiang, Jewelry Worker, Panyu, 2013)

Apart from promoting social ties and communication among different groups of workers across enterprises, the interviewed workers revealed that they received minimal support from the NGOs to continue their resistance actions:

> The NGO workers told me that I should not engage in the work stoppage, because we wouldn't be able to get anything out of these actions. They said our action caused financial loss for the factory… and that we were given a chance to get back to work … they said because we didn't apply for

exemption from doing overtime work the leaders had the right to fire us for breaching the factory rules. We were an example, showing other workers the consequence of being disobedient. The NGO workers said if they had known us earlier they could have helped us to organize a 'negotiation team' among ourselves and teach us the way to discuss issues with our leaders.

(Xiaohuang, Carton Box Manufacturing Worker, Panyu, 2013)

As with other institutions such as the State-run trade unions (see Chapter 1), the NGOs are also enmeshed in the historical and cultural structure of the everyday 'carceral network' (Foucault 1980a; see Chapter 2) that engaged *only* in activities in the "proper" ways defined by the CCP.

Thus, the NGOs, although could be viewed as independent, are just one of the 'branches' among many in the governmental bureaucracy that are subject to the 'norms' and 'discipline' constructed by the CCP:

the NGO workers said that we should resolve our unpaid social insurance issues through the 'proper' channels. Before we lodged our complaint with the Labor Bureau, the NGO appointed some of us as the worker representatives and told us to hold a meeting to discuss our issues with our leaders. The NGO workers had arranged a lawyer to help us to bargain with our leaders. Our leaders were furious and they raised their voices at us – particularly at the lawyer – and they said to the NGO workers and the lawyer if they insisted on being that nosy then they would give them some trouble. The NGO workers and lawyer said that we should all have a break before we continued the discussion… but after the break the NGO workers and lawyer just disappeared from the meeting.

(Meilin, Jewelry Worker, Panyu, 2013)

Henceforth, some NGOs had been somewhat more daring to provide workers with guidance, if not leadership, established worker committees and engaged themselves with the workers in confrontational struggles or negotiations with management in the workplaces. However, their role as 'rights protectors' and scope of activities remained limited or readjusted to what they know of proper within the legal framework. The reactions of the NGOs along with the legal workers (or lawyer) toward the threats or harassment of the workplace management revealed not only their subservient status in the bureaucratic structure, but also reflected a hierarchical obedience of subordinates to the 'perceived' superior and authority figures.

These 'high-low' hierarchical practices by the everyday workers within the 'carceral network' (Foucault 1980a) had secured the capability of the employers as well as the CCP to 'override the law' (see Chapter 2):

> the NGO workers said that we were already given a chance to get back to work after the strike action and it's our fault because we didn't get approval from the leaders to be exempt from doing overtime work. They said if we really believed it was an unlawful dismissal, they could help prepare the paperwork to sue the factory. We lost the lawsuit ... the court didn't consider the evidence that we provided... the court didn't take the side of the workers... the court ruled that the factory did not dismiss us unlawfully...
>
> (Xiaohuang, Carton Box Manufacturing Worker, Panyu, 2013)

The decision of the court indicates that the legal rights protection (***weiquan*** 維權) practices (Chapter 1) are substantially influenced by behavioral norms. These norms are conformed to the CCP discipline to ensure the maintenance of a cheap, docile labor market and 'social harmony' (***hexie*** 和諧) (see Chapter 2) in upholding the hierarchical system.

The lack of either procedural equality or an impartial and independent tribunal subsequently guaranteed that the legal rights of the workers were not upheld:

> We didn't hear anything from the court for at least five months... so we went to the court to harass the judge. The judge told us that he was just waiting for a response from our former employer to see if they were able to compensate us. The judge was trying to drag on the case for as long as possible so that we might have to give up the court case.
>
> (Qiang, Jewelry Worker, Panyu, 2013)

Strengthening Worker Passivity

The joint control exercised by the State and by the employers thus strengthened worker passivity within their given positions in the labor market as a result of the governmental discourses of 'personal quality' in their everyday 'carceral network':

> Workers are always powerless… because we're 'low-quality' and we're always at the bottom of society. Employers can always bully us and our government doesn't care about us. Even though a work strike can be an effective method to push for better pay, it doesn't have any support from the government so it can also be a means to damage our benefits easily. We never know when the government and particularly our work leaders want to exact revenge on us… it is very difficult for us to organize many of us to strike… because none of us want to go against our work leaders. Strikes only happen when the subsistence level of the whole lot of us is under threat.
>
> (Di, Honda Worker, Foshan, 2013)

The day-to-day status experiences among the workers as influenced by China's governmental discourse within its thought management system thus continued to guide them to remain silence over their grievances and act only when a 'subsistence crisis' was commonly perceived:

> after the unpaid social insurance issues… our leaders subcontracted at least half of our production work to other factories. Those orders being left for us were all complicated and time-consuming items that we couldn't make money from at all to earn our living. Our situation was getting worse, with our leaders constantly picking on us and getting us to make corrections to the same items over and over so that we were unable to move on to the next items. You know a large part of our income relied on piece rates and so we kept losing money by making constant corrections to each item… then how were we going to make enough to have a basic living? Subsistence is our only right but our leaders didn't allow us to live. We didn't know what to do to live so we stopped working.
>
> (Meilin, Jewelry Worker, Panyu, 2013)

Their defensive act toward their only deservingness, namely the 'right to subsistence', had therefore made their base of solidarity easy to break through individual incentives:

> Our leaders told us how wrong we were to create troubles for the factory and we were told to correct our wrongdoings by getting back to work immediately. They said that they were willing to increase our piece-rate by 0.01 yuan as a reward if we got back to work. One of my co-workers took that 'reward' straight away. Our leaders then invited us to dinner… and the next day straight after that dinner my co-workers started working again.
>
> (Qiang, Jewelry Worker, Panyu, 2013)

Even when some interviewees demonstrated stronger determination and resistance than the others, their lack of interest in the long-term improvement of their conditions had caused the protest actions to become insignificant:

> We were trying to get a raise of 500 or 600 yuan a month in our strike... we said we were not going to back off until we got a raise of at least 500 yuan... but you know our action lasted less than half a day with an increase of only 200 yuan. Our leaders said they would fire all of us if we continued our action; but at the same time, they gave us a supper and promised us an increase of 200 yuan if we returned to work. You see all of us were worried about losing our jobs... and you know our attitudes changed so quickly as we were having our supper – like the way we talked – we dropped our angry tone to a pretty gentle soft tone when speaking to our leaders while we were eating together. The workers then began to accept the 200 yuan increase and so the rest of us had to follow.
>
> (Yuan, Plastic Board Manufacturing Worker, Foshan, 2013)

The ineffective, short-lived protests staged by these workers highlighted not only their disunity about their goals and collective interests, but also reflected a 'filial culture' that was linked to the Confucian ideologies (see Chapter 2) within their predefined 'true-selves':

> Most of us supported our work strike in 2010 because everything was so expensive and our wages didn't allow us to live in Foshan. But after the strike we all got a pay-rise ... and from then on, we had an increase of 3% each year... though it was still very low ... we already had enough money to survive. We shouldn't keep on asking for more and more... our factory doesn't have the money to give us a raise all the time. That's why we didn't support the second strike this year [2013] he stopped the production line suddenly just because he wanted to get a raise when we already got enough [money] to live on... the strike lasted about two hours... we didn't get a raise out of this... he put us at risk as if we also wanted to go against our work leaders – that's just not right.
>
> (Zhi, Honda Worker, Foshan, 2013)

Self-Value and the Norm-Based Moralities

The value judgment between 'right' and 'wrong' acts (Foucault 1980a) for the 'worker selves' reflects the effective operation of the norm-based moralities (see Chapter 2) in relation to one another within the mindsets of the workers.

This acceptance was arguably tied to their knowledge of the 'truth' about themselves as inferior, which caused them to self-direct themselves to regulate themselves and others in accordance with their given positions in the hierarchical structure:

> many of our strikes in China are all about the threat to our subsistence… organizing a strike is a very difficult task… because we cannot afford to be angry… most of us hesitated to create trouble… as we wanted to keep our jobs… that's the reason we tried not to create any trouble. We did it previously as we could barely subsist… but we were not very determined in the 2nd strike [2009] because we had already got enough [money] to live on. Though our first strike [2006] did give us a wage increase, I still think my act was really thoughtless and irresponsible – no leaders like disobedient workers – I could easily have lost my job over that… and yet I have a family to look after… my old parents, my wife and my child.
>
> (Yuan, Plastic Board Manufacturing Worker, Foshan, 2013)

Such confessions (Foucault 1978; see Chapter 2) about 'incorrect' behaviors that were contrary to their social status, associated with the 'truth' about their responsibility for others, thus worked together to maintain their status consciousness as the "low-quality" workers and hence restricted the area of their acts:

> If I could start it all over again I wouldn't want to go against my work leaders… I don't think striking is an appropriate strategy – I don't think anyone should join a work strike at all. It's a very tiring process and it's very difficult to get everyone to stay on the same boat because everyone is selfish – we only care about ourselves.
>
> (Meilin, Jewelry Worker, Panyu, 2013)

These 'self-care' practices (Foucault 1986, 1987, 1997; see Chapter 2) in the form of 'selfishness' exercised by these workers made them 'voluntarily' subject themselves to a strict set of self-regulations that they imposed on themselves. Hence, rather than improving their living and working conditions, their self-care practices at defending their minimal subsistence level were grounded in the cultural understanding of 'proper' behaviors thus maintained their level of 'docility' within their power-knowledge relations:

> I wasn't angry about losing my fingers at work, though I couldn't work anymore and it's very difficult for me to find work again. A lot of beggars on the streets are handicapped. I considered myself lucky because it's not like I lost my two hands and legs. You know we can't afford to be angry – we can't stand up for ourselves... as long as we have food in our bellies. I wouldn't do anything to go against our leaders as long as I live. You know I didn't have meat to eat in the village but now I have. This is our mentality – we only believe in money and power – that all belongs to the leaders above us and that's why they are like kings (emperors). Workers are just workers; we have to obey the leaders. Power and rights just belong to the leaders.
>
> (Feng, Plastic Board Manufacturing Worker, Foshan, 2013)

Concluding Remarks

The findings discussed in this chapter show that while the lived experiences of this group of workers incited them to engage in resistance activities as other scholars predict (Pun and Lu 2010a, b; Chan and Hui 2012), their protest behaviors were constrained by a high-level of status consciousness.

The findings illustrate that their status consciousness was linked with the truth about their devalued societal status as low-quality workers and the truth about their normative and abnormal practices within the social hierarchy in China (see Chapter 2). Thus, as Chapters 2 and 3 show, their practices reflected the internalized 'truth' about themselves and their internal acceptance of their given destiny (or *ming*) and conditions within their 'prescribed' routines in the 'high-low' hierarchical relationships. This is because, while the experiences of these workers had provoked them to engage in protest activities, their *yayi*-based actions were grounded in their immediate economic needs in accordance with their prescribed conditions within their given positions. Their lack of interest in changing their destiny in terms of their status and conditions in the long term was a major factor that made their protest actions ineffectual. Hence, their actions were generally 'once-only' events, even when they reaped only partial or little gain.

This reflects that these workers, like their Group One colleagues continued to exercise their 'prescribed' routines and thus they also became the agents of maintaining the power-knowledge framework—consciously and subconsciously—and hence continued to maintain a high level of internal 'docility' or acquiescence to their given status within the thought management system. Thus, even while this group of workers had engaged in protest activities, their actions appeared to be influenced by an 'older rules consciousness' that affected their willingness to continue their struggles to improve their conditions for themselves and others, rather than their work-based experiences.

This cultural compliance thereby acts to endorse a natural self-regulation by the workers to internally accept the legitimacy of labor practices that—ultimately—works to serve the will of their work leaders and ultimately the 'mandate' of the Chinese State to rule by maintaining an abundant docile labor force in the socialist market economy. The question of whether everyday workers can overcome the centuries-old cultivation of docile bodies and minds to engage in activism that will lead to the formation of an active working class will be discussed in Chapter 5.

Bibliography

Chan, Anita, and Kaxton Siu. 2012. Chinese Migrant Workers: Factors Constraining the Emergence of Class Consciousness. In *China's Peasants and Workers: Changing Class Identities*, ed. Beatriz Carrillo and David Goodman. Northampton, MA: Edward Elgar Publishing Ltd.

Chan, Chris, and Elaine Hui. 2012. The Dynamics and Dilemma of Workplace Trade Union Reform in China: The Case of the Honda Workers Strike. *Journal of Industrial Relations* 54 (5): 653–668.

Chan, Chris, and Hui, Elaine. 2016. Bringing Class Struggles Back: A Marxian Analysis of the State and Class Relations in China. *Globalizations* 14 (2): 232–244.

Chen, Feng. 2000. Subsistence Crises, Managerial Corruption and Labour Protests in China. *The China Journal* 44: 41–63.

Chen, Feng. 2003. Industrial Restructuring and Workers Resistance in China. *Modern China* 29 (2): 237–262.

Cooke, Fang-Lee., Yuhua Xie, and Huimin Duan. 2016. Workers' Grievances and Resolution Mechanisms in Chinese Manufacturing Firms: Key Characteristics and the Influence of Contextual Factors. *The International Journal of Human Resource Management* 27 (18): 2119–2141.

Foucault, Michel. 1977. *Discipline and Punish: The Birth of the Prison*. New York: Vintage Books.

Foucault, Michel. 1978. *The History of Sexuality, Volume 1: An Introduction*. New York: Pantheon Books.

Foucault, Michel. 1980. *Power/Knowledge: Selected Interviews and Other Writings 1972–1977*. New York: Vintage Books.

Foucault, Michel. 1980. *Truth and Subjectivity Howison Lectures*. Berkeley: University of California.
Foucault, Michel. 1982. The Subject and Power. In *Michel Foucault: Beyond Structuralism and Hermeneutics*, ed. Hubert Dreyfus and Paul Rabinow. Chicago: University of Chicago Press.
Foucault, Michel. 1986. *The Care of the Self*. New York: Pantheon Books.
Foucault, Michel. 1987. The Ethic of Care for the Self as a Practice of Freedom: An Interview with Michel Foucault on January 20, 1984. *Philosophy & Social Critisim* 12: 112–131.
Foucault, Michel. 1997. *Ethics, Subjectivity and Truth: The Essential Works of Foucault 1954–1984*. New York: The New Press.
Gallagher, Mary. 2005. "Use the Law as Your Weapon!": Institutional Change and Legal Mobilization in China. In *Engaging the Law in China: State, Society, and Possibilities for Justice*, ed. Neil Diamant Staanley Lubman and Kelvin O'Brien. Stanford: Stanford University Press.
Gallagher, Mary. 2006. Mobilizing the Law in China: "Informed Disenchantment" and the Development of Legal Consciousness. *Law & Society Review* 40 (4): 783–816.
Gramsci, Antonio. 1988/2000. *The Gramsci Reader: Selected Writings, 1916–1935*. New York: New York University Press.
Gray, Kevin, and Youngseok Jang. 2015. Labour Unrest in the Global Political Economy: The Case of China's 2010 Strike Wave. *New Political Economy* 20 (4): 594–613.
Koo, Hagen. 2001. *Korean Workers: The Culture and Politics of Class Formation*. Londo: Cornell University Press.
Leung, Paknang, and Ngai Pun. 2009. The Radicalisation of the New Chinese Working Class: A Case Study of Collective Action in the Gemstone Industry. *Third World Quarterly* 30 (3): 551–565.
Pun, Ngai, and Huilin Lu. 2010a. A Culture of Violence: The Labor Subcontracting System and Collective Action by Construction Workers in Post-Socialist China. *The China Journal* 64: 143–158.
Pun, Ngai, and Huilin Lu. 2010b. Unfinished Proletarianization: Self, Anger, and Class Action among the Second Generation of Peasant-Workers in Present-Day China. *Modern China* 36 (5): 493–519.
Walder, Andrew. 1991. Workers, Managers and the State: The Reform Era and the Political Crisis of 1989. *The China Quarterly* 127: 467–492.

CHAPTER 5

Conclusion

> I take care not to dictate how thing[s] should be. I try instead to pose problems, to make them active, to display them in such… complexity that they can silence the prophets and lawgivers, all those who speak for others or to others. In this way, it will be possible for the complexity of the problem to appear in its connection with people's lives.
>
> (Foucualt 2001: 288)

In this chapter, I wish to bring together the analysis of the genealogy of the Chinese working class as presented in Chapter 2 to discuss the effects of governmentality on both groups of everyday workers (see Chapters 3 and 4) who are targeted for being "marginalized" as the "deserving poor" in continuously submitting themselves to their given conditions.

These effects, as presented throughout the book, are resulting from the ongoing operation of the Confucian-inspired thought management system—or a particular program of governance in Foucault's term—in the work and non-work lives of the workers. It is these lived experiences of workers generated from their historico-socio-politico understanding of the "truth" about themselves (see Chapters 2–4) that have militated against their ability and willingness to improve their conditions beyond their individual needs.

This chapter summarizes the key historical events that have shaped the development of the Chinese working-class politics as well as the academic

E. Leung, *The (Re)Making of the Chinese Working Class*, Palgrave Debates in Business History,
https://doi.org/10.1007/978-3-030-83313-8_5

debates about class and class consciousness development in Chinese labor studies, before discussing the similarities between the two groups of findings to address the research questions and propositions I posed in the opening chapter. The chapter then concludes with considering the implications of this by discussing the recent movements of resistance to the Chinese Communist Party (CCP).

The (Re-) Making of a Chinese Working Class Over the Past Decades

In Chapter 2, I have drawn on Michel Foucault's (1980a, 1982; b) genealogical method to reinvestigate the historical key events that (re-) shaped the development of the Chinese society and the working-class politics in the socialist China.

As a supposedly socialist society, the legitimacy of the Chinese Communist Party (CCP) has long rested on its claim to represent the interest of the Chinese industrial working class—the proletariat—in "liberalizing" China after 1949. In contrast to Western liberal democracies that perceive the "State" as a neutral force where class conflict as something that needs to alleviate, the CCP Chairman and the founder of the People's Republic of China (PRC) Mao Zedong understood "democracy" on the constant mobilization of the "people" and the "working class" in an ever-present class struggle to "eliminate" the traditional Confucian link between ruler and the ruled. While the traditional Confucian values were reportedly replaced by Marxism, Chapter 2 has showed how Mao had selectively modified Confucianism and Marxism into *Mao Zedong Thought* (or *Maoism*). These values were further internalized into the minds of the masses through numerous Confucian-inspired thought control programs such as *zhengfeng* 整風 (or 'Rectification Campaign') and compulsory study groups. Consistent with the works of Foucault, Chapter 2 has contextualized and subsequently untangled how, as a result of the approach to governmentality, the discourses such as "mass politics" had created hundreds of millions docile bodies and minds to automatically work for his interests.

Following the death of Mao in 1976, the analysis in Chapter 2 has depicted how the post-Mao CCP leaders modified Mao's Confucian-inspired thought control techniques for ongoing (re-) production of a docile working class both to monopolize their political power and to create an abundantly cheap labor market for export-led industrialization.

Driven by economic and political forces within and beyond China, the CCP's economic development is supported by two parallel transformations of China's labor market. That is, the conversion of millions of peasants into urban industrial and service workers and, secondly, dismantling the *iron rice bowl* (*tie fanwan* 鐵飯碗) lifetime employment for millions of State workers. These historical processes essentially reflected a neoliberal model of economic development (Harvey 2005). However, in China, the implementation of this model is dependent upon high rates of exploitation and State control of labor standards for repositioning the country as a world's factory and export leader.

Chapter 1 illustrates how studies by the Marxist exponents have posited the debates of Chinese labor activism. A major assumption in the mainstream studies is that the failure of the Chinese State to prioritize labor protections triggered the increased protest activities by workers as a "class" over the decades of economic reforms. Prior to the 2000s, nearly all studies focused on the relations between the reconstruction of the State-owned enterprises (SOEs) and State workers' protests. In so doing, these studies built the narratives around the centrality of the Chinese proletariat as the de facto "masters of the State" in Mao's period to show us a continuing class consciousness among the SOE workers in struggling against lurking "capitalist movements" in post-Mao China. Given the SOE reform has largely been completed by the early 2000s, a plethora of studies seek to understand the development of a class-for-itself by expanding the focus to include peasant workers in the non-State sector. With the mushrooming of private and foreign-invested enterprises (FIEs) that provided "sweatshop-like" conditions to peasant workers, these studies have showed us that while these workers were not historically organized into a specific working class, the formation of a class that is associated with their increased class consciousness are all sponsored by their brutal work-based lived experiences as peasant workers throughout the past decades.

Despite the view that an increase volume of protest actions represents a considerably mature level of class consciousness among workers in China, Chapter 1 has also presented alternative studies that argue workers' protests were not motivated by their common class interests, but instead focused on improving their own material status. In 1992, for instance, worker protests were triggered by job loss and reduced income that was experienced by workers arising from the restructuring of SOEs and the failure of SOEs to provide minimum living allowances and pensions. Similarly, matters such as wage arrears and low wages in foreign-invested enterprises also triggered worker protests from the mid-1990s to the present day. Hence, these protests resulted from serious and immediate economic grievances, rather than a "rising class consciousness" or a "continuous class consciousness" among the Chinese workers.

Aligned with the latter body of literature, my empirical findings have further illustrated that workers' psyche of acquiescing to the authority figures has been constraining their ability to develop a class consciousness, regardless of their experiences at, and of, work. Thus, resonating with E.P. Thompson's (1966) concept of the influences of "lived experiences" among the workers, I seek to understand how work and non-work experiences that are grounded in the Chinese sociocultural contexts have influenced the development of worker consciousness and labor activism in China. In so doing, the findings of workers in Group 1—*who have never engaged in any protest activities* (Chapter 3) and workers in Group 2 *who have engaged in protest activities* (Chapter 4) illustrate that class and class consciousness formation in China departs from the Western idea that class "happens" when workers "feel and articulate the identity of interests…" through their lived experiences (Thompson 1966: 9).

Discussing Research Propositions

In Chapters 3 and 4, I have illustrated that while the interviewed everyday workers have been experiencing forms of repressive conditions, their discourses such as '*we do whatever our leaders want*' (Group One) and '*I don't mind the leaders… insulting me… because they are our work leaders*' (Group Two) suggest that they are willing to subordinate their own interests to that of their authority figures.

In view of this contrasting picture with the mainstream literature, the theoretical propositions (see Chapter 1) that guided this study should be revisited:

Proposition 1: Worker Activism in China is Influenced by a Status Consciousness (or 'older Rules Consciousness')

Chapter 2 discusses Foucault's (2001b, 2014) analytical tools to explore the operation of power-knowledge relations that facilitates governmentality (*government of mentalities* or conduct of conduct) to guide individuals in behaving toward the *desired end* of a society. Despite its philosophical framing, governmentality also has a *conceptual-empirical orientation* (Fanoulis 2017: 10) entrenched in historicity, which facilitates the interpretation of the current research, that is, the 'history of the present'. Foucault notes that doing a 'history of the present' is based on genealogical method to grasp the unnoticed details of governance in order to analyze the effects of the power-knowledge relations in a particular society. The same chapter thereby charts the historical development and the conceptual underpinnings of the social practices and knowledge that have historically shaped the status consciousness (Koo 2001) (or 'older rules consciousness') (Perry 2009) among workers, the way they live their lives and relate to others through reinterpretation of historical events in China.

The selected historical events further illustrate how the Confucian rules, which emphasized hierarchical status and respect for authority, have been internalized in the minds of both groups of workers:

> workers are just workers – we don't have any rights – because power and rights all belong to the leaders... we cannot do anything... but to obey our leaders and do whatever we are told.
>
> (Group One, Bing, Hotel Cleaner, Hangzhou, 2011)

> Workers are always powerless... and we're always at the bottom of society... Employers can always bully us... none of us want to go against our work leaders.
>
> (Group Two, Di, Honda Worker, Foshan, 2013)

It is the effect of the Confucian 'older rules consciousness' that has (re-) shaped their thoughts and behaviors in their work and non-work lived experiences to fulfill the interests of Chinese rulers in different historical periods. It is therefore suggested that the findings of Group One and Group Two provide support for Proposition 1 and their inclination to be subservient to the Confucian hierarchical rules have also supported Proposition 2:

> *Proposition 2: The 'older rules consciousness' has affected their willingness to engage in acts that are* perceived*as contradictory to their cultural (or social) practices in China.*

It is suggested that the 'older rules consciousness' is strengthened by workers' understanding about their societal status (identity or position) and that they reinforce that status among themselves:

> *Dagong* 打工 [workers] always have a tough life… all I learnt throughout my work experience was to obey the leaders so I can earn enough to subsist.
>
> (Group One, Fang, Garment Factory Worker, Hangzhou, 2011)

> …we can't afford to be angry – we can't stand up for ourselves… as long as we have food in our bellies. Workers are just workers; we have to obey the leaders.
>
> (Group Two, Feng, Plastic Board Manufacturing Worker, Foshan, 2013)

These comments reflect that workers' sociocultural knowledge about their status in relation to themselves and their authority figures has made it disgraceful for them to engage in open and direct confrontation with their superiors. Hence, they must adapt to any conditions in order to live:

> Being a worker is not good… We must put up with whatever hardships we have; we don't have time and we don't have energy to think about any other things but our subsistence. We only want to make enough to subsist.
>
> (Group One, Yaxing, IT Worker, Shenzhen, 2011)

> We […] street cleaners (*qingjie gongren* 清佞工人) do not have 'culture' in us – we are extremely illiterate, extremely grassroots, extremely dirty. We know we shouldn't expect much. We are always at the bottom of society.
>
> (Group Two, Yao, SOE Street Cleaner, Foshan, 2013)

The findings also suggest that it is workers' internal acceptance of the 'rights' or 'mandate' of the State and their work superiors to subject them to any kind of treatment is compounded by their own self-perception of their lower societal position. This status consciousness that linked with their 'older rules consciousness' has therefore mitigated their willingness to resist against their given conditions. Because these acts are perceived as contradictory to their social and cultural practices. This mindset hence exerts a significant influence in ensuring that their actions match their given positions within the social hierarchy that supports Proposition 3:

Proposition 3: Workers' Consciousness and Their Resistant Activities Are Influenced by 'older Rules Consciousness', Rather Than Work-Based Experiences Alone.

Evidence from Group One and Group Two underlines that societal positions in China are constituted by the value of 'personal quality' that is linked to the 'truth' of educational qualification as discussed in Chapter 2. Although education is a primary criterion of stratification in most capitalist societies, the findings suggest that the workers' self-perception about their lack of education has been the main determinant of their poor treatment and working conditions:

> literate *gao suzhi* 高素質 ['high-quality'] people are always the leaders above everyone... illiterate *di suzhi*低素質 ['low-quality'] people are just like mud sitting on the ground for leaders to step on.
>
> (Group One, Bing, Hotel Cleaner, Hangzhou, 2011)

> We only want to get a raise to earn our basic living – we didn't ask for that much – and that's because we're just a bunch of low-quality people. But even if we're uneducated, illiterate and at the bottom of society, our work leaders should at least allow us to have 'full bellies'.
>
> (Group Two, Ying, SOE Street Cleaner, Foshan, 2013)

The above workers' discourses from Group One and Group Two indicate that their negative self-image about their low quality is linked to their educational deficits. Their self-recognition of a subservient status has been a major factor that constituted a strong 'sense of fatalism' (or filial piety) among themselves which steered them to submit themselves to any employment conditions. Thus, even poor working conditions have at odds triggered protest activities by Group Two workers, their actions are still tied to a 'filial culture':

> Most of us supported our work strike in 2010... we all got a pay rise... from then on ... though it was still very low... we already had enough

money to survive. We shouldn't keep on asking for more and more... as if we... wanted to go against our work leaders – that's just not right.
(Group Two, Zhi, Honda Worker, Foshan, 2013)

Without any external surveillance or forces on the part of external authorities, the self-controlled thoughts and behaviors among workers in Group One and Group Two are guided by their status consciousness that is constituted through their work and non-work lived experiences within the social hierarchy in China, thus providing support for proposition 3.

Discussing Research Questions

The above picture contradicts thus leads to considering the first research question:

Research Question 1: How Has Worker Consciousness Been Shaped in China?

In exploring how worker consciousness is shaped, Chapter 2 has drawn on Foucault's (1991) genealogical method (see Chapter 1) to analyze how the key historical events have shaped worker (or status) consciousness and practices through their lived experiences to the present day. The analysis shows that the links between their status consciousness (or awareness of their own social status) (Koo 2001) and their current knowledge about the 'truth' of their social status can be traced to events in the pre-Confucian epoch whereby the *li* 禮 hierarchical ideology (or knowledge) is internalized in the minds of Chinese workers today. Beginning with the Zhou dynasty in the thirteenth-century B.C.E., *li* and later Confucian constitutive element emphasize the concept of filial piety (*xiao* 孝) has been used to regulate how those categorized as inferiors (such as children) should behave toward their superiors and authorities (such as parents). This 'proper' conduct is the effect from the exercise of power-knowledge relations (or social relationships) (see Chapter 2) by individuals within the hierarchy or status ranking of Confucian society.

While the Confucian status system was supposedly dismantled during the events of post-1949 socialist China, it is suggested that generations of the CCP leaders have retained this traditional status hierarchy to regulate Chinese society through the construction of different status and identity categories. Contrary to the previous system of the Imperial and

Mao periods that forced the community to act in certain ways, post-Mao leaders have exercised soft control of the inferiors by revising Confucian status values into the CCP's thought management (*sixiang guanli*思想管理) approach (Brady 2008). As Chapter 2 shows, Confucian status values within the thought management system are now backed by the notion of educational qualifications through 'quality' (*suzhi* 素質) discourses, to refocus proper behavior in inferiors by redefining workers' identities. The identities of *gongren* (SOE workers工人 or government slaves宮人); *nonmingong* 農民工 (peasant workers); *mangliu* 盲流 (blind floats); *wailaigong* 外來工 (outside workers); and *dagong* 打工 (those working for bosses) have all carried a negative status. These negative labels are used not only to push workers to work in certain occupations, but to also make them think and hence behave as the 'low quality' to fit into the occupational hierarchy.

The evidence as presented in Chapter 2 and the resulting influences as illustrated in Chapters 3 and 4 further suggest that the continuous efforts of the post-Mao leaders to internalize the Confucian concept of social status through use of the quality discourses has effectively guided Groups One and Two workers to co-construct a destiny (or *ming* 命) for themselves. Thus, both groups of workers appear to have crafted an internal willingness to accept their positions and conditions as 'given':

> I felt that occupational accidents and illnesses are just some of the normal things that are *destined* to happen to low-quality people…
> (Group One, Daqing, Food Processing Worker, Foshan, 2013)

> low-quality people are *destined* to do low-paid dirty work…
> (Group Two, Yao, SOE Street Cleaner, Foshan, 2013)

The discourses above illustrate that not only have the workers' internal acceptance of their destiny lead them to abandon any desire to improve working conditions, but their destiny further defined the performance standards and goals they have for life as 'low-quality' workers:

> All working environments are dirty and unsafe for 'low-quality people… what do you think we are? You think we can choose where we want to work and can refuse to work in dirty, dangerous areas? Low-quality is low quality – low quality people live like this.
> (Group One, Ding, SOE Ready-mix Concrete Worker, Hefei, 2011)

> I've been working for this *danwei* 單位 [work unit] for 10 years but the money I earned over those years wasn't even enough to buy a toilet bowl! Low-quality people are destined to do low-pay dirty work.
>
> (Group Two, Yao, SOE Street Cleaner, Foshan, 2013)

The concepts of behavioral standards and destiny thus emerge as the 'truth' to normalize judgment (see Chapter 2) between 'right' and 'wrong' acts among the 'low-quality' workers. This maintains their proper behavior according to their social status system:

> She told the leader she didn't want to do extra work… Who did she think she is? She's just a low-quality *dagong*, but being so disobedient.
>
> (Group One, Xiaoqin, Cosmetic Sales Assistant, Shenzhen, 2011)

> …he stopped the production line suddenly just because he wanted to get a raise when we already have enough [money] to live on; he put us all at risk as if we also wanted to go against our work leaders – that's just not right.
>
> (Group Two, Zhi, Honda Worker, Foshan, 2013)

In contrast to the mainstream assumption that brutal work-based experiences have fostered a "rising class consciousness" among Chinese workers to become a class-for-itself, the evidence presented in this study suggests that workers' lived experiences of being 'the low' have guided them to engage in a strict set of self-regulatory (governance or control) rules they impose on themselves. Henceforth, they continue to live "properly" by accepting their poor working and living conditions voluntarily according to their low status.

The findings instead support the counter-narratives about worker consciousness. I have further showed that the factors constraining class and class consciousness development among both groups of workers are in fact grounded in their sociocultural understanding and commitment to behave properly to uphold their status for themselves. This section turns to the second research question:

Research Question 2: How Does the Shaping of Worker Consciousness Affect Labor Activism?

Evidence from both groups suggests that workers *desire* to act according to the 'truth' is reaffirmed by their willingness to correct their own behaviors in accordance with the commonly held standards of their particular position:

> I felt really bad about disrupting the entire production by making such a stupid mistake, so I stood up and apologized to everyone and the leaders for my disobedient act.
>
> (Group One, Ge, SOE Car Factory Worker, Hefei, 2011)

> Though our first strike [2006] did give us a wage increase, I still think my action was really thoughtless and irresponsible – no leaders like disobedient workers.
>
> (Group Two, Yuan, Plastic Board Manufacturing Worker, Foshan, 2013)

Workers' own commitment and persistence in regulating their own (and others') actions is further guided by their sense of similarity about themselves as receiving low educational qualifications. Their thoughts about themselves as being 'low quality' have further steered them to live and behave in the same way. It is the shared common understanding among the workers that all 'the low' are being the 'same' have led them to interpret and evaluate each other's actions under the doctrine of similarity. As a result, what they can or cannot do, and what they can expect from society regarding their working conditions in accordance with their lower societal position, is guided by that doctrine.

The findings thus illustrate that the doctrine of similarity to others created what Foucault (1980b, 1997) calls social truth. In that it appears to have reinforced a mindset within workers that the 'rights to subsistence' (*shengcun quan* 生存權) was "all that they were entitled to". In much the same way as Foucault's work on sexuality (1976, 1986), subjectivity (1980b, 1982), and madness and criminality (1977, 2001a, 2006), the practices of everyday workers in this study are also found to be subject to what they have come to know as the truth about themselves.

"Truth", as Foucault (1982) explains (see Chapter 2), emerged as specific forms of knowledge around the needs of particular disciplines (or practices) by defining what is 'normal' or 'abnormal', in order to naturalize the behaviors of individuals according to different categories or identities, for example, the sick and the healthy, and the criminal and the good. Behaviors in these classifications are arguably tied to cumulative meanings to identify the signs of normality and abnormality. This subtle method of control enabled a continuous measurement of individual performance, subject to a person's identity (position or status), which was interpreted and perceived by others as well as by themselves according to the dominant discourses in their everyday social relationships (Smart 1985: 104–107).

As Chapter 2 explains, Foucault describes these social relationships as power-knowledge relations that consist of a network, such as schools, hospitals, workplaces, and families, in which they together produce and reproduce the discourses of truth, in order to regulate the behaviors of self and others (1997). Foucault terms such individual engagement in self-regulation (or self-governance) in conforming to these discourses of 'truth', as the 'effects of governmentality' (or the 'conduct or conduct'), which describes the effective operations of both direct (the State or institutions per se) and indirect (the social network) forms of disciplinary power in guiding people's behaviors to the *desired end* of others. In the case of China, Chapters 2–4 show that the *desired end* for both groups of workers has been to meet the aims of the State and management to maintain an abundant docile labor force in the market economy.

The evidence as presented in Chapter 2 and then in Chapters 3 and 4 about the governmentalization of everyday Chinese workers in this study shows that the social operations of a disciplinary power include self-regulation among workers in achieving the CCP's *desire* to sustain China's docile labor force under the discourses of quality. This assertion is further supported by workers' self-recognition and acceptance of their devalued and subservient status through which they believed that their employment opportunities are minimized by their lack of education. It is this mindset (or mentality) among workers that steers them to internally accept any conditions that are prescribed for their status, causing them to obey the 'natural' rules of their work leaders in return for a liveable income.

With the embracing of the truth about their personal quality in social relationships, these workers defined and reinforced practices and norms for themselves, under which their existence as 'low-quality' workers are reflected in their 'rights to subsistence'. This idea appears to preoccupy their minds, even while they are conscious of and protested against economic issues at work. Consequently, as Chapter 4 shows, protest actions by Group Two workers spring neither from a rational effort at improving their treatment at work, nor a push for better working conditions, but simply from the 'norm-based moral sense' of their deservingness of minimal subsistence levels within the 'quality-based' status structure.

The findings suggest—and as Foucault (1987) would argue—that the 'norm-based moralities' of the two groups of workers are further reinforced by their self-care (or care of the self) practices that is associated with a sense of duty (or responsibility) in order to secure the lives for themselves and others. This effort is mostly directed at looking after others which has been repeatedly emphasized in workers' discourses (see Chapters 3 and 4). Beyond the flow of normative behaviors, care ethics are defined by the workers in terms of the areas of meanings and purposes for their existence which is opposite to the 'me first' ethics:

> ...taking care of the family is the normal responsibility for most of us in China... that's why we come out to *dagong*.
>
> (Group One, Wang, Motel Cleaner, Shenzhen, 2011)

> I could easily have lost my job over that [protest] and yet I have a family to look after my old parents, my wife and my child...
>
> (Group Two, Yuan, Plastic Board Manufacturing Worker, Foshan, 2013)

It is argued that, as Chapters 2–4 show, this double responsibility—toward others and toward the selves—along with the internalized rules (or norms) among the workers—exercise together to constitute a basis for themselves to become docile bodies and minds in the labor market. Although threats to workers' minimal subsistence triggered collective actions, these protest activities have been weighed down by their care practices of retaining their job so as to be able to look after 'others'. The matters of self-care practices which influenced their moral judgment about the rightness or wrongness of work practices, thus rarely resulted in protest activities being triggered by a strong sense of solidarity as illustrated in Chapter 4.

Consequently, while the work-based experiences have incited Group Two workers to engage in protest activities, their actions are grounded in their immediate day-to-day survival needs, which is limited to their 'prescribed' conditions in their given positions. Their lack of interest to engage in the long-term improvement of their conditions leads to the consideration of the third research question posed to this study:

> *Research Question 3: How does the shaping of worker consciousness affect their ability to develop themselves into an organized labor movement capable of improving living and working conditions for themselves and others?*

The findings suggest that protest activities are frequently sparked by deep-seated economic issues among the workers; their protest behaviors appear to be driven by their deservingness of the 'rights to subsistence' on an individual level.

However, as Chapter 4 shows, their lack of a united voice in the protests, as characterized by different individualistic demands, hardly ever brought about positive outcomes for the workers. The findings presented in Chapter 4 further suggest that the effectiveness of the protest actions by Group Two workers is undermined by their collective recognition of the truth about their positions within the quality-based hierarchy. Thus, even while they engaged in protest actions, the quiescent habits of workers are constituted by their unchanged perception of themselves as ignorant subjects, which is linked to the sense of their inferior (or 'low') position (or identity).

Much like the relation between a true *sex* and gender identity (Foucault 1986), the idea of true quality determined these workers' identities and their subsequent behavior in the marketplace. Of course, it can be argued that their daily work experiences together with the efforts of NGOs (non-government organizations) have created opportunities for workers to protect their legal rights (*weiquan* 維權) and to question their status quo. However, Chapters 3 and 4 have illustrated that their true selves are upheld by their thoughts and ongoing proper performance that are in line with what they are expected from their identities. Their knowing of the expectations of themselves is grounded in a cultural understanding of proper behaviors toward their superiors and those in authority. This self-knowledge has subsequently minimized their opportunities to permanently change their everyday working conditions.

In summing up, this study has illustrated how the centuries-long tradition of Confucian ideologies internalized a power-knowledge regime, with the result of a constructed 'truth' for both groups of workers about their status, and what they could expect from society regarding their working conditions as a result of that status. Hence, both groups of workers exhibited an internal willingness to live and behave in adherence to the given 'truth' about their 'prescribed' routines. The study therefore argues that by 'exercising' these routines, workers become agents in maintaining the power-knowledge framework—consciously and subconsciously—and thus assume a level of internal 'docility' (or acquiescence) in maintaining their status by 'voluntarily' submitting themselves to their repressive circumstances in an uncritical manner.

This cultural compliance on the part of the workers is exercised by their self-care practices toward their day-to-day survival needs in order to be able to look after themselves and hence their family members. These workers' practices are arguably fundamental to guide them to accept the legitimacy of labor practices that, ultimately, works to the benefit and the will of the State, rather than themselves. It is this aspect of workers' lived experiences that, this study suggests, significantly limits their capacity to exercise agency beyond their power-knowledge networks, and thus constraining class-consciousness and class-for-itself development among everyday workers in China.

Activism and Governmentality in China's Thought Management System

By engaging with Foucault's work, this study contributes to an understanding of the relation between worker activism and politics in China.

Through the investigation of historical events, the (re-) production of docile bodies and minds among workers is tied to the subtle forms of the replication of power-knowledge—that is, the centuries-long Confucian ideology (or knowledge) of 'superior-inferior relationships' (see Chapter 2). These relationships are embedded in the everyday lives of workers through forms of governmentality (Foucault 2014). Hence, rather than deploying coercive political rules to control individuals, China's approach to governmentality has drawn on a diversity of approaches to construct a knowledge about workers that regulates their lives with the aim that they serve as an instrument of the State with regard to economic development.

The analysis of this study thus contrast to a number of Chinese labor studies that have emphasized the relations of the work-based experiences and waves of workers' protest actions as a result of either the continuity of class consciousness from Mao's period (Lee 2007) or, more recently, a "rising class consciousness" among workers (Pun and Lu 2010; Smith and Chan 2015; Chan and Hui 2016). Instead, this study has showed how workers' self-care practices to stage resistance have been constrained by the approach to governmentality that draws on the governmental discourses of quality (*suzhi* 素質), stability maintenance (*weiwen* 維穩), well-off (*xiaokang* 小康), and harmonious society (*hexie shehui* 和諧社會) through their work and non-work-based lived experiences in their power-knowledge relations.

Pro-Democracy Movements in Hong Kong

Although self-care practices by both groups of everyday workers are linked to their self-disciplinary practices within their power-knowledge relations, the protesters of the former British colonial Hong Kong (1841–1997)[1] have illustrated to us how their self-care practices are exercised to challenge against the CCP authoritarianism.

In 1997, Hong Kong was reunified with Mainland China under the discourse of "One Country Two Systems".[2] While this discourse supposedly a mechanism that separated the ways of governing capitalist

[1] The British occupied Hong Kong under three so-called "unequal treaties". The first was the 1842 Treaty of Nanking, which resolved the Qing's defeat in the 1839–1842 Opium War, ceded Hong Kong Island to the British Crown in perpetuity. The second was the 1860 Conventions of Peking, which settled the 1856–1860s Opium War, ceded the Kowloon Peninsula to Britain permanently. Finally, Britain secured a 99-year lease of the New Territories (North of the Kowloon Peninsula) following the Qing's defeat in the 1894–1895 Sino-Japanese War which due to expire on 30 June 1997.

[2] Based on Deng Xiaoping's principle of "One Country, Two Systems", the governments of Britain and China formally signed the 1984 Joint Declaration to announce China's resumption of sovereignty over Hong Kong, including Hong Kong Island, Kowloon Peninsula, and the New Territories, in 1997. Despite the elections of the Hong Kong government or Chief Executive (CE) would be centrally controlled by the CCP, the Sino-British Joint Declaration granted the preservation of the preexisting legal, economic and social systems to retain "a high degree of autonomy" in Hong Kong for fifty years upon the city transfer to become the Special Administrative Region (SAR) of China. These assurances, following the 1989 Tiananmen Massacre (see Chapter 2), were further enshrined in the Basic Law (1990) that guaranteed the continuity of the existing individual freedom of speech, press, publication, association, assembly, and demonstration. This framework is heralded as a blueprint for Taiwan's reunification with China.

Hong Kong[3] system from China's socialism, the CCP instead concentrated its energy on the "One Country" project in decolonizing the capitalist city by embedding "China factor" (or 'Mainlandization' *Dalu hua* 大陸化) (Yew and Kwong 2014) in the social relations of Hong Kong.

Mainlandization, like the thought management system in the Mainland, consisted of a series of events and policies that aimed to politically and culturally reshape Hong Kong's "ways of life" in accordance with the values of the CCP. Since the 1980s, the CCP functioned itself as an underground organization by embedding its party members at the upper levels of the Mainland-based organizations that operated in Hong Kong. The tasks of the CCP members within these organizations, ranging from the Chinese government bodies including Hong Kong and Macau Affairs Office that operated by the CCP's mouthpiece New China News Agency (NCNA or Xinhua); to mass institutions such as China Travel Services, and to SOEs including the Bank of China (BOC) and China Resources Corporation, were to carry out extensive thought work and day-to-day influence of Hong Kong's affairs (Burns 1990). This work enabled the CCP to create the "pro-CCP forces" to restructure Hong Kong by packing the pro-CCP tycoons, their children, and their nominees into the political system so as to support the CCP-appointed government or Chief Executive (CE) by filling up half the seats of the Legislative Council (Loh 2010).

The domination of the "pro-CCP forces" in Hong Kong's political structure thus enabled the CEs since 1997 to initiate Mainlandization activities such as permitting over fifty percent of Mainland enterprises (or red companies) to dominate the Hong Kong Stock Exchange (HKEX 2021), and also relaxing the rules on Mainland immigration and tourism in Hong Kong (Haas 2017) to increase Hong Kong's dependency on Mainland China as well as to promote the use of Mandarin (or Putonghua). In addition, the pro-CCP apparatuses sought to speed up homogenization of Hong Kong into *just* another Chinese city by frequently broadcasting television clips such as "*Our Home and Country*" (心繫家國) (The Promotion of Civic Education, 2004) in promoting the

[3] Throughout the century-long British colonial rule, Hong Kong transformed from a barren rock of fishing village into one of the world's important financial centers with 7.5 million people enjoying one of the highest living standards in East Asia. See (2020) The World Bank, https://data.worldbank.org/country/hong-kong-sar-china, accessed 15 August 2020.

Chinese national anthem and the Confucian customs—for instance—filial piety and harmony; introducing "moral and national education" (MNE) (The Education Bureau 2012) in school curriculum to foster a sense of "Chinese identity" in students, and removing Hong Kong history as well as controversial historical events such as the 1989 Tiananmen Massacre (see Chapter 2) from school materials (Cheung 2018).

The collective grievances over the CCP's assimilation of the Hong Kong's "ways of life" imposed by 150 years of British colonialism and the 'care' about the fate (or destiny) of Hong Kong under the CCP's rules have triggered ongoing disruptive events by the Hong Kongers[4] (*Heung-gongyuhn* 香港人) in the city. The massive rally, with 500,000 protesters, launched on the handover day of July 1, 2003 (CNN 2003), which resulted in the withdrawal of the national security legislation (or *Article 23* of the *Basic Law*[5]) and the subsequent resignation of the first CE Tung Chee Hwa (1997–2005) (*The New York Times* 2005), was a watershed event that empowered the Hong Kong people to continuously engage in pro-democracy movements. Fear of the loss of freedom following the Article 23 event, Hong Kongers have consequently organized their annual July protests on the handover anniversary under the themes such as "*Striving for Universal Suffrage*" (BBC 2004) and "*Creating Hopes for Universal Suffrage and Democracy with an Equal and Just Hong Kong*" (*Apple Daily* 2006) to press for direct elections for their CE and the

[4] While many Hong Kong inhabitants were immigrants (or refugees) who fled the CCP rule from the Mainland to Hong Kong during the Chinese Civil Wars in the late 1940s and during the subsequent socio-political turbulence such as the 1958–1961 Great Leap Forward and the 1966–1976 Cultural Revolution, they distance themselves from the Mainlanders with their self-identification Hong Kongers (*Heunggongyuhn* 香港人) is generated from their superiority complex that they are more Westernized, civilized, and well-educated compared to those lazy, dirty, uncivilized, and uneducated *Ah Chann* 阿燦" (Chinamen); "*Dai Luk Por*" (or mainland women 大陸婆), and "*Dai Luk Lo*" (or mainland men大陸佬). The identity Hong Kongers thus indicated their desire of being "apart from China" rather than "a part of China". See Ma, Ngok (2015) 'The Rise of "Anti-China" Sentiments in Hong Kong and the 2012 Legislative Council Elections', *China Review* 15(1): 39–66.

[5] *Article 23* of the *Basic Law* specified that the Hong Kong government to prohibit "any act of treason, secession, sedition, subversion against the Central People's Government, or theft of state secrets, to prohibit foreign political organizations or bodies from conducting political activities in the Region, and to prohibit political organizations or bodies of the Region from establishing ties with foreign political organizations or bodies". See (2021) *Basic Law*, https://www.basiclaw.gov.hk/en/basiclaw/chapter2.html, accessed 11 May 2021.

Legislative Council. Despite these, tens of thousands of people flooded onto the streets to protest against the 'Moral and National Education' along with the changes in school curriculum in 2012 (*Time* 2019) while the Umbrella Movement[6] was launched to demand for the reforms of Hong Kong's electoral system in 2014 (*Apple Daily* 2015).

Five years later, a series of leaderless massive protests known as the *Anti-Extradition Law Amendment Bill* (or *Article 23* that was set out in the *Basic Law*) Movement were launched between 2019 and 2020 in response to the introduction of the *Fugitive Offenders Amendment Bill* (2019) proposed by the Hong Kong government (Reuters 2019). This extradition bill crisis is sparked by the Hong Kong resident Chan Tong-Kai who murdered his girlfriend in Taiwan before returning to Hong Kong in 2018 (The Standard 2021). Although the murderer admitted to the Hong Kong police that he had killed his girlfriend, he is not charged with murder due to the absence of an extradition treaty between Hong Kong and Taiwan. This case prompted the government to introduce an extradition bill in enabling the transfers of fugitives in Greater China, including Taiwan, Macau, and Mainland China. This in turn paved the way for any targeted criminal suspects to face trial in the Mainland. The ill-fated proposal hence triggered over a million people that come from different socioeconomic statuses ranging from medical professionals to social workers to students in protesting against the second reading of the bill on June 9, 2019; followed by another two million people on June 16, 2019 (*Apple Daily* 2020).

The refusal of the government to withdraw the bill has led to the continuation of demonstrations, before leading to violent actions against the government buildings and Chinese businesses (or red shops). On July 1, 2019, a group of protesters smashed their way into the Legislative Council building, damaging equipment, and spray-painting slogans on the walls while protesting against the bill (BBC 2019). On July 21, 2019, demonstrators were brutally attacked by a large gang of men in white shirts while police did not intervene in the attack (ABC 2019). In the same month, police responded to the protest activities with pepper spray and by firing tear gas, water cannon, and rubber bullets (and later live

[6] Umbrella Movement was a series of protests that also known as "Occupy Central" where the protesters adopted the "occupation" concept by occupying the main thoroughfares across the city for 79 days in hopes of the disruption could pressure the government to negotiate.

round of actual bullets) at the citizens or beating them with batons and fists on the streets and at the shopping malls during their arrest (Amnesty 2019). Despite the formal withdrawn of the bill on September 4, 2019 (SCMP 2019), the anti-Extradition movements have since the police's exercised of unlawful tactics against protesters evolved into waves of anti-government and anti-China movements under the slogans including "*Free Hong Kong! Democracy Now!*" and "*Five Demands Not One Less*[7]" since 2019. Violent clashes continued to grow between the police force and hundreds of thousands of protesters on the streets and even across university campuses (*The Irish Times* 2019).

At the time of this writing, the Hong Kong's pro-democracy movements appear to "die-down" a little due to the outbreak of the global coronavirus (COVID-19) pandemic as well as the *National Security Law* (2020) that is recently imposed to eject the CCP's perceived opponents. Despite collectively wearing black clothes and face masks (most notably gas masks) as a means to protest, their 'care' about the political freedom and social justice and their desire to defend the territory's autonomy have motivated the Hong Kongers to explore ongoing opportunities to struggle against their *given* conditions in new ways.

Influenced by the Kung-Fu expression "*be water*",[8] protesters took their movements to the Internet. For example, making use of online video games like *Animal Crossing: New Horizons* as a platform to protests (SCMP 2020) by importing slogans such as "*Free Hong Kong, Revolution Now*" and funeral photographs of the CCP leader Xi Jinping and the Hong Kong government Carrie Lam to get their messages heard. Meanwhile, they boycotted the red shops, and pro-CCP or pro-government merchants, businesses, and restaurants (or blue shops) by consciously supporting the like-minded, pro-democratic "yellow shops" to create a self-sufficient economy within what they called "Yellow Economic Circle".

[7] The Five Demands are: complete withdrawal of the extradition bill; retraction of the "riot" characterisation; release the arrested protesters; establishment of an independent commission of inquiry into police brutality towards protesters, and resignation of the Hong Kong government Carrie Lam and the implementation of universal suffrage for CE and Legislative Council elections.

[8] "Be water" protest tactics in Hong Kong are adopted from the philosophy of the Kung Fu movie star Bruce Lee that to be "formless, shapeless, like water can flow, or it can crash [...] be water, my friend". See Youtube (2014) Bruce Lee be as Water My Friend, https://www.youtube.com/watch?v=cJMwBwFj5nQ, accessed 3 March 2021.

The Hong Kongers' quest for freedom, involving as it does in sustaining protest actions of millions of people, is something that the Chinese docile minds and bodies in the Mainland could not do.

> "Class" consciousness is not simply understood as a matter of workers coalescing to act, but the matters of culture and history. Developing detailed accounts of these influences is important to then do as Foucault (1980a: 83) tasks us: "*...establish[ing] a historical knowledge of struggles and to make use of this knowledge tactically today*".

Bibliography

ABC. 2019. Hong Kong Pro-Democracy Protesters Beaten by Masked Attackers during Latest Civil Unrest. https://www.abc.net.au/news/2019-07-22/hong-kong-pro-democracy-protesters-beaten-by-masked-groups/11330066. Accessed 1 March 2021.

Amnesty. 2019. Hong Kong: Arbitrary Arrests, Brutal Beatings and Torture in Police Detention Revealed. https://www.amnesty.org/en/latest/news/2019/09/hong-kong-arbitrary-arrests-brutal-beatings-and-torture-in-police-detention-revealed/. Accessed 2 March 2021.

Basic Law. 2021. https://www.basiclaw.gov.hk/en/basiclaw/chapter2.html. Accessed 11 May 2021.

BBC. 2004. Liaison Office of the Central Committee of the Communist Party of China Reiterated its Rejection of Hong Kong's General Election 中聯辦重申否決港普選決定. https://www.google.com/search?q=google+translate&oq=google+translate&aqs=chrome.0.69i59j69i64.2908j0j7&sourceid=chrome&ie=UTF-8. Accessed 15 March 2021.

BBC. 2019. Hong Kong: Protesters Storm and Deface Parliament on Handover Anniversary. https://www.bbc.com/news/world-asia-china-48821640. Accessed 1 March 2021.

Brady, Anne-Marie. 2008. *Marketing Dictatorship: Propaganda and Thought Work in Contemporary China*. Lanhamry, MD: Rowman & Littlefield Publishers.

Burns, John. 1990. The Structure of Communist Party Control in Hong Kong. *Asian Survey* 30 (8): 748–765.

Chan, Chris, and Elaine Hui. 2016. Bringing Class Struggles Back: A Marxian Analysis of the State and Class Relations in China. *Globalizations* 14 (2): 1–13.

Cheung, Karen. 2018. Hong Kong History Will Not Be Separate Topic In New Curriculum; No Room for Tiananmen Massacre or '67 Riots. https://hongkongfp.com/2018/05/25/hong-kong-history-will-not-separate-topic-new-curriculum-no-room-tiananmen-massacre-67-riots/. Accessed 11 May 2021.

CNN. 2003. Huge Protest Fills HK Streets. https://edition.cnn.com/2003/WORLD/asiapcf/east/07/01/hk.protest/. Accessed 8 April 2021.

Fanoulis, Evangelos. 2017. *The Democratic Quality of European Security and Defence Policy: Between Practices of Governance and Practices of Freedom*. New York: Routledge.

Foucault, Michel. 1976. *The History of Sexuality*. New York: Penguin Books.

Foucault, Michel. 1977. *Discipline and Punish: The Birth of the Prison*. New York: Vintage Books.

Foucault, Michel. 1980. *Power/Knowledge: Selected Interviews and Other Writings 1972–1977*. New York: Vintage Books.

Foucault, Michel. 1980. *Truth and Subjectivity Howison Lectures*. Berkeley: University of California.

Foucault, Michel. 1982. The Subject and Power. In *Michel Foucault: Beyond Structuralism and Hermeneutics*, ed. Hubert Dreyfus and Paul Rabinow. Chicago: University of Chicago Press.

Foucault, Michel. 1986. *The Care of the Self*. New York: Pantheon Books.

Foucault, Michel. 1987. The Ethic of Care for the Self as a Practice of Freedom: An Interview with Michel Foucault on January 20, 1984. *Philosophy & Social Critisim* 12: 112–131.

Foucault, Michel. 1997. *Ethics, Subjectivity and Truth: The Essential Works of Foucault 1954–1984*. New York: The New Press.

Foucault, Michel. 2001a. *Madness and Civilization: A History of Insanity in the Age of Reason*. New York: Vintage Books.

Michel, and Foucault. 2001b. *Power: The Essential Works of Foucault 1954–1984*. London: Penguin Books.

Foucault, Michel. 2006. *History of Madness*. New York: Routledge.

Foucault, Michel. 2014. *On The Government of the Living: Lectures at the College De France 1979–1980*. New York: Palgrave Macmillan.

Foucault, Michel, and Paul Rabinow. 1991. *The Foucault Reader: An Introduction to Foucault's Thought*. Harmondsworth: Penguin.

Foucualt, Michel. 2001. *Power: The Essential Works of Foucault 1954–1984*. London: Penguin Books.

Haas, Benjamin. 2017. How China Changed Hong Kong: Views from the City. https://www.theguardian.com/world/2017/jun/28/how-china-changed-hong-kong-views-city-handover-1997-uk-residents. Accessed 15 October 2020.

Harvey, David. 2005. *A Brief History of Neoliberalism*. New York: Oxford University Press.

HKEX. 2021. China Dimension. https://www.hkex.com.hk/Market-Data/Statistics/Consolidated-Reports/China-Dimension?sc_lang=en#select1=0&select2=1. Accessed 25 August 2020.

Hong Kong's Embattled Leader Steps Down. 2005. https://www.nytimes.com/2005/03/10/international/asia/hong-kongs-embattled-leader-steps-down.html. Accessed 10 April 2021.

Hong Kong Police Launch Tear Gas as Protestors Fire Arrows. 2019. https://www.irishtimes.com/news/world/asia-pacific/hong-kong-police-launch-tear-gas-as-protestors-fire-arrows-1.4085500. Accessed 2 March 2021.

Koo, Hagen. 2001. *Korean Workers: The Culture and Politics of Class Formation*. Londo: Cornell University Press.

Lee, Ching Kwan. 2007. *Against the Law: Labor Protests in China's Rustbelt and Sunbelt*. Berkeley: University of California Press.

Loh, Christine. 2010. *Underground Front: The Chinese Communist Party in Hong Kong*. Hong Kong: Hong Kong University Press.

Ma, Ngok. 2015. The Rise of "Anti-China" Sentiments in Hong Kong and the 2012 Legislative Council Elections. *China Review* 15 (1): 39–66.

Mom Sends Pink 'Gift' to Suspect. 2021. https://www.thestandard.com.hk/section-news/section/4/227567/Mom-sends-pink-'gift'-to-suspect. Accessed 3 March 2021.

Moral and National Education Curriculum Guide: Primary 1 to Secondary 6. 2012. https://www.edb.gov.hk/attachment/en/curriculum-development/moral-national-edu/MNE%20Guide%20(ENG)%20Final_remark_09102012.pdf. Accessed 15 March 2021.

Perry, Elizabeth. 2009. A New Rights Consciouness? *Journal of Democracy* 20 (3): 17–20.

Pun, Ngai, and Huilin Lu. 2010. Unfinished Proletarianization: Self, Anger, and Class Action among the Second Generation of Peasant-Workers in Present-Day China. *Modern China* 36 (5): 493–519.

Press Release. 2004. https://www.info.gov.hk/gia/general/brandhk/311204c3.htm. Accessed 1 May 2021.

Reuters. 2019. Why Hong Kong's Extradition Law Changes are Fueling Fears. https://www.reuters.com/article/us-hongkong-politics-extradition-idUSKCN1T70OA. Accessed 1 March 2021.

SCMP. 2019. Hong Kong Leader Carrie Lam announces Formal Withdrawal of the Extradition Bill and Sets Up a Platform to Look into Key Causes of Protest Crisis. https://www.scmp.com/news/hong-kong/politics/article/3025641/hong-kong-leader-carrie-lam-announce-formal-withdrawal. Accessed 2 March 2021.

SCMP. 2020. Animal Crossing Removed In China amid Flood of Hong Kong Protest Art. https://www.scmp.com/abacus/games/article/3079426/animal-crossing-removed-china-amid-flood-hong-kong-protest-art. Accessed 1 March 2021.

Smart, Barry. 1985. *Michel Foucault*. London: Tavistock Publications Limited.

Smith, Chris, and Jenny Chan. 2015. Working for Two Bosses: Student Interns as Constrained Labour in China. *Journal of Human Relations* 68 (2): 305–326.

The Anger of Hong Kongers 港人怒吼. 2020. https://tw.inv.appledaily.com/StandwithHongKong/. Accessed 1 May 2021.

The First Anniverssary of Umbrella Movement 傘運一周年. 2015. https://hk.appledaily.com/local/20150928/WCFJ5HSE3GEBOB5DBVZYFDIBXM/. Accessed 20 April 2021.

7.1 The Parade adds the Theme of Fighting for Justice (7.1遊行增加爭取公義主題). 2006. https://hk.appledaily.com/local/20060413/VAGC56NVQMBFTXVKJX6VX6GFSI/. Accessed 3 March 2021.

The New York Times. 2005. Hong Kong's Embattled Leader Steps Down. https://www.nytimes.com/2005/03/10/international/asia/hong-kongs-embattled-leader-steps-down.html. Accessed 10 April 2021.

The World Bank. 2020. https://data.worldbank.org/country/hong-kong-sar-china. Accessed 15 August 2020.

Thompson, E.P. 1966. *The Making of the English Working Class*. New York: Vintage Books.

Time. 2019. A Brief History of Protest in Post-Handover Hong Kong. https://time.com/5606212/hong-kong-history-mass-demonstrations-protest/. Accessed 14 April 2021.

Yew, Chiew Ping, and Kin-ming Kwong. 2014. Hong Kong Identity on the Rise. *Asian Survey* 54 (6): 1088–1112.

Youtube. 2014. Bruce Lee be as Water My Friend. https://www.youtube.com/watch?v=cJMwBwFj5nQ. Accessed 3 March 2021.

The manufacturer's authorised representative in the EU is Springer
Nature Customer Service Centre GmbH, Europaplatz 3, 69115 Heidelberg,
Germany. If you have any concerns regarding our products, please
contact ProductSafety@springernature.com

Printed and bound by CPI Group (UK) Ltd, Croydon, CR0 4YY
30/09/2026
02225702-0001